Edited and designed
by David Dew

Contributors

Richard Birch	James Hill	Dave Orton
Tom Bull	Paul Kealy	Mark Scully
Scott Burton	Tony McFadden	Mark Storey
Dave Edwards	Keith Melrose	Alan Sweetman
Nicholas Godfrey	Kevin Morley	Simon Turner
Dylan Hill	Lee Mottershead	Nick Watts

Cover artwork by Nathen Bines
Inside artwork by Stefan Searle and Nigel Jones

Published in 2017 by Racing Post Books, Raceform, 27 Kingfisher Court, Hambridge Road, Newbury, RG14 5SJ

ISBN: 978-1910497111

LOWDOWN FROM THE TRAINERS

RACING POST EXPERTS

A-Z OF KEY HORSES

STATISTICS

THE LOWDOWN CHARLIE APPLEBY & SAEED BIN SUROOR

Thunder and Wuheida head Classic squad for two stables full of talent

LAST year was very much a tale of two stables as far as Godolphin's retained trainers in Newmarket were concerned.

While Charlie Appleby sent out only two more winners than Saeed Bin Suroor, his 70 successes put him more than £600,000 ahead of his colleague, *writes Scott Burton*.

Appleby's big-race winners included Hawkbill's Coral-Eclipse and Wuheida's all-the-way success under a determined William Buick in the Prix Marcel Boussac on Arc day.

Bin Suroor's yard struggled with the virus that affected several yards in the town for much of the summer, although he did get on the Group 1 scoresheet at Saint-Cloud on the last day of October when Thunder Snow put five lengths on his rivals in the Criterium International over seven furlongs.

And the Godolphin stalwart pulls no punches when it comes to his feelings about that 2016 campaign.

"Last year was really disappointing with the horses being sick," he says. "The reality is that for the last three years the quality of the horses has not been high enough to run in the big races. The yearlings come to us and we run what we get but, while some improve, most of them win a small race and then that's it. They're not Group 1 horses and Godolphin needs to have high standards. But I'm optimistic for the future."

Thunder Snow finished fourth to Churchill in the Dewhurst Stakes at Newmarket but is only 2lb shy of the winner judged on his subsequent defeat of South Seas at Saint-Cloud. Having proved he can handle dirt in the UAE 2,000 Guineas, the son of Helmet now has a range of pathways open to him for the spring.

"We'll see how he goes in the UAE Derby before talking to Sheikh Mohammed and make a decision," says Bin Suroor. "Options are open for him between the Classics in England, France or Ireland. It will depend how he comes out of the race first. If he were to win very impressively then the Kentucky Derby could come into it but you need to take the best there and they need to be 100 per cent."

Bin Suroor engaged Christophe Soumillon to ride Thunder Snow at Saint-Cloud and

....

Appleby tends to start the turf season well. In 2015 during March and April, he sent out 38 winners from 104 runners (37%, +3.30pt) while last year during April and May, he sent out 15 winners from 48 runners (31%, +53.73pt)

'Appleby's big-race winners included Hawkbill's Coral-Eclipse and Wuheida's all-the-way success in the Prix Marcel Boussac on Arc day'

DID YOU KNOW?

Saeed Bin Suroor has recorded top-level victories in 12 different countries. That's quite a record. In Britain he's won 25 different Group 1s, some as many as seven times, and his overall Group 1 tally isn't far off 200. He's been champion trainer four times, but before his training career began he was a policeman.

maintained the winning partnership in the UAE Guineas.

He says: "Soumillon knows the horse well and there's a chance he'll stay associated with the horse, although that depends on whether he's available."

Top Score would not have figured highly in the stable's pecking order based on seven starts at two in Europe – although he was only just touched off by Dreamfield at Newmarket in October – but a Middle Eastern winter has certainly seen the son of Hard Spun thrive.

Bin Suroor's runners aged two and three are worth following over trips ranging from 5f to 6f. Juveniles have provided a steady profit (47-172, 27%, +6.76pt), as have the Classic generation (11-46, 24%, +11.39pt). His older horses do best between 1m3f and 1m4f (22-93, 24%, +25.25pt)

Two wins over seven furlongs on the Meydan turf – the latter a Listed success at the expense of Fly At Dawn and Bin Suroor's talented filly Really Special – earned Top Score a place alongside Thunder Snow on the teamsheet for World Cup night.

"He's improved a lot mentally since he arrived in Dubai," says Bin Suroor. "He runs in the UAE Derby and we'll see how far he stays. The mile and a quarter is a question mark and he showed plenty of speed over short of a mile. We have to find out about his stamina but he always tries hard and we think he can do well."

Four colts with Classic credentials

Bin Suroor has made four further entries for the 2,000 Guineas in addition to Thunder Snow and Top Score.

Of those, **Bin Battuta** has not been seen since finishing seventh to the Appleby-trained Boynton in the Group 2 Superlative Stakes at Newmarket last July.

"I was disappointed with him because he was very good early on and then suffered a setback in that race," says the trainer. "He's entered in the Guineas but I think he'll be suited by a mile and a quarter or a mile and a half. He'll run in a Derby Trial."

Big Challenge is another who holds Guineas and Derby engagements. He won his only start when scoring at Nottingham in November, while **Leshlaa** could not have been more impressive when bolting up on his debut at Kempton the same month.

Bin Suroor says: "Big Challenge has done very well both mentally and physically. He obviously needs to run in the big races. Leshlaa is doing well and I like him. Like a lot of mine, you'll see him out early, perhaps more so than last year. We need to find out which ones are good enough to run in the Classics."

Bin Suroor's Guineas sextet is rounded off by **Dream Castle** – not to be confused with Godolphin's Classic hopeful Dreamfield trained by John Gosden – who failed to reach the track in 2016 but who boasts an eyecatching pedigree by Frankel out of the

Flying Childers winner Sand Vixen.

"He was very backward last year and I didn't want to rush him," says Bin Suroor. "He's done only half speeds so far but I like him and I think he has a future."

With regards to the Fillies' Classic, Bin Suroor has made three entries, headed by **Really Special**, winner of the Zetland Stakes before heading to Dubai over the winter.

The trainer says of the trio: "**Dubai One** stayed in Newmarket over the winter and is doing well. Really Special will travel back to Newmarket and they'll both run in trials. A good trip for Really Special could be a mile and a quarter or a mile and a half. **Extra Mile** is doing well and she was another who needed time at two."

Although unraced at two, Extra Mile is bred for the trip, being another Frankel, this time out of Bin Suroor's multiple Group winner Local Time.

The trainer's disappointing 2016 means there are fewer older horses than normal to get the pulse racing, while some are also recovering from their exertions in Australia.

Beautiful staying plan

One name to note in Cup races back in Britain is **Beautiful Romance**, winner of the Middleton Stakes at York early last season over an extended mile and a quarter who seems to have relished an increased emphasis on stamina since.

Having finished seventh in the Melbourne Cup, she accounted for Almoonqith in the Zipping Classic at Sandown before making a fine Dubai debut when proving too strong for Vazirabad over a mile and a half.

"She won really well on her first try in

DID YOU KNOW?

Charlie Appleby's 70 winners in Britain last year was not a personal best, but in his short career at the helm with Godolphin it was probably the most successful in terms of big-race winners. He won three Group 1s in three different countries, including the prestigious Eclipse with Hawkbill. He also won some top handicaps, notably Australia's Geelong Cup with former hurdler Qewy.

Appleby excited by super filly

If Thunder Snow gives Bin Suroor a classy challenger for Classic honours on the colts' side, then Appleby makes no secret of how excited he is about **Wuheida**, whose victory in a furiously run Marcel Boussac came off the back of a solitary maiden success.

Appleby clearly has the Investec Oaks in mind for the filly, but her Group 1-winning form at two entitles her to be campaigned with Newmarket in mind to begin with.

"Wuheida has wintered well and done everything asked of her," says Appleby. "She will most likely go straight to the Guineas. She'll probably be seen at her best when stepping up in trip."

Sobetsu – who like Wuheida is

Dubai," says Bin Suroor. "The plan is that she'll go for the Dubai Gold Cup. She's improved with age and she could be one for all of those mile and six, two-mile races."

WHEN YOU BET ON RACING, YOU CAN BET ON RACING POST racingpost.com/mobile

CHARLIE APPLEBY
NEWMARKET, SUFFOLK

	No. of Hrs	Races Run	1st	2nd	3rd	Unpl	Per cent	£1 Level Stake
2-y-o	46	131	32	26	22	50	24.4	-30.88
3-y-o	40	114	25	19	16	54	21.9	+5.84
4-y-o+	33	86	13	16	6	51	15.1	+9.06
Totals	**119**	**331**	**70**	**61**	**44**	**155**	**21.1**	**-15.98**
2015	*186*	*663*	*151*	*113*	*96*	*303*	*22.8*	*+3.40*
2014	*171*	*549*	*102*	*84*	*82*	*281*	*18.6*	*-40.05*

BY MONTH

2-y-o	W-R	Per cent	£1 Level Stake	3-y-o	W-R	Per cent	£1 Level Stake
January	0-0	0.0	0.00	January	0-2	0.0	-2.00
February	0-0	0.0	0.00	February	0-0	0.0	0.00
March	0-0	0.0	0.00	March	0-0	0.0	0.00
April	0-0	0.0	0.00	April	5-10	50.0	+16.10
May	2-5	40.0	+0.25	May	6-20	30.0	+16.38
June	4-10	40.0	+1.40	June	5-23	21.7	-4.98
July	9-27	33.3	+4.90	July	5-22	22.7	+5.63
August	5-25	20.0	-9.70	August	1-8	12.5	-5.90
September	6-32	18.8	-12.13	September	1-15	6.7	-12.63
October	3-26	11.5	-19.45	October	2-13	15.4	-5.75
November	3-6	50.0	+3.85	November	0-1	0.0	-1.00
December	0-0	0.0	0.00	December	0-0	0.0	0.00

4-y-o+	W-R	Per cent	£1 Level Stake	Totals	W-R	Per cent	£1 Level Stake
January	1-2	50.0	+1.00	January	1-4	25.0	-1.00
February	0-3	0.0	-3.00	February	0-3	0.0	-3.00
March	0-3	0.0	-3.00	March	0-3	0.0	-3.00
April	1-5	20.0	+8.00	April	6-15	40.0	+24.10
May	1-8	12.5	+13.00	May	9-33	27.3	+29.63
June	2-20	10.0	+2.00	June	11-53	20.8	-1.58
July	4-26	15.4	-11.94	July	18-75	24.0	-1.41
August	1-10	10.0	-19.60	August	7-43	16.3	-19.60
September	2-6	33.3	+6.50	September	9-53	17.0	-18.26
October	1-3	33.3	+0.50	October	6-42	14.3	-24.70
November	0-0	0.0	0.00	November	3-7	42.9	-1.00
December	0-0	0.0	0.00	December	0-0	0.0	0.00

DISTANCE

2-y-o	W-R	Per cent	£1 Level Stake	3-y-o	W-R	Per cent	£1 Level Stake
5f-6f	11-38	28.9	-4.32	5f-6f	1-9	11.1	-6.90
7f-8f	18-86	20.9	-29.30	7f-8f	12-59	20.3	-3.75
9f-13f	3-7	42.9	+2.75	9f-13f	11-43	25.6	+11.49
14f+	0-0	0.0	0.00	14f+	1-3	33.3	+5.00

4-y-o	W-R	Per cent	£1 Level Stake	Totals	W-R	Per cent	£1 Level Stake
5f-6f	0-17	0.0	-17.00	5f-6f	12-64	18.8	-28.22
7f-8f	4-15	26.7	+28.50	7f-8f	34-160	21.3	-4.55
9f-13f	4-27	14.8	-8.34	9f-13f	18-77	23.4	+5.90
14f+	5-27	18.5	+5.90	14f+	6-30	20.0	+10.90

TYPE OF RACE

Non-Handicaps	W-R	Per cent	£1 Level Stake	Handicaps	W-R	Per cent	£1 Level Stake
2-y-o	28-120	23.3	-34.38	2-y-o	4-11	36.4	+3.50
3-y-o	16-53	30.2	+28.84	3-y-o	9-61	14.8	-23.00
4-y-o+	5-35	14.3	+3.00	4-y-o+	8-51	15.7	+25.90

RACE CLASS

	W-R	Per cent	£1 Level Stake
Class 1	11-77	14.3	-13.72
Class 2	13-78	16.7	+23.13
Class 3	7-36	19.4	-6.30
Class 4	14-67	20.9	-27.90
Class 5	25-72	34.7	+9.82
Class 6	0-1	0.0	-1.00
Class 7	0-0	0.0	0.00

FIRST TIME OUT

	W-R	Per cent	£1 Level Stake
2-y-o	10-46	21.7	-11.40
3-y-o	11-40	27.5	+19.27
4-y-o+	6-33	18.2	-3.35
Totals	27-119	22.7	+4.52

Wuheida (second left) has Charlie Appleby dreaming of Classic success after Group 1 victory at Chantilly

SAEED BIN SUROOR
NEWMARKET, SUFFOLK

	No. of Hrs	Races Run	1st	2nd	3rd	Unpl	Per cent	£1 Level Stake
2-y-o	53	111	32	23	13	43	28.8	+11.88
3-y-o	41	130	26	26	15	63	20.0	-23.09
4-y-o+	29	78	10	13	5	50	12.8	-27.44
Totals	123	319	68	62	33	156	21.3	-38.65
2015	131	392	105	67	51	169	26.8	+16.14
2014	135	405	93	69	45	198	23.0	-23.97

BY MONTH

2-y-o	W-R	Per cent	£1 Level Stake	3-y-o	W-R	Per cent	£1 Level Stake
January	0-0	0.0	0.00	January	1-2	50.0	+3.00
February	0-0	0.0	0.00	February	1-1	100.0	+0.22
March	0-0	0.0	0.00	March	0-2	0.0	-2.00
April	1-2	50.0	+0.63	April	1-16	6.3	-8.50
May	5-7	71.4	+5.92	May	2-20	10.0	-14.75
June	1-6	16.7	-3.50	June	6-20	30.0	-5.28
July	3-15	20.0	+10.00	July	3-25	12.0	-12.15
August	0-1	0.0	-1.00	August	0-2	0.0	-2.00
September	2-15	13.3	-10.20	September	3-14	21.4	+9.50
October	10-37	27.0	+8.58	October	5-14	35.7	+3.38
November	9-27	33.3	-1.28	November	3-8	37.5	+7.00
December	1-1	100.0	+2.75	December	1-6	16.7	-1.50

4-y-o+	W-R	Per cent	£1 Level Stake	Totals	W-R	Per cent	£1 Level Stake
January	2-7	28.6	-3.19	January	3-9	33.3	-0.19
February	0-1	0.0	-1.00	February	1-2	50.0	-0.78
March	0-0	0.0	0.00	March	0-2	0.0	-2.00
April	1-6	16.7	+1.50	April	3-24	12.5	-6.37
May	3-16	18.8	+3.00	May	10-43	23.3	-5.83
June	0-12	0.0	-12.00	June	7-38	18.4	-20.78
July	0-14	0.0	-14.00	July	6-54	11.1	-16.15
August	0-0	0.0	0.00	August	0-3	0.0	-3.00
September	3-12	25.0	+4.50	September	8-41	19.5	+3.80
October	0-8	0.0	-8.00	October	15-59	25.4	+3.96
November	1-2	50.0	+1.75	November	13-37	35.1	+8.75
December	0-0	0.0	0.00	December	2-7	28.6	-1.50

DISTANCE

2-y-o	W-R	Per cent	£1 Level Stake	3-y-o	W-R	Per cent	£1 Level Stake
5f-6f	18-46	39.1	+13.02	5f-6f	3-13	23.1	-4.40
7f-8f	14-60	23.3	+3.86	7f-8f	8-55	14.5	-20.21
9f-13f	0-5	0.0	-5.00	9f-13f	13-57	22.8	-0.98
14f+	0-0	0.0	0.00	14f+	2-5	40.0	+2.50

4-y-o	W-R	Per cent	£1 Level Stake	Totals	W-R	Per cent	£1 Level Stake
5f-6f	2-9	22.2	+0.12	5f-6f	23-68	33.8	+8.74
7f-8f	1-25	4.0	-16.00	7f-8f	23-140	16.4	-32.35
9f-13f	7-43	16.3	-10.55	9f-13f	20-105	19.0	-16.53
14f+	0-1	0.0	-1.00	14f+	2-6	33.3	+1.50

TYPE OF RACE

Non-Handicaps	W-R	Per cent	£1 Level Stake	Handicaps	W-R	Per cent	£1 Level Stake
2-y-o	28-101	27.7	+10.26	2-y-o	4-10	40.0	+1.63
3-y-o	15-67	22.4	-15.96	3-y-o	11-63	17.5	-7.13
4-y-o+	5-25	20.0	+12.00	4-y-o+	5-53	9.4	-30.43

RACECLASS / FIRST TIME OUT

	W-R	Per cent	£1 Level Stake		W-R	Per cent	£1 Level Stake
Class 1	9-72	12.5	-13.50	2-y-o	13-53	24.5	+4.30
Class 2	10-66	15.2	-26.18	3-y-o	5-41	12.2	-16.50
Class 3	9-47	19.1	-4.46	4-y-o+	9-29	31.0	+18.06
Class 4	15-56	26.8	+8.47	Totals	27-123	22.0	+5.86
Class 5	24-77	31.2	-5.23				
Class 6	1-1	100.0	+2.25				
Class 7	0-0	0.0	0.00				

Bin Suroor's juveniles more than pay their way in nurseries (15-38, 39%, +11.88pt), while three-year-olds generally perform well in maidens (71-241, 29%, +4.23pt)

by Dubawi – was another to earn direct promotion from maiden winner to Group 1 runner last autumn, a gamble which appeared justified after a ten-length romp at Newmarket.

Appleby reveals there was an excuse for her distant fifth behind Rhododendron back on the Rowley Mile on future champions day.

He says: "Sobetsu broke her maiden impressively but disappointed in the Fillies' Mile. She subsequently returned a dirty scope post-race but has spent the winter in Dubai and has done well. Her preparation will be geared towards the Guineas."

The stable also has **Grecian Light** – twice placed at Group level last year – and **Fashion**

Theory among their Newmarket entries.

Appleby also has two for the 2,000 Guineas at this stage, both of whom are worthy of a place on the basis of their two-year-old form.

Boynton looked a very bright prospect when landing the Group 2 Superlative Stakes at the expense of War Decree, fighting to regain the lead having been headed inside the final furlong.

The son of More Than Ready was unable to confirm that superiority under a 3lb penalty at Glorious Goodwood in what looked a strong renewal of the Vintage Stakes (Thunder Snow was second), and Appleby says: "Boynton had a minor setback in the autumn. He's coming along nicely and it's possible he'll have a tilt at the Guineas as long as he continues progressing the way he is."

Salsabeel progressing well

If time could be against Boynton then the second colt from Moulton Paddocks to hold the 2,000 Guineas engagement, **Salsabeel**, is the subject of a glowing report card.

By Exceed And Excel out of Tokyo Rose, who won the Listed Prix Ceres for Henri Alex Pantall over seven furlongs on her final start, stamina for a mile is not guaranteed on pedigree. But Salsabeel was showing no signs of stopping when just failing to reel in Rodaini in the Listed Flying Scotsman Stakes at Doncaster's St Leger meeting.

"Salsabeel has done very well physically and mentally," says Appleby. "The form from his two-year-old year is strong and I'm hopeful he can measure up to a Guineas preparation."

Blue can make his point

One colt who has proved himself more than capable at Group 1 level is **Blue Point**, who found only The Last Lion too strong in the Middle Park and then chased home Churchill and Lancaster Bomber just two weeks later in the Dewhurst, where the final 100 yards appeared beyond the son of Shamardal.

That means Blue Point – a winner of the Group 2 Gimcrack at York's Ebor meeting last August – starts the year vying with Caravaggio as the highest-rated three-year-old sprinter in Europe, and Appleby has no intention of being distracted from that path.

"Blue Point spent the winter in Dubai, and the plan is to start him back in the Group 2 Sandy Lane Stakes in May," says Appleby, who will be hoping the Haydock race can act as a springboard to the Commonwealth Cup.

Appleby also has a host of high-class campaigners among his older horses.

Jungle Cat has proved himself a redoubtable presence on the sprinting scene at Meydan, while **Endless Time** deserves to score at Group level after fine seconds in the Prix Vermeille (behind Left Hand) and the Prix Royal-Oak (Vazirabad).

SUPER STATS

Appleby has a fine strike-rate on each of the British all-weather tracks, with his best records coming at Kempton (63-242, 26%, +10.01pt) and Lingfield (44-145, 30%, +9.59pt)

Appleby's turf runners are generally best followed on Newmarket's Rowley Mile course (29-134, 22%, +41.67pt), Goodwood (15-78, 19%, +5.96) and at Pontefract (12-33, 36%, +1.32pt)

Appleby's older horses racing over 1m1f to 1m2f return a handsome level-stake profit and strike-rate (21-74, 28%, +26.33pt)

William Buick rode most of Appleby's winners last year for a profit (33-161, 22%, +4.25pt), while Adam Kirby's mounts provided the best level-stake returns (4-16, 25%, +17.85pt)

Saeed Bin Suroor is respected on the all-weather, turning over level-stake profits at Chelmsford (20-58, 34%, +3.68pt), Kempton (45-173, 26%, +26.80pt), Lingfield (25-87, 29%, +3.77pt), Newcastle (8-20, 40%, +3.80pt) and Wolverhampton (36-98, 37%, +7.40pt)

The bulk of Bin Suroor's turf success comes at Newmarket with his figures on the July course catching the eye (31-134, 23%, +13.27pt). Raids to Brighton (7-16, 44%, +4.20pt) and Windsor (16-38, 42%, +16.08pt) are always worth watching out for too

*All statistics cover the last five years

Quality team and big ambitions could see more records broken

THERE is no doubt the 2016 Flat season will be remembered fondly by Clive Cox. The trainer sent out 65 winners – his best return to date – and also registered a career best in terms of total prize-money, passing the £1.5 million mark for the first time.

Two big contributors to that impressive haul were My Dream Boat and Profitable, who both bagged Group 1 glory, winning the Prince of Wales's Stakes and King's Stand Stakes respectively at Royal Ascot, *writes Tony McFadden*.

"It was our most successful season in terms of winners and prize-money, and with a Group 1 double at Royal Ascot as well, so it was great," says the trainer.

Cox has long had a reputation as an excellent handler of sprinters, and has enjoyed success at the highest level with the likes of Reckless Abandon and Lethal Force, so he admits he took particular satisfaction from landing one of the most prestigious ten-furlong races in the calendar with My Dream Boat, who he inherited as a 76-rated maiden the previous year.

"We've enjoyed success with sprinters – we've had six Group 1 wins in sprints – so it's a great privilege to also have a middle-distance horse at the top level," Cox explains.

My Dream Boat, who ran with credit in the Eclipse, Irish Champion Stakes and Champion Stakes, will once again be aimed at the major middle-distance races, and could be asked to step up beyond ten furlongs for the first time.

"**My Dream Boat** is training really well," Cox says. "I'm very much looking forward to him this year and I think there's every possibility we'll step him up to a mile and a half. He started off in the Gordon Richards Stakes at Sandown last year and I think that might be a good starting point again. He's in great form."

Targets for My Dream Boat will be dictated by conditions, with Cox adamant the colt needs a bit of juice in the ground to be seen at his best. "He's definitely more at home on an easier surface," the trainer explains. "He's not as effective when the ground is quick."

Cox runners return their best level-stake figures at Haydock (6-44, 14%, +16.25pt) and York (3-24, 13%, +27.75pt), but the strike-rates are higher at Bath (21-102, 21%, +10.30pt) and Brighton (7-25, 28%, +6.24pt)

'We've enjoyed success with sprinters – we've had six Group 1 wins in sprints – so it's a great privilege to also have a middle-distance horse at the top level'

An exciting development for Cox is the addition of a new high-profile owner to the stable.

"**Profitable** will run in the Godolphin colours, whom we are very pleased and proud to have onboard," the trainer says. "He'll follow a very similar plan to last year. He started out with a win in the Palace House Stakes at Newmarket on 2,000 Guineas day and, all being well, the intention is to go back."

Profitable has run with credit on both occasions he's tackled six furlongs – not beaten far in the 2015 Commonwealth Cup or last year's July Cup – but is believed to be at his blistering best over the minimum trip.

"In my opinion he is definitely a better horse over five furlongs," Cox says. "We ran him in the July Cup last year but his form suggests his preference is five [furlongs]."

Cox has a wealth of talent to call upon in the three-year-old division, but there is little doubt as to which horse the trainer expects to be the flagbearer.

Harry sets the heart racing

"I really hope we've got a great team to go to war with this year, and **Harry Angel**, in particular, is very exciting," Cox says. "He sets the heart racing.

"We've had some really nice ones like Lethal Force and Reckless Abandon, to mention two, but he's equally exciting at this stage – he's full of promise."

Having shaped with bundles of potential when finishing a narrow runner-up on his debut last May, Harry Angel justified strong support in the Group 2 Mill Reef Stakes, winning in the style of a horse capable of cutting it at the highest level. He received quotes for the 2,000 Guineas, but a sprinting campaign seems more likely.

"I did win a race over a mile and a quarter

CLIVE COX
LAMBOURN, BERKS

	No. of Hrs	Races Run	1st	2nd	3rd	Unpl	Per cent	£1 Level Stake
2-y-o	37	107	16	11	8	72	15.0	-32.95
3-y-o	40	215	32	29	31	123	14.9	-18.45
4-y-o+	23	113	17	14	13	69	15.0	-0.05
Totals	100	435	65	54	52	264	14.9	-51.45
2015	87	399	44	42	57	256	11.0	-72.00
2014	82	385	62	59	49	215	16.1	-15.29

BY MONTH

2-y-o	W-R	Per cent	£1 Level Stake	3-y-o	W-R	Per cent	£1 Level Stake
January	0-0	0.0	0.00	January	0-9	0.0	-9.00
February	0-0	0.0	0.00	February	1-4	25.0	+3.50
March	0-0	0.0	0.00	March	1-4	25.0	0.00
April	0-0	0.0	0.00	April	1-14	7.1	-5.00
May	2-7	28.6	-1.88	May	5-30	16.7	-3.13
June	0-6	0.0	-6.00	June	5-35	14.3	+0.32
July	5-19	26.3	-8.13	July	7-39	17.9	+6.88
August	1-15	6.7	-4.00	August	7-34	20.6	-3.50
September	4-25	16.0	-1.50	September	4-30	13.3	+5.75
October	2-16	12.5	-12.43	October	0-11	0.0	-11.00
November	1-12	8.3	-4.00	November	0-3	0.0	-3.00
December	1-7	14.3	+5.00	December	1-2	50.0	-0.27

4-y-o+	W-R	Per cent	£1 Level Stake	Totals	W-R	Per cent	£1 Level Stake
January	1-6	16.7	-1.50	January	1-15	6.7	-10.50
February	0-6	0.0	-6.00	February	1-10	10.0	-2.50
March	1-4	25.0	-0.25	March	2-8	25.0	-0.25
April	4-7	57.1	+29.25	April	5-21	23.8	+24.25
May	5-18	27.8	+9.75	May	12-55	21.8	+4.74
June	3-18	16.7	+6.20	June	8-59	13.6	+0.52
July	2-18	11.1	-4.00	July	14-76	18.4	-5.25
August	1-10	10.0	-7.50	August	9-59	15.3	-15.00
September	0-9	0.0	-9.00	September	8-64	12.5	-4.75
October	0-10	0.0	-10.00	October	2-37	5.4	-33.43
November	0-4	0.0	-4.00	November	1-19	5.3	-7.00
December	0-3	0.0	-3.00	December	2-12	16.7	-3.27

DISTANCE

2-y-o	W-R	Per cent	£1 Level Stake	3-y-o	W-R	Per cent	£1 Level Stake
5f-6f	13-64	20.3	-16.95	5f-6f	14-87	16.1	-26.93
7f-8f	3-41	7.3	-14.00	7f-8f	11-84	13.1	+3.88
9f-13f	0-2	0.0	-2.00	9f-13f	7-42	16.7	+6.60
14f+	0-0	0.0	0.00	14f+	0-2	0.0	-2.00

4-y-o	W-R	Per cent	£1 Level Stake	Totals	W-R	Per cent	£1 Level Stake
5f-6f	7-43	16.3	+9.75	5f-6f	34-194	17.5	-34.13
7f-8f	3-32	9.4	-14.50	7f-8f	17-157	10.8	-24.62
9f-13f	7-34	20.6	+8.70	9f-13f	14-78	17.9	+13.30
14f+	0-4	0.0	-4.00	14f+	0-6	0.0	-6.00

TYPE OF RACE

Non-Handicaps	W-R	Per cent	£1 Level Stake	Handicaps	W-R	Per cent	£1 Level Stake
2-y-o	13-89	14.6	-41.95	2-y-o	3-18	16.7	+9.00
3-y-o	11-65	16.9	+4.80	3 y o	21-150	14.0	-23.25
4-y-o+	6-20	30.0	+49.00	4-y-o+	11-93	11.8	-43.80

RACE CLASS

	W-R	Per cent	£1 Level Stake
Class 1	10-39	25.6	+55.75
Class 2	0-30	0.0	-30.00
Class 3	11-44	25.0	+21.13
Class 4	10-110	9.1	-57.83
Class 5	29-179	16.2	-36.97
Class 6	5-33	15.2	-3.52
Class 7	0-0	0.0	0.00

FIRST TIME OUT

	W-R	Per cent	£1 Level Stake
2-y-o	2-37	5.4	-23.50
3-y-o	3-40	7.5	-15.75
4-y-o+	8-23	34.8	+32.45
Totals	13-100	13.0	-6.80

Profitable (far side): last year's Palace House Stakes winner will race in the colours of Godolphin this season

DID YOU KNOW?

Clive Cox had a successful career as a jump jockey, riding the best part of 100 winners. He then became assistant trainer to Mikey Heaton-Ellis and took over the licence at Barbury Castle in 1999. The following year Cox moved to John Francome's Beechdown Stables in Lambourn, from where his first big winner came in 2003 when New Seeker won the Britannia Handicap at Royal Ascot.

with his brother, but he gives me every indication he's a Commonwealth Cup type, so we will work backwards from there," Cox says. "I'm not sure where he'll start yet as he has a Group 2 penalty – we'll see how he trains during the next month."

Marvellous in fine shape

Also likely to have the Commonwealth Cup on his agenda is **Tis Marvellous**, who was an impressive winner of the Group 2 Prix Robert Papin before running below expectations in the Prix Morny and Flying Childers last season.

"Tis Marvellous was very impressive at Maisons-Laffitte but we probably just got stuck in the fast lane a little bit earlier than ideal with him," Cox says. "He's wintered really well and has a wonderful temperament."

Another with solid Group-race form is **Barroche**, third in a Chantilly Group 3 on her final start of a successful campaign.

"She's a very honest and courageous performer – I like her temperament," the trainer says. "She's a good, strong scopey filly who can go forward as a three-year-old. She likes quick ground."

Kodiline is also thought to be at his best when conditions are sound underfoot.

"He won well on top of the ground at Windsor and was then placed in a Listed race," says Cox. "We'll be looking forward to seeing him at the height of summer on a quick surface. He showed a lot of ability at two and has matured mentally."

Unexposed and exciting

In addition to those who have already proven themselves capable of cutting it at pattern-race level, Cox also has a number of completely unexposed three-year-olds who are open to substantial improvement.

One such type is **Pavillon**, who caught the eye when sweeping from last to first to overcome clear signs of inexperience on her debut at Kempton in November.

"She was impressive and is from a nice family," Cox says. There should be plenty to come and she's exciting."

Home-bred **Graphite Storm** followed a Windsor maiden win with an impressive nursery success at Newbury, and this well-regarded colt ought to make an impact from a mark of 86.

"Sadly his sire Delegator is no longer with us, but he's certainly left us with a very nice one in this fellow," Cox says. "He's still very much a baby so we'll take it a step at a time, but I'm very pleased with what he's shown so far. He displayed a lot of courage and ability last year and has wintered well."

Another who has benefited from a winter on his back is twice-raced maiden winner **Dark Power**.

"He's a very big, scopey individual and did well to win as a two-year-old. He's bred along an identical cross to Lethal Force – by Dark Angel out of a Desert Style mare."

Genie could be a real hit

Even more lightly raced is **The Jean Genie**, who shaped well on her only start, finishing an encouraging second over a mile at Haydock.

"She's out of a mare who won an Oaks trial so she'll get further in due course, but I don't think she'd want the ground too soft," Cox explains. "It was a very pleasing debut and she's entitled to improve. She's a very nice filly to look forward to."

February Wolverhampton winner **Flood Warning** could be one to follow in handicaps.

"She had a hold-up as a two-year-old but won well and is on a rating of 76. She should be able to move forward from that."

Supplementing the exciting bunch of youngsters is a solid crop of older horses, with many still open to progress.

Listed winner **Priceless** is one such potential improver, having struck on her first attempt at five furlongs, suggesting there could be more to come over the minimum trip.

"She signed off really well with a win at Doncaster," Cox says. "She took a while to come to herself in the spring and progressed as the season went on, but she was also helped by dropping back to the minimum distance at Doncaster."

There are also high hopes for **Zonderland**,

who ran well in the 2,000 Guineas and struck at Group 3 level.

"He's been really well," Cox says. "He's a very exciting prospect having won the Sovereign Stakes and finished second in the Celebration Mile. He's always been a scopey, impressive individual and I hope we'll see further progress from him."

Worth another chance

Bobby Wheeler may have disappointed on two occasions after running so well at Glorious Goodwood, but he could prove to be a different proposition after undergoing a gelding operation.

"He's out of a Group 1-winning mare and from a great family, so I hope he can take a step forward," says his trainer. "He's matured since we've had him gelded."

It could also be worth forgiving **Go On Go On Go On** for a tame final effort on her final start as she had looked progressive previously.

"She was exciting when she won at Bath and had gone off the boil at Doncaster. She wouldn't want the ground too easy."

Another thought to be most effective on a sound surface is **Laidback Romeo**, who won his final two starts and is now rated highly enough to contest valuable handicaps.

"He looks great and he'll be ready for when we have some decent, summer ground," Cox says.

Yard favourite **Seeking Magic** *(right)* made his debut as a two-year-old and is still going strong at the age of nine.

"He's as good as ever," Cox says. "He's a favourite round the yard. He's still a real livewire and it's great to see him performing at such a level. He's so consistent the handicapper never gives him much grace."

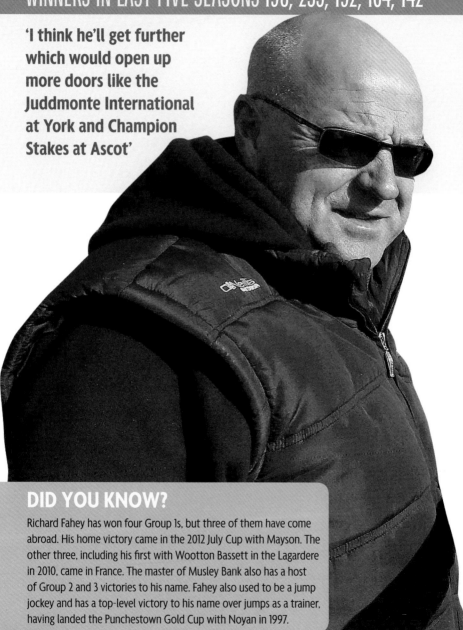

WINNERS IN LAST FIVE SEASONS 198, 235, 192, 164, 142

'I think he'll get further which would open up more doors like the Juddmonte International at York and Champion Stakes at Ascot'

DID YOU KNOW?

Richard Fahey has won four Group 1s, but three of them have come abroad. His home victory came in the 2012 July Cup with Mayson. The other three, including his first with Wootton Bassett in the Lagardere in 2010, came in France. The master of Musley Bank also has a host of Group 2 and 3 victories to his name. Fahey also used to be a jump jockey and has a top-level victory to his name over jumps as a trainer, having landed the Punchestown Gold Cup with Noyan in 1997.

'The best I've trained' – Ribchester earmarked for the top mile races

IT promises to be yet another big season for Richard Fahey. Since launching his training career 20 years ago his meteoric rise up the ladder has provided one of Flat racing's success stories.

Surpassing his 2015 season when he equalled Richard Hannon snr's record of 235 winners in a calendar year was always going to prove an uphill quest, but he nonetheless managed to end 2016 with 198 winners, a cool £3 million in prize-money, third place in the trainers' title and a Group 1 winner courtesy of the Godolphin-owned super-colt Ribchester in France, *writes Richard Birch*.

He starts the present campaign with an exciting bunch of two-year-olds, a strong team of jockeys, including former dual champion Paul Hanagan – who Fahey regards as "a close friend as well as a top rider" – and a healthy blend of Group-race performers and useful handicappers.

Ribchester, star of the Musley Bank stable last year when his victories included the Group 1 Prix Jacques le Marois at Deauville in August, is being primed to reappear on Dubai World Cup night at Meydan in the Group 1 Dubai Turf.

"I'm very happy with him," Fahey says. "Dubai looks a good starting point followed by the Lockinge at Newbury.

"We'll consider all the top mile races, but I think he'll get further which would open up more doors like the Juddmonte International at York and Champion Stakes at Ascot. He's the best horse I've trained."

Ribchester trained on supremely well from two to three, winding up his second season by going head to head with the brilliant Ballydoyle filly Minding in Ascot's Queen Elizabeth II Stakes, and Fahey is clearly hoping his **Queen Kindly**, a smart juvenile last year, follows suit.

The daughter of wonder-horse Frankel landed three of her first four starts, including the Group 2 Lowther Stakes at York, and there was no lack of stable confidence when she locked horns with the blisteringly quick odds-on favourite Lady Aurelia in Newmarket's Group 1 Cheveley Park Stakes in September.

Neither ran up to market expectations that day, Queen Kindly managing only fourth to 25-1 scorer Brave Anna, and it will be interesting to see how she develops in 2017.

....

Fahey's runners are best followed on turf – with healthy level-stake profits at Pontefract (44-207, 21%, +65.24pt), Catterick (37-152, 24%, +27.92pt), Leicester (23-117, 20%, +38.16pt) and Musselburgh (36-183, 20%, +26.57pt)

RICHARD FAHEY
MUSLEY BANK, N YORKS

	No. of Hrs	Races Run	1st	2nd	3rd	Unpl	Per cent	£1 Level Stake
2-y-o	101	456	58	64	71	262	12.7	-82.10
3-y-o	94	544	75	59	69	339	13.8	-42.94
4-y-o+	99	739	65	71	83	520	8.8	-271.05
Totals	**294**	**1739**	**198**	**194**	**223**	**1121**	**11.4**	**-396.09**
2015	296	1691	235	220	199	1036	13.9	-84.39
2014	279	1502	192	206	176	922	12.8	-70.08

BY MONTH

2-y-o	W-R	Per cent	£1 Level Stake	3-y-o	W-R	Per cent	£1 Level Stake
January	0-0	0.0	0.00	January	1-16	6.3	-9.50
February	0-0	0.0	0.00	February	3-17	17.6	+0.50
March	0-1	0.0	-1.00	March	2-20	10.0	-12.39
April	3-11	27.3	+12.23	April	12-49	24.5	+2.89
May	5-38	13.2	+34.25	May	5-70	7.1	-40.13
June	6-51	11.8	-19.85	June	15-84	17.9	+10.08
July	10-91	11.0	-40.63	July	9-79	11.4	+7.75
August	11-90	12.2	-20.83	August	11-62	17.7	+16.60
September	9-66	13.6	-14.72	September	6-50	12.0	-6.75
October	10-61	16.4	-12.80	October	5-49	10.2	-8.00
November	4-30	13.3	-1.75	November	3-24	12.5	-3.00
December	0-17	0.0	-17.00	December	3-24	12.5	-1.00

4-y-o+	W-R	Per cent	£1 Level Stake	Totals	W-R	Per cent	£1 Level Stake
January	6-32	18.8	+9.75	January	7-48	14.6	+0.25
February	3-25	12.0	-13.75	February	6-42	14.3	-13.25
March	4-24	16.7	+0.08	March	6-45	13.3	-13.31
April	7-70	10.0	-28.25	April	22-130	16.9	-13.13
May	8-103	7.8	-61.63	May	18-211	8.5	-67.51
June	14-85	16.5	+35.00	June	35-220	15.9	+25.23
July	8-108	7.4	-49.38	July	27-278	9.7	-82.26
August	5-88	5.7	-42.50	August	27-240	11.3	-46.73
September	4-84	4.8	-56.39	September	19-200	9.5	-77.86
October	3-61	4.9	-42.00	October	18-171	10.5	-62.80
November	2-35	5.7	-24.00	November	9-89	10.1	-27.00
December	1-24	4.2	+2.00	December	4-65	6.2	+1.00

DISTANCE

2-y-o	W-R	Per cent	£1 Level Stake	3-y-o	W-R	Per cent	£1 Level Stake
5f-6f	38-300	12.7	-40.26	5f-6f	26-206	12.6	-66.31
7f-8f	20-155	12.9	-40.84	7f-8f	39-246	15.9	+58.88
9f-13f	0-1	0.0	-1.00	9f-13f	10-89	11.2	-32.50
14f+	0-0	0.0	0.00	14f+	0-3	0.0	-3.00

4-y-o	W-R	Per cent	£1 Level Stake	Totals	W-R	Per cent	£1 Level Stake
5f-6f	21-210	10.0	-61.13	5f-6f	85-716	11.9	-167.70
7f-8f	25-267	9.4	-88.50	7f-8f	84-668	12.6	-70.46
9f-13f	16-206	7.8	-81.18	9f-13f	26-296	8.8	-114.68
14f+	3-56	5.4	-40.25	14f+	3-59	5.1	-43.25

TYPE OF RACE

Non-Handicaps	W-R	Per cent	£1 Level Stake	Handicaps	W-R	Per cent	£1 Level Stake
2-y-o	41-319	12.9	-54.81	2-y-o	17-137	12.4	-27.29
3-y-o	19-98	19.4	-0.91	3-y-o	56-446	12.6	-42.02
4-y-o+	13-81	16.0	+42.00	4-y-o+	52-658	7.9	-263.42

RACECLASS   FIRST TIME OUT

	W-R	Per cent	£1 Level Stake		W-R	Per cent	£1 Level Stake
Class 1	7-90	7.8	-21.50	2-y-o	15-101	14.9	-12.40
Class 2	22-284	7.7	-84.13	3-y-o	12-94	12.8	-28.48
Class 3	18-255	7.1	-142.63	4-y-o+	11-99	11.1	-33.25
Class 4	48-437	11.0	-79.80				
Class 5	73-469	15.6	-46.98	Totals	38-294	12.9	-74.13
Class 6	30-204	14.7	-20.06				
Class 7	0-0	0.0	0.00				

Fahey's juveniles do well at Chester (14-67, 21%, +12.21pt), three-year-olds are strong at Thirsk (15-77, 19%, +33.27pt) while the trainer's older horses do well at Redcar (12-58, 21%, +32.16pt)

"She's a ball of speed and isn't particularly big, even though she's grown over the winter," Fahey reports.

"We'll try her over seven furlongs in the Fred Darling at Newbury, but I'm conscious she might be a sprinter. We'll find out by a process of trial and error."

Melesina, another notable winner for Fahey last year when securing Deauville's Group 3 Prix des Reservoirs in October, has since acquitted herself with credit in finishing fourth in the same grade in Dubai.

"Oisin Murphy felt she should have won that race at Meydan," the trainer reveals. "She's in good form and could run in the Nell Gwyn at Newmarket. A bit further down the line, a step up to 1m2f in York's Musidora could be on the agenda."

Mr Lupton is a prime candidate for good sprints after signing off his three-year-old career with a ninth of 13 to The Tin Man in the Group 1 British Champions Sprint at Ascot.

"He enjoyed a good season, winning a nice handicap at York in the summer," Fahey recalls.

"He's done very well over the winter, and we'll start him off in the Cammidge Trophy at Doncaster."

Growl ready for the top table

Ahead of Mr Lupton at Ascot was the lower-rated **Growl**, who belied 50-1 odds by finishing second, beaten just a length.

After starting last season rated 89, Growl progressed enormously throughout 2016 and begins the new campaign on a mark of 114.

"He did fantastically well last year," Fahey says. "There's a race which has been upgraded at York over seven furlongs which should suit him, and he'll be aimed at the top sprints too. He's dining at the top table now."

Don't Touch, another to have contested that Ascot race – he finished fifth – could be stepped up to 7f this year.

The son of Dutch Art enjoyed a memorable year in 2015, when his five successes included the Ayr Gold Cup, but he took time to adapt to a rise in grade last season.

Mr Lupton (right): Fahey's smart sprinter has done well over the winter and looks a prime candidate for more success this season

Hopes are high, though, that he can make further progress this term. "I was pleased with his run at Ascot," Fahey says. "I'm keen to try him at 7f. There should be more to come from him."

Playboy to act the part

Birchwood, winner of the Group 2 Superlative Stakes at Newmarket's July meeting during his juvenile days, managed to add only a Listed Chester event last year to his CV. Fahey describes that campaign as tricky, but is hopeful there are better times ahead in 2017.

"Birchwood was a bit of a playboy last year, but seems mentally more mature this spring," the trainer reveals. "We could drop him back to six furlongs."

The stable houses a number of aspirants for Doncaster's Lincoln Handicap on April 1. They include eight-year-old **Gabrial**, whose rating has dropped to 108 from a career-high of 114 following a winless second half of 2016.

"Gabrial was a bit disappointing last season and he didn't enjoy Dubai over the winter," Fahey says. "We'll start him off in the Lincoln, a race he won two years ago."

The four-year-old **Stamp Hill**, a winner over 6f and 7f, could also be Doncaster-bound.

"There could be a big one in him," Fahey predicts. "We'll see about stepping him up to a mile. He enjoys a bit of dig in the ground."

Other Fahey entries for the Lincoln include wonderful servant **Heaven's Guest**, winner of nine races including valuable handicaps at Ascot and Newmarket, **Another Touch** and **Dolphin Vista**.

"We had a frustrating winter with Another Touch in Dubai," Fahey laments. "He was reserve four times, but never got a run.

"Dolphin Vista doesn't mind soft ground, and we've had him gelded. He looks well

and I'm happy with him. I'd really like to get him in the Lincoln."

Third Time Lucky, winner of the Cambridgeshire in 2015, again ran a blinder in the Newmarket cavalry charge to finish fourth to Spark Plug in the latest renewal.

You wouldn't rule out further big handicap success this season for him, even though he will start the turf campaign with a rating of 101. The 5lb penalty he picked up for scoring at Wolverhampton in February means Fahey is reluctant to send him to Town Moor for the Lincoln. "Can he win a Lincoln off 106?" Fahey muses. "Probably not. We'll have to look at other targets for him."

Van Gogh looking a picture

The trainer clearly has a soft spot for **Miss Van Gogh**, a five-year-old mare with a marked preference for plenty of cut in the ground, who has already won five handicaps for the Malton yard.

"She's in great order," the trainer says. "The plan is to get her out early when she should get the conditions she enjoys. She's come down a bit in the weights, and will win a handicap off her present mark."

Powerallied, a Dr Marwan Koukash-owned four-year-old, loves Chester and should always be noted on his forays round that unique circuit, while Fahey also offers encouragement for **Gabrial's Kaka** *(left)* hero of the Newbury Spring Cup three years ago, who has been training well.

The Paco Boy four-year-old **Garcia**, who impressed many observers when landing the valuable Haydock Silver Bowl last May, could progress further this season from a starting point of 95. With just six runs behind him – three of them wins – he remains lightly raced.

The tough and genuine filly **Mayfair Lady** is on a black-type mission in 2017, something Fahey believes she thoroughly deserves.

Six performers on the up

Private Matter, a Cheveley Park Stud-owned three-year-old who starts off on a mark of 106 following victory in a Maisons-Laffitte Listed event in October, is just one of a number of second-season performers Fahey expects to improve.

"He's done really well over the winter," the trainer confirms. "We've gelded him and it could prove to be the making of him. I'm not sure where he'll start off but the Free Handicap at Newmarket is a possibility."

The twice-raced **Areen Heart**, allocated an opening mark of 81 after justifying odds-on favouritism in a Beverley maiden in September, is another.

"I've been very pleased with the work he's done so far this year," Fahey enthuses. "He could progress through the handicap ranks."

Royal Ascot hopes are harboured for Elzaam colt **Andok**, winner of two of his three races as a juvenile.

Although only second on his final start at Doncaster in October, the 87-rated Andok once again showed well-above-average ability in chasing home Masham Star, and looks the type of three-year-old handicapper Fahey will place to great advantage.

"We like him," Fahey says. "I was disappointed he got beat at Doncaster, but expect him to get better. The Britannia is a race I have in mind for him at this stage."

Senator, a gelded son of Frankel, boasts similar results to Andok, having won at Leicester and Carlisle before getting turned over on his final start, but is rated higher on 91.

"Things didn't go right for him in a Listed race at the St Leger meeting," Fahey says. "We've gelded him over the winter."

The three-year-old **Marie Of Lyon** receives a favourable mention. "She's a filly we like, and I think she's well handicapped on 88 if she can put it all together," Fahey says.

Temerity, a winner at Ayr in July, also possesses a good deal of ability. "On pedigree she could progress," Fahey says.

It's a team rich in quality, strong in overall depth and, as ever, Fahey can be relied upon to get the very best out of them.

SUPER STATS

Fahey's southern raids enjoy most success at Epsom (13-85, 15%, +26.88pt) and Windsor (8-37, 22%, +29.50pt)

Over the past five seasons, Fahey's three-year-olds have returned the best level-stake profits over distances of 1m3f to 1m4f (17-128, 13%, +29.46pt) but last year they did best over distances from 7f to 1m (39-243, 16%, +61.88pt)

It's always worth noting when Fahey drops one into either a seller (25-88, 28%, +12.53pt) or a claimer (21-101, 21%, +24.43pt)

Fahey knows how to place his juveniles in handicaps – his runners in nurseries provide a handsome profit (69-436, 16%, +60.58pt)

Tony Hamilton rode most winners for the yard last term, followed by apprentice Adam McNamara but better returns were provided by the mounts of David Nolan (20-143, 14%, +0.17pt) and Patrick Mathers (14-117, 12%, +15.25pt)

The rides of Paul Hanagan have returned a profit over the past five seasons (80-501, 16%, +38.68pt). He'll be riding plenty of winners now he's stable jockey once again

June is often a strong month for Fahey. He returned plenty of winners and a sizeable level-stake profit for the month in 2014 (32-218, 15%, +40.43pt) and last year (35-220, 16%, +25.23pt)

Confidence behind Jack Hobbs shining on the world stage

JOHN GOSDEN **might not have any obvious candidates for the Classics this year according to the early ante-post lists but the same could be said in the spring of 2015 before Golden Horn went on to win the Epsom Derby, Coral Eclipse and Prix de l'Arc de Triomphe to hand the Clarehaven handler his second trainers' title.**

As ever, there is a mix of the new and old at the Bury Road establishment in Newmarket with the likes of **Jack Hobbs** carrying the torch for the senior brigade much as he did 12 months ago before the wheels came off on his reappearance in the Group 2 Jockey Club Stakes at Newmarket, *writes David Milnes.*

Nursed back to health following a hip fracture that day, the previous year's Irish Derby winner looked right back to his best when finishing third on his most recent appearance in the Group 1 Champion Stakes at Ascot in October.

Jack Hobbs has long been pencilled in to start off 2017 in the Group 1 Dubai Sheema Classic at Meydan at the end of March, and a clear run through the rest of the year would see him prove a major force in the top middle-distance contests around the world.

Gosden says: "Jack Hobbs had an interrupted campaign last year but ran very well in his one race in the autumn. He's in good order now and we're looking towards the Sheema Classic and then races like the King George at Ascot in the summer."

Another five-year-old still around is the admirable mare **Journey**, who is owned by one of Gosden's oldest supporters George Strawbridge.

When last seen, the daughter of Dubawi went one better than the previous season by landing her first Group 1 in the Champion Fillies & Mares Stakes at Ascot in October – and she could have a similar programme this time around.

Her trainer says: "Journey finished last year very well when winning at Newmarket and Ascot and has come through the winter in good shape. She'll be pointed at the mile-and-a-quarter and mile-and-a-half races and will take on fillies and colts this year. She does particularly well in the autumn when there's some give in the ground."

Another female who could be in for a big year is one-time Oaks fancy **So Mi Dar**, who was forced to miss the Epsom Classic last season with a foot problem but returned in the autumn to win a Listed contest at Yarmouth and may have been unlucky when third in the Group 1 Prix de l'Opera at Chantilly on her only subsequent start.

'So Mi Dar ran well in the autumn. She seems in good order and we'll be looking to races like the Group 2 Middleton Stakes at York'

The four-year-old could be set to make her reappearance at York in May where she won the Group 3 Musidora Stakes last year.

Gosden says: "So Mi Dar ran well in the autumn although she didn't get a smooth passage when third on Arc day in France. She seems in good order and we'll be looking to races like the Group 2 Middleton Stakes at York with her. I think a mile and a quarter is perfect for her at this stage and we'll think about going further later."

Another filly on a sharp upward curve last summer was **Persuasive**. She won five races on the spin, including the Listed

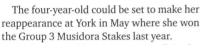

Gosden sent out a personal best of 141 winners last season, striking at 23% and returning a level-stake profit of +2.14pt

Sandringham Handicap at Royal Ascot and the Group 3 Atalanta Stakes at Sandown until meeting her match at Group 1 level at Leopardstown on her final start.

Her trainer says: "Persuasive finished the year very well when second to Alice Springs in the Matron Stakes. We'll look at the top mile races for her. Another one to mention in this bracket is **Nathra**, who has also wintered very well. Both fillies will be aimed towards the Group 2 Duke of Cambridge Stakes at Royal Ascot."

Patient approach could pay off

Of the four-year-old colts, **Royal Artillery** does not have many miles on the clock and could be a big player over a mile and a quarter this year. The son of War Front is built to improve with age but was no mug at three when he won the Group 3 Rose of Lancaster Stakes at Haydock before finishing an honourable third to Almanzor in a Deauville Group 2.

Gosden says: "Royal Artillery's last two runs were his best, particularly when finishing third to a Prix du Jockey Club winner who then went on to win the Champion Stakes in Britain and Ireland. He's a very big horse and we've given him plenty of time. We might start him somewhere like Sandown in the Group 3 Gordon Richards."

Unlike 2015, the yard did not manage a Classic success last season, although many thought Gosden had his best chance in the St Leger with **Muntahaa** until he refused to settle and ran out of gas in the straight to finish fourth to Harbour Law.

The grey wore a hood all last year and looks sure to test the strength of owner Hamdan Al Maktoum's new jockey Jim Crowley.

The trainer says: "Muntahaa was very progressive last year when he didn't have a bundle of luck in running in the King Edward VII Stakes at Royal Ascot, and he's better than he showed in the Leger when he ran too free. We'll look to start him back in the Group 3 John Porter Stakes at Newbury in April."

DID YOU KNOW?

John Gosden is the son of Towser Gosden, who was a prominent trainer in that previously mighty training base of Lewes in East Sussex. Gosden snr had to weather the Great Depression and the second world war in his time as a trainer. However, he still managed to train some great horses in his time, including Derby winner Charlottown as a juvenile and Aggressor, who won the King George VI & Queen Elizabeth Stakes in 1960.

JOHN GOSDEN
NEWMARKET, SUFFOLK

	No. of Hrs	Races Run	1st	2nd	3rd	Unpl	Per cent	£1 Level Stake
2-y-o	94	203	53	29	27	94	26.1	+28.34
3-y-o	92	314	75	64	37	138	23.9	-17.76
4-y-o+	25	96	13	14	14	55	13.5	-8.44
Totals	**211**	**613**	**141**	**107**	**78**	**287**	**23.0**	**+2.14**
2015	*191*	*577*	*133*	*101*	*76*	*266*	*23.1*	*+2.29*
2014	*195*	*613*	*132*	*93*	*81*	*305*	*21.5*	*+22.70*

BY MONTH

2-y-o	W-R	Per cent	£1 Level Stake	3-y-o	W-R	Per cent	£1 Level Stake
January	0-0	0.0	0.00	January	4-14	28.6	-3.09
February	0-0	0.0	0.00	February	0-6	0.0	-6.00
March	0-0	0.0	0.00	March	2-6	33.3	+0.20
April	0-0	0.0	0.00	April	14-53	26.4	-2.84
May	1-8	12.5	-3.50	May	11-56	19.6	-19.16
June	4-21	19.0	+8.42	June	8-56	14.3	-28.52
July	6-21	28.6	-1.52	July	10-39	25.6	+23.61
August	3-12	25.0	-5.70	August	12-29	41.4	+19.29
September	7-32	21.9	-5.90	September	5-24	20.8	-1.98
October	17-53	32.1	+40.42	October	8-26	30.8	+3.22
November	9-39	23.1	-5.13	November	1-5	20.0	-2.50
December	6-17	35.3	+1.25	December	0-0	0.0	0.00

4-y-o+	W-R	Per cent	£1 Level Stake	Totals	W-R	Per cent	£1 Level Stake
January	1-3	33.3	-0.90	January	5-17	29.4	-3.99
February	1-5	20.0	0.00	February	1-11	9.1	-6.00
March	0-2	0.0	-2.00	March	2-8	25.0	-1.80
April	2-8	25.0	-0.17	April	16-61	26.2	-3.01
May	2-15	13.3	+4.00	May	14-79	17.7	-18.66
June	0-12	0.0	-12.00	June	12-89	13.5	-32.10
July	2-15	13.3	0.00	July	18-75	24.0	+22.09
August	1-4	25.0	+8.00	August	16-45	35.6	+21.59
September	2-13	15.4	+6.38	September	14-69	20.3	-1.50
October	1-14	7.1	-9.00	October	26-93	28.0	+34.64
November	1-5	20.0	-2.75	November	11-49	22.4	-5.25
December	0-0	0.0	0.00	December	6-17	35.3	0.00

DISTANCE

2-y-o	W-R	Per cent	£1 Level Stake	3-y-o	W-R	Per cent	£1 Level Stake
5f-6f	13-44	29.5	+17.69	5f-6f	6-22	27.3	-1.88
7f-8f	34-138	24.6	+12.90	7f-8f	31-120	25.8	+12.48
9f-13f	6-21	28.6	-2.26	9f-13f	37-168	22.0	-29.37
14f+	0-0	0.0	0.00	14f+	1-4	25.0	+1.00

4-y-o	W-R	Per cent	£1 Level Stake	Totals	W-R	Per cent	£1 Level Stake
5f-6f	0-7	0.0	-7.00	5f-6f	19-73	26.0	+8.81
7f-8f	3-24	12.5	+8.50	7f-8f	68-282	24.1	+33.88
9f-13f	9-54	16.7	-4.44	9f-13f	52-243	21.4	-36.07
14f+	1-11	9.1	-5.50	14f+	2-15	13.3	-4.50

TYPE OF RACE

Non-Handicaps	W-R	Per cent	£1 Level Stake	Handicaps	W-R	Per cent	£1 Level Stake
2-y-o	50-189	26.5	+32.43	2-y-o	3-14	21.4	-4.09
3-y-o	52-216	24.1	-44.79	3-y-o	23-98	23.5	+27.03
4-y-o+	11-82	13.4	+16.00	4-y-o+	2-14	14.3	+12.50

RACE CLASS / FIRST TIME OUT

	W-R	Per cent	£1 Level Stake		W-R	Per cent	£1 Level Stake
Class 1	23-150	15.3	-26.49	2-y-o	21-94	22.3	+8.46
Class 2	10-45	22.2	-3.75	3-y-o	23-92	25.0	-15.27
Class 3	15-49	30.6	+31.03	4-y-o+	5-25	20.0	+18.93
Class 4	34-141	24.1	+34.05				
Class 5	58-223	26.0	-31.46	Totals	49-211	23.2	+12.12
Class 6	1-5	20.0	-1.25				
Class 7	0-0	0.0	0.00				

Gosden's highest returns over the last five years have come at Haydock (30%, +36.62pt) and Newmarket's July course (20%, +37.46pt)

So Mi Dar: likely to be heading back to York for the Middleton Stakes

Ardad (2): could have Royal Ascot's King's Stand Stakes on his agenda

As he was unraced as a youngster, **Wings Of Desire** should have plenty more to give after his fourth to Harzand in the Epsom Derby and subsequent second to Highland Reel in the King George.

Gosden says: "Wings Of Desire is in good order and we plan to start him off over a mile and a quarter this season. We think he stays a mile and a half but his best form is at shorter."

Classic candidates

There are a host of hopefuls on the fringe of the Classic picture at Clarehaven this year, including a mix of once-raced winners and unexposed types who are likely to progress.

If Gosden has a 2,000 Guineas hope it still could be the Frankel colt **Seven Heavens** despite his flop when finishing last of seven to Churchill in the Group 1 Dewhurst Stakes at Newmarket on his final start in October.

Unbeaten in two races before that, Seven Heavens will need to settle better if he is going to turn the tables on Aidan O'Brien's ante-post favourite for the first Classic.

Gosden says: "Seven Heavens was too keen for his own good in the Dewhurst but if he learns to settle better he remains promising. We might start him in the Listed Free Handicap at the Craven meeting."

Dreamfield has an entry in the 2,000 Guineas but could be in line for a crack at the Group 1 Commonwealth Cup at Royal Ascot, a race Gosden had hoped to win with the injury-hit Shalaa a year ago.

The trainer says: "Dreamfield was unbeaten in two last year and it will be interesting to see what trip he wants this year – his sire Oasis Dream screams six furlongs while his dam says further."

Another Frankel colt of interest is **Cracksman**, who ran out a handsome winner of his only start in October at Newmarket. Gosden says: "He won in decent style for a horse who was very unfurnished. He's done well through the winter and could start in the Group 3 Craven Stakes or Listed Feilden Stakes at Newmarket."

In the same bracket is a son of Giant's Causeway named **Utmost**, who won over

seven furlongs at Leicester at the backend. "He's a big rangy horse whose form has worked out nicely, and we also could be looking at the Craven or Feilden with him," says Gosden.

"Also with this profile is **Chessman**, who won his only start on the all-weather. We could run him in the three-year-old-only handicap on the Friday of the Greenham meeting at Newbury."

Ardad is at the other end of the stamina scale but could be in line for an early return to Royal Ascot where he prospered a year ago.

He was the yard's first two-year-old winner last season and went on to land the Listed Windsor Castle Stakes before scooping the Group 2 Flying Childers Stakes at Doncaster in September.

Gosden says: "Ardad had a grand season last year and was the last one off the bridle in the Prix de l'Abbaye on his final start. There's a Group 2 for three-year-olds only at York we could look at, and then we could point him at the Group 1 King's Stand."

Also in the Classic generation, but over longer distances, Gosden is not short of ammunition, and says: "**Monarchs Glen** is a likeable fellow who won his second start. We could see him starting out in something like the Group 3 Classic Trial at Sandown. **Glencadam Glory** is just starting back and, as he has a mark of 86, we might start him off in handicaps. The same applies to **Middle Kingdom**, who won nicely on the all-weather at Newcastle before Christmas."

High hopes for Coronet

Of the fillies, top of the pile of the Epsom Oaks hopes is **Coronet**, who was unbeaten in two starts last year, most recently when overcoming stablemate Cunco in the Listed Zetland Stakes at Newmarket in October. Coronet is 12-1 with most firms to give Gosden his second Oaks win after Taghrooda in 2014.

The trainer says: "She won her maiden and her Listed race very well and will be pointed at the Group 3 Musidora Stakes at York, although she'll have an entry in the Group 1

Prix Saint-Alary in France at the same time.

"We'll start her at a mile and a quarter but at the same time we'd have no fear about going a mile and a half."

Dabyah wintered well

It is a long time since Gosden won the 1,000 Guineas, but if he has a candidate this year it may well be **Dabyah**, who was last seen finishing third in the Group 1 Prix Marcel Boussac.

Of the filly, who is a general 12-1 chance, Gosden says: "Dabyah has done well through the winter and we'd be looking to start her in the Group 3 Dubai Duty Free Stakes at Newbury where she won a conditions event last year."

Other females of note include Newmarket maiden winner **Astronomy's Choice**, who has an Irish Oaks entry but could yet be campaigned over shorter.

Her trainer says: "She's a nice filly who won well at Newmarket. We could go to the Listed Pretty Polly Stakes with her or start her off over shorter."

Gosden has some other names to remember, and says: "We also have **Icespire**, a powerful filly by Frankel who won her maiden at Salisbury. Another in this bracket is **Shutter Speed**, who won nicely at Yarmouth in October. She's grand but there are mixed messages from her pedigree so we may start her off over a mile or a mile and a quarter."

The trainer also makes mention of two recent all-weather winners it could pay to follow this summer, adding: "**Daban** and **Precious Ramotswe** are fillies we like and both have reasonable handicap marks to start off with."

Dabyah: likely starting point is the Dubai Duty Free at Newbury

SUPER STATS

Rare visits to Catterick (2-3, 67%, +1.58pt) and Chepstow (3-6, 50%, +0.30pt) are worth watching for

Gosden's juveniles are best followed at Haydock (10-27, 37%, +11.37pt) and Nottingham (9-39, 23%, +11.81pt). Three-year-olds can be backed with confidence at Newmarket (July) (19-92, 21%, +21.68pt) and Salisbury (6-24, 25%, +23.67pt). Older horses do well at Sandown (5-19, 26%, +11.25pt)

Last season, Gosden's juveniles did particularly well at Doncaster (5-11, 45%, +11.25pt) while his three-year-olds excelled on Kempton's Polytrack (8-19, 42%, +21.10pt)

The mounts of Robert Havlin gave an excellent return last season (55-211, 26%, +48.38pt) while those ridden by Tom Queally also posted attractive figures (5-11, 45%, +6.41pt)

Juveniles are best backed over sprint trips (5f-6f) (30-129, 23%, +13.29pt) while those aged three and older can be backed blind over trips in excess of 1m3f (112-439, 26%, +66.82pt)

Juveniles can be backed with confidence in maidens (126-566, 22%, +12.14pt) while two- (7-26, 27%, +7.41pt) and three-year-olds (25-115, 22%, +6.09pt) return level-stake profits. Older horses do best in handicaps (25-101, 25%, +42.18pt)

Ladbrokes

BEST ODDS GUARANTEED

Available in-shop for 2 hours each day

THE LOWDOWN WILLIAM HAGGAS

Rivet leads way for yard big on numbers and high on quality recruits

I **N 2016 William Haggas had more runners and more winners than ever before. He embarks on the 2017 turf campaign with his Somerville Lodge Stables boasting his biggest string yet – and perhaps also more quality.**

The super-shrewd Haggas recorded a total of 201 horses in Raceform's *Horses In Training*, making his yard officially the strongest numerically in Newmarket. He insists that is not the case but he does not dispute the high hopes held for his bumper squad.

"I have some very nice horses this year," he says. "I like the look of them and they seem healthy, but I said that at the same time last year and three weeks later they couldn't do a thing."

Assuming no such setbacks are suffered, Haggas has every reason to be hopeful, not least with his 2016 Group 1 hero **Rivet**, who sandwiched a below-par effort in the Dewhurst Stakes with two major wins at Doncaster, first in the Champagne Stakes and then the Racing Post Trophy.

With Coolmore and Lester Piggott among Rivet's owners, it is no surprise significant targets are on the Fastnet Rock colt's agenda.

"He'll be trained with Classic races in mind

and I think he has every chance of being competitive," says Haggas.

"I'd like to have a prep with him, either in the Greenham – although I'm loath to go back to seven furlongs – or possibly the new race at Newcastle on Good Friday. It's obviously a contest designed to attract him and other Group 1 winners, as he would be unpenalised, and the track and trip would suit.

"Winning it wouldn't do anything for his future value, but it would be an opportunity to get a start into him before a bigger race, so it's very much on my radar.

"After that I'd like to run him in a Guineas. As for the Derby, his brother, who is our only guide, is trained in Hong Kong by John Moore, who feels he'll get 1m4f standing on his head."

Classics, or certainly Classic trials, are also being considered for National Stakes third Lockheed and Derby entry Across Dubai, a pleasing winner on his debut at Lingfield in October.

"**Lockheed** ran well in the National Stakes but then not so well at Newmarket, although I don't think he liked the track," says Haggas. "He could be a Guineas outsider here or a German Guineas type. I also think he'll get 1m2f.

"Pat Cosgrave liked **Across Dubai** when he won first time out. He wants fast ground and a minimum of 1m2f. He'll go for one of

'He'll be trained with Classic races in mind and I think he has every chance of being competitive. A trial first is very much on my radar'

the Classic trials, possibly the Dee Stakes."

The yard's three-year-old fillies are headed by an exciting new recruit, the Tsui-family owned Sea Of Grace, who posted a Group 3 victory for her former trainer John Oxx at the Curragh in August. She holds a prominent position in the Qipco 1,000 Guineas market, for which an entry is also held by Radley Stakes winner Cristal Fizz.

Not entered for the Rowley Mile Classic, but clearly smart, are Radley runner-up Glitter Girl and Sandown Listed winner On Her Toes.

"**Sea Of Grace** is a filly I like," says

....

Haggas set a personal best in terms of total winners last year with 137 winners on the board. He also broke the £2 million prize-money barrier for the third season in a row

Haggas. "The aim is to run her in the Nell Gwyn and then the Guineas.

"**Cristal Fizz** did well to beat Glitter Girl in the Radley as she's inexperienced and she looked like she wanted a mile. I'd think she'll run in a Guineas of some description."

Haggas adds: "**Glitter Girl** (*below*) will go for the Fred Darling. She doesn't mind cut in the ground and gets the trip well. She is also very useful and genuine.

"**On Her Toes** didn't run after the Sweet Solera but she has done well and will be out early, probably in the Nell Gwyn or Fred Darling. I see her as a Sandringham filly."

Smart sprinter can bounce back

Already on something of a retrieval mission is **Mubtasim**, who failed to meet expectations in two major Group events, either side of a valuable sales race success at Doncaster.

"Mubtasim is a good sprinter who has done well over the winter," says Haggas.

"The disappointment was that every time I raised him in class he didn't deliver, but I think he had genuine excuses in the Gimcrack and Middle Park.

"I think he'll start off in something like the Carnarvon Stakes at Newbury. That said, my feeling is he's better on top of the ground, so if we happen to have a dry period he could come out sooner than that in the Pavilion at Ascot."

WILLIAM HAGGAS
NEWMARKET, SUFFOLK

	No. of Hrs	Races Run	1st	2nd	3rd	Unpl	Per cent	£1 Level Stake
2-y-o	58	183	40	36	18	89	21.9	-36.44
3-y-o	79	327	81	64	57	125	24.8	-61.60
4-y-o+	19	86	16	7	14	49	18.6	+19.25
Totals	156	596	137	107	89	263	23.0	-78.79
2015	144	533	113	86	50	282	21.2	-39.17
2014	138	520	113	68	72	267	21.7	+9.50

BY MONTH

2-y-o	W R	Per cent	£1 Level Stake
January	0-0	0.0	0.00
February	0-0	0.0	0.00
March	0-0	0.0	0.00
April	0-0	0.0	0.00
May	0-4	0.0	-4.00
June	2-11	18.2	-3.75
July	6-25	24.0	-9.89
August	6-28	21.4	-10.22
September	12-39	30.8	+18.95
October	8-47	17.0	-20.65
November	4-19	21.1	-2.00
December	2-10	20.0	-4.89

3-y-o	W-R	Per cent	£1 Level Stake
January	1-12	8.3	-10.80
February	0-0	0.0	0.00
March	2-5	40.0	+0.50
April	6-25	24.0	-10.36
May	9-44	20.5	-7.47
June	11-51	21.6	-10.72
July	13-62	21.0	-21.93
August	14-48	29.2	-10.41
September	21-54	38.9	+18.42
October	2-21	9.5	-10.50
November	2-4	50.0	+2.67
December	0-1	0.0	-1.00

4-y-o+	W-R	Per cent	£1 Level Stake
January	2-3	66.7	+11.00
February	0-3	0.0	-3.00
March	2-3	66.7	+7.75
April	1-5	20.0	0.00
May	1-12	8.3	0.00
June	2-9	22.2	-1.25
July	2-15	13.3	+6.50
August	0-10	0.0	-10.00
September	3-11	27.3	+5.50
October	3-12	25.0	+5.75
November	0-1	0.0	-1.00
December	0-2	0.0	-2.00

Totals	W-R	Per cent	£1 Level Stake
January	3-15	20.0	+0.20
February	0-3	0.0	-3.00
March	4-8	50.0	+8.25
April	7-30	23.3	-10.36
May	10-60	16.7	-11.47
June	15-71	21.1	-15.72
July	21-102	20.6	-25.32
August	20-86	23.3	-30.63
September	36-104	34.6	+42.87
October	13-80	16.3	-25.40
November	6-24	25.0	+1.67
December	2-13	15.4	-3.00

DISTANCE

2-y-o	W-R	Per cent	£1 Level Stake	3-y-o	W-R	Per cent	£1 Level Stake
5f-6f	19-101	18.8	-26.38	5f-6f	16-79	20.3	-23.63
7f-8f	21-81	25.9	-9.06	7f-8f	32-128	25.0	-25.58
9f-13f	0-1	0.0	-1.00	9f-13f	31-116	26.7	-15.14
14f+	0-0	0.0	0.00	14f+	2-4	50.0	+2.75

4-y-o	W-R	Per cent	£1 Level Stake	Totals	W-R	Per cent	£1 Level Stake
5f-6f	1-10	10.0	-4.00	5f-6f	36-190	18.9	-54.01
7f-8f	9-42	21.4	+0.50	7f-8f	62-251	24.7	-34.14
9f 13f	6-26	23.1	+30.75	9f-13f	37-143	25.9	+14.61
14f+	0-8	0.0	-8.00	14f+	2-12	16.7	-5.25

TYPE OF RACE

Non-Handicaps	W R	Per cent	£1 Level Stake	Handicaps	W-R	Per cent	£1 Level Stake
2-y-o	36-153	23.5	-20.85	2-y-o	4 30	13.3	-15.59
3-y-o	40-169	23.7	-55.50	3-y-o	41-158	25.9	-6.09
4-y-o+	7-33	21.2	+43.00	4-y-o+	9-53	17.0	+5.50

RACECLASS / FIRST TIME OUT

	W-R	Per cent	£1 Level Stake		W-R	Per cent	£1 Level Stake
Class 1	13-81	16.0	-14.43	2-y-o	6-58	10.3	-11.50
Class 2	12-70	17.1	-4.38	3-y-o	16-79	20.3	-25.41
Class 3	9-59	15.3	-11.67	4-y-o+	5-19	26.3	+9.25
Class 4	39-155	25.2	-7.85	Totals	27-156	17.3	-27.66
Class 5	59-209	28.2	-33.04				
Class 6	5-22	22.7	-6.43				
Class 7	0-0	0.0	0.00				

In the south, Haggas's inmates are best backed at Goodwood (17-67. 25%, +12.71pt), Sandown (16-58, 28%, +12.88pt) and Yarmouth (29-85, 34%, +21.12pt)

Another to have flopped in Pattern company is the Queen's four-runner Newmarket maiden winner **Seniority**, subsequently last of ten in the Solario Stakes.

"He won a weakish maiden and then ran badly on softish ground," says Haggas. "He wants top of the ground and will get a mile well. He's done well since you last saw him and isn't a bad horse."

Executive could be staying force

Nor is **Executive Force**, who beat only one home in the Horris Hill Stakes but had started favourite.

"After finishing second in a Dundalk Listed race he got stuck in the ground at Newbury," explains his trainer. "Personally, I think the fact the race came a bit quick after his trip to Ireland was more of a factor than the ground.

"I know he's by Sepoy, but he may well stay further, as there's bags of stamina on the damside and his half-sister Beautiful Romance has already won over 1m6f in Dubai this year. He may be one for the Hampton Court at Royal Ascot."

Like Executive Force's sibling, **Second Thought** has been active in 2017, scoring over 7f in Listed company at Lingfield in early March.

Haggas says: "The 6f final on All-Weather Championship Finals day will probably be his target, although it appeared 7f, and I suspect

even a mile, was within his capability last time.

"He's useful and possesses a turn of foot, which is so hard to find. He could possibly develop into a Jersey Stakes horse."

Among the other Somerville Lodge three-year-olds, **Pennsylvania Dutch** – who suffered a setback after winning on his debut at Haydock – is likely to go handicapping, while Newcastle backend winner **Mojito** is described as "a nice horse with bags of scope."

Two others to note are a dark filly and an even darker colt. **Dynamic** was a highly encouraging third in a Newbury maiden in October but picked up a winter injury that will rule her out until August.

"That's a shame, as I do think she's lovely," says Haggas. "She's one to look out for when she returns."

Yet to race is the Queen's Derby entry **Call To Mind**, a Galileo colt out of the high-class Memory.

Haggas says: "He's a brother to our good horse Recorder but very different to him, in that he's going to stay well. He's a lovely mover and he's got a good mind as well. I could see him becoming a nice horse over 1m2f and 1m4f."

Recorder, also owned by the Queen, has been absent since taking

Second Thought: could be heading to Lingfield on Good Friday

his record to two wins from three starts in the 2015 Acomb Stakes. He is one of many exciting older horses in the Haggas camp.

"He missed the whole of last year after picking up a problem at two, but he's back," says the royal trainer. "We've always planned to run him in the Lockinge. He's had a serious injury, and as a trainer you're always mindful of that, but he's been given plenty of time."

Mutakayyef still on the up

The Lockinge is also the plan for Haydock Group 3 victor **Hathal**. However, for stable star **Mutakayyef**, whose biggest triumph so far in Ascot's Group 2 Summer Mile was followed by excellent Group 1 thirds behind global superstars Postponed in the Juddmonte International and Tepin at Woodbine, all roads lead to Goodwood.

"He could easily be better again this year as, despite being six, he's been lightly raced and it's taken me five years to work out what makes him tick," says Haggas.

"I feel he's a fast ground miler and I'm keen to go for the Lockinge and Queen Anne after he's run in Dubai on World Cup night. However, both the Lockinge and Queen Anne are staged on straight tracks, whereas he loves racing a bit tight around a turning track, so my view is the Sussex Stakes will be his race."

An even more valuable and celebrated prize could await **Dal Harraild**, whose three-year-old season featured important wins in a hot Glorious Goodwood handicap and Newmarket's Listed Godolphin Stakes. The dream is he may conceivably become his stable's first runner in the Melbourne Cup.

"This is a lovely horse and one who could develop into a Cup performer in Australia," says Haggas. "He really improved last year and strikes me as perfect for Australia. I've never had a runner in the country but I've followed the sport there closely.

"To start with we'll need to feel our way a bit, but I do know he's much better on fast ground. What I don't know is how far he'll stay. However, we'll make entries everywhere as I think he's an exciting high-class horse with a bit of foot.

"I'd like to get him to Ascot, but whether he'll stay the Gold Cup trip, I'm not sure. I also don't see any reason why he couldn't be a Hardwicke horse."

Also bound for the royal meeting is this year's Meydan Group 1 third **Muffri'Ha**.

"I think she'll end up in the Duke of Cambridge as she likes a straight track and is probably better with a lead," notes Haggas, whose boxes are occupied by a number of interesting older sprinters, including last year's Greenham Stakes winner **Tasleet**.

More Group races on the radar

"This is definitely a Group horse," insists Haggas. "I think the Lennox will be right up his street. He wants to go right-handed over 6f or 7f. My job is to make him into a stallion as he'd be borderline at the moment.

An old favourite will be back for more action over the minimum trip this season, as Haggas reports: "**Muthmir** didn't have much of a break two winters ago because he was trained for Dubai, but he's had a good holiday this time and he's much better for it. He could have a good year but he's rubbish on anything but firm ground.

"**Gravity Flow** also wants fast ground. Her target is the Summer Stakes at York. She'll probably start at Nottingham in mid-May or maybe even Bath before that. She needs to improve again but did nothing but improve last year."

Established classy handicappers to watch out for include **Squats** – "one of those rare animals who runs a stone better at Ascot" – **Afjaan**, who will be trained for the Victoria Cup and then Royal Hunt Cup, and Stewards' Cup third **Raucous**. "He's been gelded since last year and that looks to have done him a lot of good," says Haggas.

Another name to remember is lightly raced four-year-old **Victory Bond**, a promising sixth in the Dante Stakes last May.

"He's useful and has a chance of doing well," says Haggas. "He's rated 100 but I think he's definitely a stakes horse. Whether we try to nick a handicap along the way, we'll see."

SUPER STATS

When Haggas runners are sent north they are best followed at Haydock (26-81, 32%, +25.26pt), but he maintains high strike-rates at Catterick (5-7, 71%, +1.89pt), Musselburgh (8-17, 47%, +19.16pt) and Redcar (11-21, 52%, +11.26pt)

The Haggas juveniles do best at Doncaster (9-29, 31%, +17.28pt) and York (11-42, 26%, +10.84pt) while older horses provide the best returns at Goodwood (5-16, 31%, +22.25pt)

Take note when he sends three-year-olds to Carlisle (6-13, 46%, +6.20pt), Pontefract 7-21, 33%, +5.79pt) and Redcar (8-15, 53%, +6.65pt)

Juveniles from the yard are best backed over distances ranging from 7f to a mile (70-348, 20%, +10.26pt), while three-year-olds come into their own at 1m3f-plus (44-152, 29%, +42.30pt)

Older Haggas horses can be backed blind in handicaps (43-214, 20%, +42.17pt)

September is often a good month for the Newmarket trainer, and that was certainly the case in 2016 when he sent out 36 winners from 104 runners (35%, +42.88pt)

Three riders stood out for the yard last year, with the mounts of Pat Cosgrave (57-218, 26%, +20.37pt), Ben Curtis (13-32, 41%, +14.23pt) and Frankie Dettori (12-28, 43%, +7.72pt) providing healthy level-stake profits

THE LOWDOWN RICHARD HANNON

They're queuing up to fill the boots of retired heavy-hitters

THE Group 1 stars were not busy lighting up Richard Hannon's yard last season, but 173 winners and nearly £3 million in prize-money shows he was still able to deliver handsomely on thinner ammunition.

Now a promising-looking bunch of two-year-olds and a pair of likely sorts for the 2,000 Guineas has the trainer, crowned champion in 2014, enthused about prospects for the coming campaign, *writes Mark Storey*.

The departure of Mehmas to stud after a smart two-year-old season which climaxed with success in the Richmond Stakes has left a hole widened by the retirement of Nations Alexander, a one-time 1,000 Guineas hope, and Group 1 winner Toormore.

St Leger runner-up Ventura Storm, who won the Group 1 Premio Jockey Club in Milan, is also no longer part of the roster having been bought to race in Australia.

But with the likes of Classic hopes **Larchmont Lad** and **Barney Roy** causing a ripple of excitement around Hannon's Wiltshire headquarters there are no worries about filling the void.

"We're looking for another champion," says Hannon. "We've got a bunch of two-year-olds we really like. They look a lot sharper group than last year and hopefully we can find one or two stars among them.

"I think we have two real nice Guineas horses. Whether they'll win a Guineas, I don't know, but hopefully they're good enough to be Group 1 horses."

Victory over Whitecliffsofdover in Newmarket's Group 3 Tattersalls Stakes, on his third and final start of the season, identified Larchmont Lad as a Classic contender, but Hannon is just as enthused by Barney Roy, who experienced a racecourse just once last season, winning a Haydock maiden convincingly in September.

"Barney Roy will probably go to the Greenham as it's just up the road," Hannon says. "He's run once and won very impressively. We always thought he was a really nice horse – the work he did before he ran was extremely impressive.

"He's only cantered this year but he does plenty. He's not keen but he's just very enthusiastic so doesn't need a lot more. I'm very hopeful he'll turn into a Guineas horse.

"Larchmont Lad will probably go to the Craven as he's already won on that track. He was unlucky not to win at Doncaster when he got to the front and got tired, but then he won a Group 3. He's been up there and done it at a high level and he doesn't have to find much more to prove himself a lively Guineas horse.

"I didn't think there was any need to run

'He's done exceptionally well over the winter, putting on a lot of weight. We can't wait to get going with him'

Hannon enjoyed a fruitful May last term (36-196, 18%, +68.61pt). It was a similar story during the same month in his debut season in 2014 (31-180, 17%, +40.64pt)

him in deep ground at the backend of the season when he had done plenty, and he's done exceptionally well over the winter, putting on a lot of weight. We can't wait to get going with him."

Instinct tells Hannon that his challenge for the first

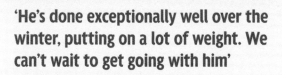

Classic of the season on May 6 could be strong.

"In years when you go into it with six to eight Guineas horses you ain't going to win the Guineas," he says. "But if you have one or two who stand out that far, which we seem to have this year, then I think you have more chance of winning it."

Promising type for fillies' Classic

The loss of Nations Alexander has diminished the Qipco 1,000 Guineas assault but Hannon is sweet on a daughter of Invincible Spirit who was beaten a neck by Kilmah in a Goodwood Group 3 on her third start.

He says: "We've got a nice filly called **Promising** who is still a maiden. She had a nice break over the winter and looks great. She's rated 100-odd and I'll probably start her off in a maiden somewhere and then look at the Guineas trials. I would say she would be my only one around that level. She looks like she's trained on."

Royal Ascot has already been pencilled in for Listed Epsom winner **Legendary Lunch**, whose best piece of juvenile form came when splitting Ardad and subsequent Middle Park winner The Last Lion in the Flying Childers. Hannon says: "We'll work back from the Commonwealth Cup. He'll probably go for the Pavilion Stakes at Ascot before."

Despite landing less prize-money in 2016

Legendary Lunch: Epsom winner is
likely to have Royal Ascot on his agenda

RICHARD HANNON
EAST EVERLEIGH, WILTS

	No. of Hrs	Races Run	1st	2nd	3rd	Unpl	Per cent	£1 Level Stake
2-y-o	153	622	87	93	83	357	14.0	-83.92
3-y-o	117	593	80	74	63	375	13.5	-11.50
4-y-o+	27	142	6	16	19	101	4.2	-108.50
Totals	297	1357	173	183	165	833	12.7	-203.92
2015	305	1382	195	178	172	834	14.1	-52.22
2014	303	1404	206	198	195	804	14.7	-82.35

BY MONTH

2-y-o	W-R	Per cent	£1 Level Stake	3-y-o	W-R	Per cent	£1 Level Stake
January	0-0	0.0	0.00	January	7-23	30.4	+13.82
February	0-0	0.0	0.00	February	2-17	11.8	-6.00
March	0-1	0.0	-1.00	March	1-12	8.3	-9.13
April	4-18	22.2	-9.31	April	8-73	11.0	-17.46
May	15-56	26.8	+17.08	May	20-118	16.9	+60.53
June	9-75	12.0	-28.63	June	11-97	11.3	-24.34
July	15-103	14.6	-13.50	July	15-91	16.5	+31.15
August	19-102	18.6	-4.40	August	5-56	8.9	-30.67
September	7-112	6.3	-64.25	September	2-50	4.0	-39.67
October	10-101	9.9	+9.00	October	6-34	17.6	+9.25
November	4-31	12.9	+16.00	November	3-10	30.0	+13.00
December	4-23	17.4	+4.08	December	0-12	0.0	-12.00

4-y-o+	W-R	Per cent	£1 Level Stake	Totals	W-R	Per cent	£1 Level Stake
January	1-5	20.0	0.00	January	8-28	28.6	+13.82
February	0-1	0.0	-1.00	February	2-18	11.1	-7.00
March	1-6	16.7	-1.50	March	2-19	10.5	-11.63
April	1-19	5.3	-14.50	April	13-110	11.8	-41.27
May	1-22	4.5	-9.00	May	36-196	18.4	+68.61
June	0-19	0.0	-19.00	June	20-191	10.5	-71.97
July	1-29	3.4	-27.00	July	31-223	13.9	-9.35
August	0-12	0.0	-12.00	August	24-170	14.1	-47.07
September	0-16	0.0	-16.00	September	9-178	5.1	-119.92
October	1-10	10.0	-5.50	October	17-145	11.7	+3.75
November	0-3	0.0	-3.00	November	7-44	15.9	+10.00
December	0-0	0.0	0.00	December	4-35	11.4	-12.00

DISTANCE

2-y-o	W-R	Per cent	£1 Level Stake	3-y-o	W-R	Per cent	£1 Level Stake
5f-6f	50-338	14.8	-62.24	5f-6f	16-139	11.5	-29.56
7f-8f	35-275	12.7	-20.18	7f-8f	41-294	13.9	+42.43
9f-13f	2-9	22.2	-1.50	9f-13f	21-157	13.4	-31.13
14f+	0-0	0.0	0.00	14f+	2-3	66.7	+6.75

4-y-o	W-R	Per cent	£1 Level Stake	Totals	W-R	Per cent	£1 Level Stake
5f-6f	1-35	2.9	-30.00	5f-6f	67-512	13.1	-121.80
7f-8f	3-67	4.5	-56.00	7f-8f	79-636	12.4	-33.75
9f-13f	2-40	5.0	-22.50	9f-13f	25-206	12.1	-55.13
14f+	0-0	0.0	0.00	14f+	2-3	66.7	+6.75

TYPE OF RACE

Non-Handicaps	W-R	Per cent	£1 Level Stake	Handicaps	W-R	Per cent	£1 Level Stake
2-y-o	74-482	15.4	-42.92	2-y-o	13-140	9.3	-41.00
3-y-o	29-185	15.7	-6.82	3-y-o	51-408	12.5	-4.00
4-y-o+	4-54	7.4	-31.00	4-y-o+	2-88	2.3	-70.50

RACECLASS / FIRST TIME OUT

RACECLASS	W-R	Per cent	£1 Level Stake	FIRST TIME OUT	W-R	Per cent	£1 Level Stake
Class 1	16-152	10.5	-41.38	2-y-o	17-153	11.1	+0.50
Class 2	11-142	7.7	-72.17	3-y-o	16-117	13.7	+9.49
Class 3	14-131	10.7	-35.29	4-y-o+	3-27	11.1	-13.00
Class 4	45-366	12.3	-76.54				
Class 5	68-443	15.3	+8.30	Totals	36-297	12.1	-3.01
Class 6	19-122	15.6	+14.15				
Class 7	0-1	0.0	-1.00				

Hannon utilises several jockeys throughout the year although Tom Marquand returned the best level-stake profit last year of those who rider regularly for him (26-209, 12%, +11.53pt)

DID YOU KNOW?

than during his first two years of training, in many ways Hannon proved his mettle last term by hammering in winners at all levels on lesser resources.

"It's always a good sign when you don't quite have the stars but you're still getting the winners," he says. "Stars are very hard to find and it's very easy when you've got them. You miss them when they're not there and you have to go to the other ranks and hope they can perform."

High hopes for Eqtiraan

One three-year-old Hannon hopes could be a moneyspinner is the Solario Stakes third **Eqtiraan**, who has been gelded.

He says about the son of Helmet: "I think the world of him, always have done. He could be anything and hopefully he'll win a few nice races through the year. He's not handicapped that badly so that might be an option.

"And I like a horse called **Majeste**, who's been working very well and is going to run in the Free Handicap. He was fourth in the Champagne Stakes when my horses weren't running well but he still did okay.

"**Giant's Treasure** is entered in the

Derby but hasn't run yet and has a long way to go before being a Derby horse. But he's one we might take to one of the nice maidens at Newmarket or Newbury.

Repton wasn't beaten far in the Vintage Stakes. I hope he'll be a black-type horse but he's got a way to go to prove that."

Nearly a third of Hannon's winners last season were on the all-weather and the trainer has decent expectations for one who ended his juvenile campaign with victory at the sixth attempt when tried beyond a mile for the first time at Wolverhampton.

He says: "I've got a very nice handicapper called **Whip Nae Nae**, who improved last year, winning a maiden on his last start. He's done very well – he's a big horse who's thrived over the winter. I'm pleased with him."

One of the most intriguing of Hannon's older crop is **Eltezam**, who has been sidelined since finishing little more than three lengths fourth to Shalaa in the 2015 July Stakes.

He says about the son of Kodiac: "He's a nice horse who was third in the Coventry two seasons ago. He had a year off with an injury and I can start him off in a conditions race."

Kool Lockinge aim

After a year in Australia with trainer Chris Waller the 2015 Craven winner **Kool Kompany** *(right)* returned to the yard last autumn with a neck second in a Listed contest at Salisbury. Hannon says: "He might start in a Group 2 at Sandown and then hopefully on to the Lockinge. It's good to have him back."

Tupi, also five, is winless since 2015 but glimmers of form and a drop to six furlongs have Hannon thinking there could be a decent prize in him. He says: "He's talented on his day. He's not been showing it but he's one who could easily bounce back."

No horse won more often for Hannon last season than the Team Wallop-owned **Oh This Is Us,** who scored five times, the pick being a £100,000 handicap at Goodwood over seven furlongs last May. Hannon says: "He ran well twice in Dubai over the winter and goes for the Lincoln on April 1 which could suit him. I'm looking forward to him."

Tabarrak has not been out of the first two in five career starts, twice beaten a neck, form that points to a profitable season for the four-year-old who was last seen winning an Ascot handicap last May.

"He had an easy end to last year," says Hannon. "He's very talented but has had one or two problems with his feet. He's back and moving very well.

"**Danehill Kodiac** and **Steel Of Madrid** are two very similar horses who I'm pleased with and will both be going for middle-distance races all year. Steel Of Madrid was a near-miss in a few nice races last season but will certainly win a few this year."

Humphrey Bogart, who is recovering from a tendon injury and not expected to be back until the summer, gave owners Chelsea Thoroughbreds a memorable day out at Epsom when finishing fifth in the Derby.

Hannon says: "**Tony Curtis** is another who's done well for the same owners. They have three very nice two-year-olds, an Acclamation, a Footstepsinthesand and a Camelot filly, to look forward to.

"We didn't sell Tony Curtis at the end of last year and he looks like he might be a bit stronger this year. He's won a Listed contest and run well in a Group 3 so hopefully he'll be bang there in those kinds of races."

Aiming to boost tally

Hannon is not shy about naming his target for 2017. "The aim would be to beat last year," he says. "We've got a lot of nice horses, nice two-year-olds, and there are some decent maidens from last year.

"Other than Mehmas and Larchmont Lad we probably struggled a bit with the two-year-olds last year. But we did all right with what you might say was a sub-standard crop. If we have a similar season with a few top-quality winners, it will be a very good year."

SUPER STATS

There aren't many tracks where Hannon regularly churns out a level-stake profit but rare visits north to Beverley (2-3, 67%, +2.17pt), Hamilton (1-2, 50%, +7.00pt), Redcar (4-13, 31%, +5.58pt) and Thirsk (3-5, 60%, +4.88pt) have been turning a profit

Hannon turns out no more than a steady flow on the all-weather but his best figures on the sand are at Southwell, where he has sent out seven winners from 28 runners (25%, +5.88pt)

Hannon juveniles are prolific on Newmarket's July course (26-140, 19%, +10.08pt). Three-year-olds do better on the Rowley Mile (18-98, 18%, +70.50pt) and at Doncaster (10-60, 17%, +29.98pt)

It's not easy to break down a specific distance over which Hannon's runners excel, but his three-year-olds boasted a solid record over trips ranging from 7f to a mile last year (42-303, 14%, +48.81pt)

The hint should be taken when Hannon drops one into selling company, a grade in which he has sent out 11 winners from 40 runners (28%, +19.20pt)

Timmy Murphy posted some solid figures for the yard from limited opportunities in 2016 (7-22, 32%, +16.67pt)

Don't expect fireworks early on but do watch for three exciting fillies

FROM the days of Double Trigger, the stamps of a Mark Johnston horse have been toughness and generosity under pressure. It would be difficult to find much contrast in that regard between the 1995 Gold Cup winner and last year's stable flagbearer, Middle Park winner The Last Lion, but extremely hard to draw any further similarities.

Johnston will start 2017 without The Last Lion, whom he described as among the best and toughest he has trained, after he was sent to stud in Ireland, *writes Keith Melrose*.

"We've been there before with horses who have gone to stud," says the trainer. "It's sad not to have him but at the same time that's life and we need to push on and find another like him."

It is the only attitude to be expected from Johnston, whose stoicism has been tested that little bit further by the retirement of two of last year's star three-year-old fillies, Fireglow and Lumiere.

The second-named in particular was a horse for which Johnston could not hide his admiration. "As a two-year-old she was fantastic," he says. "She was a bit in and out last year, but very good on the better days. She's gone to visit Dubawi."

It is his juveniles and three-year-old fillies Johnston hopes are to bring him the greatest joy this season but, as he explains, it would be unwise to expect the sort of explosive start we have seen in the last couple of seasons from his two-year-olds.

"Having done it two years in a row, there's an element of pressure to do it again," he says. "However, to put it into perspective, when we galloped our first two-year-olds recently we galloped 20 horses. On the first day we galloped two-year-olds last year we galloped 56.

"It's a massive difference," he adds. "We have far fewer horses for Darley, and Sheikh Hamdan Bin Mohammed is down from 60 two-year-olds to 23, and they've all come in later. So it's going to be very difficult to get the same number out early, but we won't be

A tally of 195 winners in 2016 was the first time Johnston had fallen short of the 200-winner mark since 2011, although he did break the £2.7 million prize-money barrier for the fourth consecutive season

'When we galloped our first two-year-olds recently we galloped 20 horses. On the first day last year we galloped 56 two-year-olds'

hanging back. It's worked so well for us the last two years."

There is one race, however, that remains symbolic of the early Johnston offensive and he does remain determined to keep up recent form.

"The programme is very different from the last two years with Easter being so late, and the Brocklesby is back to being the first two-year-old race," he says.

"We've won that the last two years, with The Last Lion last year, and we'll be looking for that elusive horse to win it again.

"I used to say I didn't really want to win the Brocklesby, as it's a funny race that the handicappers can end up rating very high, but then I doubt they got the winner high enough last year."

Johnston also offers guarded praise of the changes to the two-year-old programme rolled out last year, vastly increasing the number of novice stakes run.

"I found the novice stakes programme very good," he says. "The only problem I had with it is the penalty structure. I don't think any horse won more than two novice races on the trot. We're still a long way from the days of Provideo when two-year-olds could bring up a big sequence. I'd rather something like that than the reliance on handicaps we have, which punishes the best horses."

With The Last Lion retired, hopes for the Newmarket classics look to rest with a band of three fillies.

Classic aspirations

"We talk about Miss Infinity, Baileys Showgirl and Kilmah all in the one breath, as they're

all more or less identically rated and are all heading for Guineas trials and it'll be a juggle as to which one, or more, make it to Newmarket," says Johnston.

"**Kilmah** will possibly start off in the Nell Gwyn. I'd like to think she'll be better at a mile, and you can put a line through her last run at Doncaster because she got really upset in the stalls and we don't know why – she's never had stalls problems.

"She's rated 101 just now and that would make her an outsider for the Guineas, but take out her last run and she's a Group 3 winner on the way up and if she wins a trial I'd think that would earn her a place there."

Of **Miss Infinity**, he says: "She did her running over six and seven furlongs last year but will probably stay a bit further. She got her black type by winning a Listed race at Vichy and then went abroad again to Baden-Baden where she was second to Navarra King, who unfortunately died but at the time was seen as one of Germany's top two-year-olds. I thought she might have been a little unlucky – she was carried across the track – so that was a great run, as was her third in the Rockfel when she was sent off 25-1 outsider.

"If you run her in a Guineas straight off that then she's an outsider again, but she deserves to run in a trial to see if she's worth a shot."

He adds of **Baileys Showgirl**: "She ran abroad most of the time, so she might be easy to miss, but she won a Listed race at Chantilly and was placed in a couple of Group races, albeit she was below form in a Group 1 on her last start."

Among the colts there is unlikely to be a Johnston runner in the 2,000 Guineas, but Classics are not exactly off the table for their

Kilmah: could be heading to the 1,000 Guineas if she can win a Classic trial

representative from Frankel's first crop, **Frankuus**.

"There's a good claim about Frankuus," says Johnston. "He was the cheapest Frankel yearling sold in 2015 and he became the highest-rated Frankel colt!

"His last run in France was disappointing, but before that everything had gone right. He's rated 106 and there's an outside chance we'll keep him to a mile and go to the Guineas or the French Guineas, but it's more likely we'll start him off in a Derby trial and try to work him up to a mile and a half.

"He's not necessarily bred to stay that far – he's out of a Linamix mare and of course the jury's out about Frankel and how far his progeny will stay. Frankuus won over nine furlongs at Chantilly and it always looked to us like he'll stay, irrespective of the speed Frankel had."

Exceptional but frustrating

In general, the three-year-olds from Kingsley House start the season with boundless promise but something to prove after stuttering towards the end of their two-year-old campaigns.

The strongest example might be **Yalta**, whose Glorious Goodwood win was so impressive that he was put in the Nunthorpe.

"Yalta has been frustrating, but on the best of his form he's been exceptional," says Johnston. "He never quite did it again after Goodwood and we never really got to the

bottom of why, but if he can recover anything like that form he's a top-class sprinter.

"The form is solid because he had The Last Lion and Global Applause behind him – they met a couple of times and were well matched. Yalta didn't just beat them, he beat them by three lengths in a very fast time.

"We'll probably have the Commonwealth Cup as a first major target and work back from there to see if he's up to it."

There is a remarkably similar story to tell of **Bear Valley**: "We've agonised a lot about him over the winter. He looked exceptional at Goodwood, beating Montataire by four lengths. We took him to York very confident, but he flopped and beat only one horse in three starts after Goodwood.

"He's bred to stay, but his best form was over seven furlongs and he showed so much speed at Goodwood that I'm not sure about his best trip now. Above all, we need to get that form back."

Montataire is also trained by Johnston, who says: "He had quite a few runs last year, nine in all, but we think he might be a middle-

....

July is usually a strong month for Johnston. He returned a healthy level-stake profit for the month in 2014 (40-203, 20%, +25.44pt), 2015 (47-213, 22%, +36.10pt) and 2016 (38-233, 16%, +24.03pt)

MARK JOHNSTON
MIDDLEHAM MOOR, N YORKS

	No. of Hrs	Races Run	1st	2nd	3rd	Unpl	Per cent	£1 Level Stake
2-y-o	112	540	94	84	73	288	17.4	-56.45
3-y-o	96	614	71	93	74	376	11.6	-195.23
4-y-o+	29	259	30	28	29	172	11.6	-65.63
Totals	**237**	**1413**	**195**	**205**	**176**	**836**	**13.8**	**-317.31**
2015	*199*	*1208*	*204*	*167*	*148*	*689*	*16.9*	*-6.77*
2014	*212*	*1344*	*207*	*177*	*189*	*771*	*15.4*	*-65.32*

BY MONTH

2-y-o	W-R	Per cent	£1 Level Stake	3-y-o	W-R	Per cent	£1 Level Stake
January	0-0	0.0	0.00	January	5-23	21.7	-2.70
February	0-0	0.0	0.00	February	4-15	26.7	-4.40
March	3-3	100.0	+4.82	March	4-28	14.3	-18.45
April	3-24	12.5	-15.76	April	7-68	10.3	-42.24
May	11-52	21.2	+0.25	May	7-75	9.3	-38.79
June	23-74	31.1	+17.31	June	8-96	8.3	-48.04
July	15-84	17.9	-28.05	July	16-109	14.7	+42.58
August	12-82	14.6	-43.36	August	8-62	12.9	-36.94
September	10-67	14.9	+17.46	September	7-62	11.3	-10.00
October	10-82	12.2	+28.91	October	2-43	4.7	-17.00
November	5-41	12.2	-25.02	November	0-16	0.0	-16.00
December	2-31	6.5	-13.00	December	3-17	17.6	-3.25

4-y-o+	W-R	Per cent	£1 Level Stake	Totals	W-R	Per cent	£1 Level Stake
January	0-11	0.0	-11.00	January	5-34	14.7	-13.70
February	0-8	0.0	-8.00	February	4-23	17.4	-12.40
March	4-18	22.2	+3.00	March	11-49	22.4	-10.63
April	2-25	8.0	-18.13	April	12-117	10.3	-76.13
May	3-41	7.3	-24.17	May	21-168	12.5	-62.71
June	4-34	11.8	-2.50	June	35-204	17.2	-33.23
July	7-40	17.5	+9.50	July	38-233	16.3	+24.03
August	3-34	8.8	-18.59	August	23-178	12.9	-98.89
September	2-20	10.0	-11.75	September	19-149	12.8	-4.29
October	2-15	13.3	-1.50	October	14-140	10.0	+10.41
November	2-7	28.6	+8.50	November	7-64	10.9	-7.50
December	1-6	16.7	+9.00	December	6-54	11.1	+5.75

DISTANCE

2-y-o	W-R	Per cent	£1 Level Stake	3-y-o	W-R	Per cent	£1 Level Stake
5f-6f	52-290	17.9	-55.94	5f-6f	7-83	8.4	-60.26
7f-8f	39-231	16.9	+6.40	7f-8f	35-264	13.3	-36.62
9f-13f	3-19	15.8	-6.90	9f-13f	26-245	10.6	-92.85
14f+	0-0	0.0	0.00	14f+	3-22	13.6	-5.50

4-y-o	W-R	Per cent	£1 Level Stake	Totals	W-R	Per cent	£1 Level Stake
5f-6f	1-1	100.0	+3.33	5f-6f	60-374	16.0	-112.87
7f-8f	5-66	7.6	-45.13	7f-8f	79-561	14.1	-75.35
9f-13f	21-158	13.3	-7.84	9f-13f	50-422	11.8	-107.59
14f+	3-34	8.8	-16.00	14f+	6-56	10.7	-21.50

TYPE OF RACE

Non-Handicaps	W-R	Per cent	£1 Level Stake	Handicaps	W-R	Per cent	£1 Level Stake
2 y o	75-398	18.8	-77.66	2-y-o	19-142	13.4	+21.22
3-y-o	16-129	12.4	-71.47	3-y-o	55-485	11.3	-123.76
4-y-o+	3-32	9.4	-5.00	4-y-o+	27-227	11.9	-51.63

RACE CLASS

	W-R	Per cent	£1 Level Stake
Class 1	10-107	9.3	-35.47
Class 2	22-277	7.9	-90.97
Class 3	30-176	17.0	-13.17
Class 4	60-347	17.3	-48.51
Class 5	60-391	15.3	-75.72
Class 6	13-113	11.5	-50.46
Class 7	0-2	0.0	-2.00

FIRST TIME OUT

	W-R	Per cent	£1 Level Stake
2-y-o	19-112	17.0	-23.47
3-y-o	12-96	12.5	-41.70
4-y-o+	2-29	6.9	-19.50
Totals	33-237	13.9	-84.67

Of Johnston's riders, Adam Kirby has posted the best stats since 2013 (23-101, 23%, +16.15pt) although the most impressive haul last year was that of PJ McDonald (10-61, 16%, +21.25pt)

Yalta: form tailed off after his stunning Goodwood win, but he could yet prove a potent force in the sprinting division

distance horse and we hope stepping up in trip might be the key to him. There are no specific targets, but he was a Listed winner on his best run at Salisbury last season and so we're probably looking at Pattern races."

The buffer zone between Pattern races and handicaps will also be the starting point for a whole host of other Johnston charges, whose depth below the very top level is always impressive.

"**Permian** ended the season on something near to a high, finishing third in a Listed race at Newmarket," says Johnston. "That was over a mile and a quarter and he'll stay further this year. His rating is 100, which for a three-year-old puts him right in the gap. We'll be entering him and the others like him in handicaps and stakes races and seeing how these races look.

"**Comedy School** will be out early in the season. She was another who came along nicely in the autumn, but finished with a poor run. I thought the ground was appalling at Doncaster that day, so maybe that's a run to forgive. You'd imagine she'll be best at six or seven furlongs."

"**Rusumaat** went away for a break in the winter. He'll be stepping up to seven furlongs, which we've more or less agreed with Angus Gold, maybe even a mile. We'd like to think he'll be better over further. He's rated 93 and so we'll try him in some good handicaps."

Johnston also nominates **Sutter County**, one of his earliest two-year-old winners last year who has been active on the all-weather during the winter as one who might yet make the jump up.

Sky is still the limit

Talk eventually turns, however, to a long-absent three-year-old Johnston still harbours high hopes for. "**Love Dreams** has been very frustrating," he says. "We thought a huge amount of him – he's a magnificent, grand-looking horse and we'd have had him up there as among our best two-year-olds. He won his first two and was declared for the July Stakes, but he was pulled out lame with a problem just below his knee.

"We thought it was a foot abscess at first as there was nothing to see, but he's been off the track with the same problem ever since. He's not even back cantering as we speak, so I don't know when we'll start him back. It wouldn't be before May, but the main thing is to get him back fit and well. I thought he was heading for the top and I hope he still is.

"He's got a mark of 91 and we weren't thinking much about handicaps at the time, but once you've got a handicap mark I'm loath to give it away, so it's another option that's open to us."

Unexposed and full of potential

Johnston also picked out a few three-year-olds who, though yet to make a real splash, have the profile to make up into the good handicappers that his yard produces seemingly at will.

"I'll be getting a lot of those sorts of horses out as soon as there are races for them on the turf. That's a good time to get them started," he says.

"**Time To Study** is one who might be interesting. We got held up with him, through no fault of our own. He won at Carlisle in September, but the handicapper wouldn't give him a rating and so we had nowhere to run him until November. He's a Motivator and has won over ten furlongs already, so he'll be one for middle-distances and might end up good enough for something like a King George V Handicap.

"**Mister Manduro** has had just three starts and has been improving. He's rated 85 and could end up as a nice middle-distance handicapper. **Makkaar** is a nice handicapper to look forward to, while **Masham Star** has done well at Meydan and won at Newcastle on his last start in Britain. He's a top-class handicapper and could end up higher."

Old favourites back for more

Johnston also has more old favourites than most running in the best handicaps and many of them will be back again this season.

Fire Fighting has not had an all-weather or Dubai campaign, but will return. "He's been on the go such a long time – it's been so long by his standards since he ran!" says Johnston.

"He'll be back for the turf and it'll be more of the same. He's virtually out of even top handicaps now off 112, so there'll be some conditions races and Group 3s for him as well. He's won Listed races but he tends to come unstuck in Group company, to date at least. You'd think rated 112 that he'd be up to winning a Group 3 if everything falls right."

Oriental Fox will also be back for more: "He's been brilliant in these big handicaps and I'm sure it'll be a similar sort of route again. He'll probably go to the Queen Alexandra and if he keeps showing he can do it we'll keep trying in good races. He starts the year on a mark of 103, 6lb below his peak, so he's no forlorn hope."

There is also **Yorkidding**, who progressed through the ranks last season. "She's very well bred and you could argue on what she's done that she might have been off to stud by now," says Johnston.

"But she was the first horse her owner had and he's keen to keep going with the one who's given him the most fun. We sent her abroad a couple of times in search of some black type and she got it in a Listed race at Baden-Baden, when the trip was probably too sharp for her. We'll come back looking at some big handicaps and for some big black type."

Oriental Fox: nine-year-old will be back to ply his trade in valuable handicap company

SUPER STATS

Goodwood is one of Johnston's favourite tracks and his runners on the Sussex Downs return a big level-stake profit (34-240, 14%, +53.38pt). Only his runners at Yarmouth boast a comparable figure during the same time frame (12-60, 20%, +56.08pt)

Johnston juveniles do well at Hamilton (16-57, 28%, +18.11pt) and Musselburgh (16-69, 23%, +10.21pt). Goodwood aside, three-year-olds do best on Newmarket's July course (21-99, 21%, +45.68pt), Haydock (14-92, 15%, +28.08pt) and Ripon (16-90, 18%, +39.54pt). His older horses are best followed on the Rowley Mile (6-42, 14%, +53.35pt)

You have to go age specific at certain tracks to make the most of backing Johnston's string on the all-weather. Juveniles do best at Chelmsford (13-66, 20%, +2.80pt), three-year-olds are best followed at Southwell (17-76, 22%, +25.08pt) while his older horses can be backed blind at Wolverhampton (26-106, 25%, +20.05pt)

Unsurprisingly, it is in staying races where Johnston returns the best level-stake profits. His older horses running over trips of 1m5f-plus can be backed with confidence (34-217, 16%, +39.32pt)

Guineas ace ready to help talented trainer to another golden season

IT IS extremely rare for a trainer to gain a first Classic success within five years of starting up, but Hugo Palmer achieved exactly that with Galileo Gold in last season's 2,000 Guineas.

Indeed, Palmer has come a long way since Making Eyes gave him his first stakes winner in 2012, and there's every reason to think that his stable, based at Kremlin Cottage in Newmarket, will continue to flourish this season, *writes Tom Bull.*

An average strike rate of nearly 20 per cent is testament to how adept the trainer is at placing his horses and, with some proven Group performers as well as once-raced maiden winners, there is plenty to look forward to in the coming months.

As for his greatest achievement so far, Palmer will be aware that the form of the 2,000 Guineas won by **Galileo Gold** did not work out as well as might have been expected. However, the son of Paco Boy soon bolstered the view he was a miler out of the top drawer with a victory in the St James's Palace Stakes followed by a neck second in the Sussex Stakes.

Palmer says, "Galileo Gold is in great shape – he seems a much more settled, relaxed horse. It's a huge relief he's wintered well and at the moment all roads lead to the Lockinge."

"It doesn't take a genius to plan the route out for these top milers, and he'll be aimed at the Sussex Stakes again as well as the QEII and possibly the Prix Jacques le Marois."

Another Group winner from last year who has big-race targets is the Godolphin-owned **Best Of Days**. The three-year-old has won two of his three starts with his best performance when winning the Royal Lodge at the end of September. A 33-1 chance for the Derby, Palmer believes he might well have the attributes for Epsom.

"He's done extremely well over winter. He's much stronger and has just started pace work. Winning the Royal Lodge was a massive highlight, and, while that was over a mile, we think he's much more of a middle-distance type who will flourish in a test like the Derby.

"Although we might give him a Guineas entry, I'd imagine he'll start off at either York or Lingfield for one of the Derby trials. At this stage, he's got Epsom written all over him."

A colt Palmer thinks may have done well in the Derby had he been entered is **Crimean Tatar**. Now a four-year-old, the son of Sea The Stars has the right pedigree for stardom, and his trainer is mapping out an ambitious campaign for the unbeaten dual winner.

Palmer reveals: "Crimean Tatar is very exciting. There aren't many around who are rated 109 after just two starts and I'm of the

'He's done extremely well over winter. I'd imagine he'll start off at York or Lingfield in a Derby trial – at this stage he's got Epsom written all over him'

feeling that if I never win the Derby he might have been the one who got away. He gives the impression there's an awful lot more to come – I'm torn whether or not to go slowly with him or shoot for the stars. At the moment the plan is to start in the John Porter at Newbury before a possible tilt at the Hardwicke at Royal Ascot."

One horse who did contest a

....

Palmer set personal bests in 2015 in terms of winners (34) and prize-money (just over £1 million) but he more than doubled those figures last term with 71 winners and more than £2 million with his string returning a level-stake profit of +13.28pt

Classic at Epsom last season is **Architecture**, who finished second to Minding in the Oaks. Despite having earned over £200,000 in prize-money, it is hard to believe Palmer's filly has only a maiden success to her name, and winning a more valuable race appears to be the first port of call this season.

"Architecture has done very well since her maiden win but I'm conscious of the fact that's all she's accomplished. She needs to be a stakes winner for her breeding and I'm looking at a nice race at Goodwood on Guineas weekend before maybe something more prestigious like the Yorkshire Oaks."

First Classic still the plan

Escobar led ante-post lists for the 2,000 Guineas after an impressive win in the Listed Washington Singer at Newbury last August but disappointed in the Tattersalls Stakes and has not been seen since. However, Palmer

> Palmer sends out plenty of winners on the sand, returning level-stake profits at Chelmsford (11-44, 25%, +23.50pt), Newcastle (7-22, 32%, +6.28pt) and Wolverhampton (12-42, 29%, +22.15pt)

clearly still thinks the colt is good enough to compete at the highest level this year.

The trainer says: "Escobar was really promising but scoped slightly dirty after his run at Newmarket. However, I think the problem was more than that as he had three runs in quick succession and maybe that came too early in his career.

"A Guineas trial is a possibility for him – perhaps the Greenham at Newbury – but he'll probably head straight to the Classic without a prep. He grew up a lot over the winter and physically he looks like he could

DID YOU KNOW?

Hugo Palmer used to train for the Racing Post. Our adopted filly Born To Run ran five times for the master of Kremlin Cottage. Palmer has improved his winners' tally every season since 2012. His personal best of 71 in Britain last term included a 2,000 Guineas victory with Galileo Gold. And Kremlin Cottage has a knack of producing Classic winners. It was where Luca Cumani trained his two Epsom Derby colts from. How fitting then that Palmer's first Group winner, Aktabantay, was bred by Luca and Sara Cumani.

HUGO PALMER
NEWMARKET, SUFFOLK

	No. of Hrs	Races Run	1st	2nd	3rd	Unpl	Per cent	£1 Level Stake
2-y-o	58	174	33	33	25	82	19.0	-32.01
3-y-o	36	136	31	15	19	71	22.8	+49.49
4-y-o+	8	34	7	6	5	16	20.6	-4.20
Totals	**102**	**344**	**71**	**54**	**49**	**169**	**20.6**	**+13.28**
2015	*52*	*197*	*34*	*32*	*30*	*101*	*17.3*	*-20.00*
2014	*36*	*148*	*24*	*25*	*15*	*84*	*16.2*	*-2.00*

BY MONTH

2-y-o	W-R	Per cent	£1 Level Stake	3-y-o	W-R	Per cent	£1 Level Stake
January	0-0	0.0	0.00	January	1-6	16.7	+4.00
February	0-0	0.0	0.00	February	0-3	0.0	-3.00
March	0-0	0.0	0.00	March	1-6	16.7	-3.25
April	2-8	25.0	+2.25	April	6-19	31.6	+16.75
May	1-12	8.3	-8.25	May	3-18	16.7	+5.00
June	2-7	28.6	-3.69	June	2-20	10.0	-8.50
July	5-23	21.7	+8.83	July	5-21	23.8	-4.63
August	6-29	20.7	-4.77	August	3-7	42.9	+20.25
September	10-36	27.8	-3.98	September	6-15	40.0	+21.50
October	5-40	12.5	-15.90	October	2-15	13.3	-1.00
November	2-14	14.3	-1.50	November	1-4	25.0	+2.00
December	0-5	0.0	-5.00	December	1-2	50.0	+0.38

4-y-o+	W-R	Per cent	£1 Level Stake	Totals	W-R	Per cent	£1 Level Stake
January	0-0	0.0	0.00	January	1-6	16.7	+4.00
February	1-2	50.0	0.00	February	1-5	20.0	-3.00
March	0-2	0.0	-2.00	March	1-8	12.5	-5.25
April	1-4	25.0	-0.25	April	9-31	29.0	+18.75
May	2-8	25.0	-2.75	May	6-38	15.8	-6.00
June	1-2	50.0	+2.00	June	5-29	17.2	-10.19
July	0-5	0.0	-5.00	July	10-49	20.4	-0.80
August	1-5	20.0	-3.20	August	10-41	24.4	+12.28
September	0-2	0.0	-2.00	September	16-53	30.2	+15.52
October	1-4	25.0	+9.00	October	8-59	13.6	-7.90
November	0-0	0.0	0.00	November	3-18	16.7	+2.00
December	0-0	0.0	0.00	December	1-7	14.3	+0.38

DISTANCE

2-y-o	W-R	Per cent	£1 Level Stake	3-y-o	W-R	Per cent	£1 Level Stake
5f-6f	13-76	17.1	-33.51	5f-6f	3-12	25.0	+1.50
7f-8f	19-91	20.9	+6.12	7f-8f	10-56	17.9	+6.00
9f-13f	1-7	14.3	-4.63	9f-13f	16-64	25.0	+25.49
14f+	0-0	0.0	0.00	14f+	2-4	50.0	+16.50

4-y-o	W-R	Per cent	£1 Level Stake	Totals	W-R	Per cent	£1 Level Stake
5f-6f	0-0	0.0	0.00	5f-6f	16-88	18.2	-32.01
7f-8f	3-9	33.3	+2.00	7f-8f	32-156	20.5	+14.12
9f-13f	3-19	15.8	-13.20	9f-13f	20-90	22.2	+7.66
14f+	1-6	16.7	+7.00	14f+	3-10	30.0	+23.50

TYPE OF RACE

Non-Handicaps	W-R	Per cent	£1 Level Stake	Handicaps	W-R	Per cent	£1 Level Stake
2-y-o	31-149	20.8	-14.73	2-y-o	2-25	8.0	-17.27
3-y-o	13-67	19.4	+3.79	3-y-o	18-69	26.1	+45.70
4-y-o+	4-15	26.7	+22.00	4-y-o+	3-19	15.8	-11.20

RACE CLASS

	W-R	Per cent	£1 Level Stake
Class 1	10-60	16.7	+9.20
Class 2	7-36	19.4	+7.00
Class 3	7-31	22.6	+5.20
Class 4	18-90	20.0	+0.96
Class 5	27-116	23.3	-7.20
Class 6	2-11	18.2	-1.88
Class 7	0-0	0.0	0.00

FIRST TIME OUT

	W-R	Per cent	£1 Level Stake
2-y-o	11-58	19.0	+19.25
3-y-o	7-36	19.4	+1.92
4-y-o+	2-8	25.0	-2.25
Totals	20-102	19.6	+18.92

Escobar (second right): very highly regarded and could head straight to the 2,000 Guineas without a prep

be a Group 1 horse. I'd rather take the chance to see whether he is."

More to come from Master

A stalwart of Palmer's yard is the hardy and consistent **Gifted Master**. A run of five straight victories between 2015 and 2016 was the result of meticulous placing from his trainer and the gelding's resolute disposition. Unsurprisingly, he is a stable favourite. As far as his targets for this season are concerned, Palmer wants his four-year-old to build on an unspectacular seasonal debut in Dubai.

"Gifted Master will take a little bit of thought as his comeback run in a Group 2 in Dubai was satisfactory without being thrilling. He's due to run again on dirt on World Cup night and if gets in the Godolphin Mile we'll have a crack at that.

"Unfortunately, every time we've run in a Group 2 we've been beaten about four lengths and consequently as the season progresses we might think about going to North America. He's very versatile as he can go over seven furlongs or a mile on a variety of different grounds."

Another who is almost top level over seven furlongs and still could be is **Home Of The Brave**.

Every time the son of Starspangledbanner has ventured into Group 1 company he has been slightly disappointing, but the manner in which he won the John of Gaunt Stakes and finished a close second in the Group 2 Lennox Stakes last season suggests he should be able to make his mark at the top level.

Palmer says: "He's stronger than he's ever been but I'm not sure quite where we'll go. I'm keen to try him over a mile as he ran very well in Gleneagles' Guineas and he's muscled up since he was last in action.

"Seven furlongs is probably his best trip but I've always been eager to have a go at the longer distance and it's possible he'll go to the Lockinge with Galileo Gold. He goes very well fresh so there'd be no reason to run him beforehand."

Baydar to step up in class

One of the success stories of last season was **Baydar**, who defied the handicapper on numerous occasions, winning five times

Baydar wins his fifth race and will now head into Listed company

before proving a shade disappointing in a Listed race towards the backend of the season. The four-year-old built up a good relationship with Josephine Gordon, who has now been given a permanent position with the yard, and Palmer expects the pair to blossom again this year.

"Baydar is another who seems to have improved over the winter which is good to see," says Palmer. "He could join Crimean Tatar in the John Porter or stick at ten furlongs.

"He's virtually unbeaten over that distance and I certainly think he'll be up to Listed level, although a lot of the handicaps at the trip are worth more than Pattern races. Something like the Gordon Richards could be a good starting point."

Melbourne dream

One of the more remarkable winners of last season was **Wall Of Fire**, who landed the Mallard Stakes at Doncaster on his final start with a phenomenal late surge, getting up in the final furlong after having looked beaten half a mile earlier. Stamina is clearly his game

> Palmer's juveniles do well on the sand. They have posted profit at Chelmsford (3-21, 14%, +2.00pt), Kempton (6-42, 14%, +4.33pt), Newcastle (5-14, 36%, +9.03pt) and Wolverhampton (6-16, 38%, +13.35pt). On the turf, youngsters should be noted at Doncaster (3-21, 14%, +2.00pt) and Haydock (4-10, 40%, +0.27pt)

and, with that in mind, his trainer is looking at the staying route for the son of Canford Cliffs.

"He'll start in the Dubai Gold Cup. His work recently has been really good and he's come forward a lot. It's difficult to tell from how he is at home whether he's improved as he has such a funny running style. He's been bought by some Australian owners off Carmichael Jennings and they have one eye on the Melbourne Cup, but he'll need to go up a few pounds and hopefully he'll be capable of doing just that."

Another who carried the Jennings silks last season was **To Be Wild**. An inauspicious fifth on his debut was quickly followed by two impressive victories, one in a Ffos Las maiden and the other in a competitive handicap at Doncaster, where he bolted up by four lengths. Unsurprisingly, his trainer has big plans for him this year.

"To Be Wild is another exciting stayer but he likes to get his toe in, so fast ground wouldn't be up his street. A mile and a half seems to suit him well but it does look as though he could take off if campaigned over even further so I imagine he'll get all the big entries, races like the Yorkshire and Lonsdale Cups."

French plan for smart sprinter

At the completely opposite end of the distance scale is **Afandem**, possibly Palmer's best sprinter. The three-year-old displayed a preference for foreign shores last season, with wins in a Listed race at Vichy and a Group 3 at Chantilly.

His trainer says: "Afandem is not very big – in fact he's nearly as wide as he is tall. He's a proper speed machine and, considering how successful he was in France last year, I think he may end up spending a lot of his time there.

"A possible starting point could be Maisons-Laffitte or Deauville. It can be difficult for three-year-old sprinters over there though, so we could try our hand in something like the Abernant or the Palace House first."

The future is clearly bright for Kremlin Cottage, and the master trainer is also keen on a number of lightly raced sorts. Among those he mentions to keep in mind are Chelmsford maiden winner **Omeros** and **Fleabiscuit**, who finished down the field in the Fillies' Mile on her second start. Others include **Unforgetable Filly**, who finished third in the Oh So Sharp Stakes, and **Koropick**, who displayed some smart form last season.

Along with the considerable firepower of the older generation, these may well help Palmer to his most successful season yet.

SUPER STATS

On the turf, Palmer has been best followed at Lingfield (6-15, 40%, +17.32pt) and Newbury (6-25, 24%, +22.50pt)

Three-year-olds excel on Chelmsford's Polytrack (7-18, 39%, +22.50pt) but on turf they are best at York (4-10, 40%, +30.00pt) and Newmarket's July course (4-14, 29%, +4.20pt). The few older horses Palmer has at his disposal do best on Kempton's Polytrack (3-11, 27%, +18.00pt)

Palmer juveniles have a decent strike-rate and profit in maidens (48-213, 23%, +19.34pt) but three-year-olds do best in handicaps (32-160, 20%, +69.95pt)

Jim Crowley rode most winners for the stable last year (20-82, 24%, +13.26pt), followed by Josephine Gordon (11-41, 27%, +14.42pt)

Palmer often looks for the elite in the saddle, and the mounts of James Doyle (7-29, 24%, +8.20pt), William Buick (4-17, 24%, +12.00pt), Frankie Dettori (3-15, 20%, +9.00pt) and Ryan Moore (2-5, 40%, +0.38pt) all returned a profit in 2016

Palmer returned a small loss in July last year (10-49, 20%, -0.80pt) but posted profitable figures for the month in 2015 (8-28, 29%, +1.12pt), 2014 (4-17, 24%, +4.91pt) and 2013 (2-9, 22%, +6.00pt). April has also been a strong month for him for the last two years: 2015 (4-12, 33%, +26.50pt) and 2016 (9-31, 29%, +18.75pt)

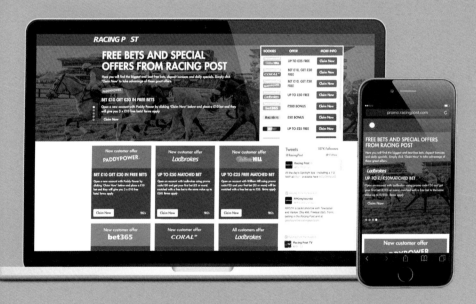

THE LOWDOWN ROGER VARIAN

Postponed primed for team brimming with promise in all corners

THERE are few handlers who possess the ability to take on a Group 1 horse from another yard and improve it, but that's exactly what Roger Varian has achieved with his stable star Postponed.

Since joining the Newmarket trainer, the son of Dubawi has won a Juddmonte International, a Dubai Sheema Classic and a Coronation Cup – and there is little to suggest the top-level winning machine won't continue to dismantle his opponents this season, *writes Tom Bull.*

With Belardo retired, Varian is relying on his six-year-old to fly the Group 1 flag for the older brigade this campaign, and he doesn't feel that an unexpected defeat in the City Of Gold in Dubai at the start of March is a sign of things to come.

"The City Of Gold turned into a messy race and Postponed produced a solid performance, finishing second behind a race-fit rival. I expect him to improve for the run and I think he'll go to the Sheema Classic with every chance of becoming the first horse to win the race twice."

As far as targets in the near future are concerned, Varian says: "We enjoyed a stellar season with him last year, winning the Coronation Cup and the Juddmonte International after his victories in Dubai, and I expect we'll follow a similar path this time, although his main summer target will be the King George, the race he won in 2015 but was unfortunately forced to miss last year with a respiratory infection. That said, we won't be making any firm plans until after the Sheema Classic."

Over the last couple of seasons, Sheikh Mohammed Obaid Al Maktoum has bolstered Varian's stable by sending him some established Group performers, and the powerful owner once again has some lovely prospects to look forward to. One of those is **Certificate**, who produced some excellent performances last year and has the potential to progress further.

Varian says: "He won twice last season, including a £100,000 pot at Goodwood, and acquitted himself well at stakes level, finishing second in an above-average Listed race at Redcar before backing up quickly to finish fourth in the Group 2 Challenge Stakes at Newmarket, shaping well having raced towards the centre of the course and away from where the action developed.

"He's by Pivotal, but he relishes fast ground and he looks a real 7f specialist. Now rated 110, he'll return at stakes level, potentially in the Listed King Richard III Stakes at Leicester in April."

'We enjoyed a stellar season with him last year and I expect we'll follow a similar path this time, although his summer target will be the King George'

With 97 winners on the board in 2016, Varian just fell short of notching a century for the second successive season, but his prizemoney haul of over £2.3 million was a personal best

Autumn overseas plan

Another horse who has been plying his trade at around Listed level is **Barsanti**. A big improver last term, the five-year-old moved from a mark of 75 to 110 under Varian's careful handling, and it would be of little surprise if the son of Champs Elysees is capable of even more this year.

"Barsanti improved out of sight last year, winning four times and being Listed placed on his three other starts. We tried him over 1m6f last season, but his optimum trip looks to be 1m4f, and he could even drop back to 1m2f. He enjoys fast ground and a flat track and he could be the sort to travel abroad in the autumn. He'll likely make his reappearance in April or May at stakes level."

It's not a normal winter season if Varian doesn't produce a prolific all-weather winner,

and it looks as though he's found a really top-class prospect in **Ennaadd**.

The four-year-old has only had six starts but he has won four of them (all on a synthetic surface) and he was particularly impressive when returning from a break to sluice up in a Kempton Listed race in November.

His trainer says: "Ennaadd was forced to miss most of last summer with a niggling injury, but he returned with a bang when winning the Listed Hyde Stakes. He bolted up in a really good time and looked a horse of considerable class.

"He qualified for the AW Mile Final by winning there and that's been the plan since. He's working well in the build-up to Good Friday and I hope he can prove a Group horse on the turf this summer."

One who has already demonstrated classy

Group form on turf is **Mount Logan**. Another moved from Cumani to Varian, he immediately found improvement, winning a Listed contest on his first outing for the trainer. Now gelded, there could be even more to come from the six-year-old.

"Mount Logan has shown a real affinity for Goodwood, winning the Listed Tapster Stakes in May last year, which was his third course win," says Varian.

"He then ran a blinder to finish fourth in the Group 2 Hardwicke Stakes at Royal Ascot before arguably registering a career-best in conditions company at Doncaster, blowing his rivals away by six lengths. We probably ran him back too quickly on his final start as he's best fresh. He can switch between 1m2f and 1m4f, and he'll probably follow a similar route as he's lost his Listed penalty now."

Mount Logan (left): Listed winner should be able to hold his own in Group company having finished fourth in the Hardwicke Stakes

Well-regarded filly on the up

With the likes of Nahrain and Ambivalent, Varian has demonstrated he is capable of training fillies to a very high level, and in **Nezwaah** he could have another destined for the top.

The daughter of Dubawi has shown good form in some decent stakes races, and her trainer thinks she could step up even further this campaign.

"I think a lot of this filly and she looked very good on occasions last year, particularly when bolting up in the Listed Hoppings Stakes at Newcastle. Things didn't go right for her on her final start in a Group 1 at Woodbine, where she was beaten only two lengths having been denied a clear run from the inside draw, but I think she's better than that.

"She could start out in the Group 2 Dahlia Stakes at Newmarket or the Group 2 Middleton Stakes at York and I hope she'll be back in top-flight company before long. Her dam won over 1m4f and, while this filly has plenty of speed, we might try her over that trip at some stage this season."

Another filly Varian hopes can reach great heights is **Spangled**. Despite being the daughter of top sprinter Starspangledbanner, the five-year-old appears to be better over slightly longer distances, and her trainer hopes she can fill into her frame this season.

"The Group 3 Sceptre Stakes at Doncaster was the plan all last season for her and thankfully it paid off as she secured a game neck success. She's the heaviest horse in the yard and has a giant frame, so we think she'll improve again physically, and we hope she's capable of mixing it at Group 1 and Group 2 level.

"She's shown her best form over 7f on fast ground, but she'll likely have another crack at a mile at some stage this season. She could start back under a penalty in the Group 3 Chartwell Stakes at Lingfield before having her sights raised."

Getting a win is the priority

Although **Ajman Princess** could never quite get that elusive victory under her belt last year, she nevertheless displayed some very smart form and the first aim this year is to finish first past the post.

Varian says: "Ajman Princess is one of the highest-rated maidens in Britain and she's been unlucky not to win a race. She ran a screamer when second in the Ribblesdale at Royal Ascot and you can forget her run in the Irish Oaks when she had difficulties at the start and a number of my string were under the weather.

ROGER VARIAN
NEWMARKET, SUFFOLK

	No. of Hrs	Races Run	1st	2nd	3rd	Unpl	Per cent	£1 Level Stake
2-y-o	59	135	18	25	11	79	13.3	-26.91
3-y-o	73	281	53	33	35	160	18.9	-82.88
4-y-o+	35	138	26	14	19	78	18.8	-31.56
Totals	**167**	**554**	**97**	**72**	**65**	**317**	**17.5**	**-141.35**
2015	*126*	*474*	*100*	*78*	*65*	*229*	*21.1*	*+10.13*
2014	*139*	*471*	*78*	*81*	*70*	*241*	*16.6*	*-37.77*

BY MONTH

2-y-o	W-R	Per cent	£1 Level Stake	3-y-o	W-R	Per cent	£1 Level Stake
January	0-0	0.0	0.00	January	3-5	60.0	+2.56
February	0-0	0.0	0.00	February	3-6	50.0	-0.04
March	0-0	0.0	0.00	March	1-6	16.7	+3.00
April	0-0	0.0	0.00	April	5-30	16.7	-15.08
May	1-6	16.7	-4.43	May	7-62	11.3	-32.92
June	2-11	18.2	-3.83	June	11-58	19.0	-1.85
July	1-9	11.1	-5.25	July	5-18	27.8	+0.62
August	0-0	0.0	0.00	August	1-10	10.0	-8.00
September	7-26	26.9	+16.92	September	6-36	16.7	-18.51
October	4-57	7.0	-31.20	October	7-33	21.2	-5.77
November	3-20	15.0	+6.88	November	2-10	20.0	-4.25
December	0-6	0.0	-6.00	December	2-7	28.6	-2.63

4-y-o+	W-R	Per cent	£1 Level Stake	Totals	W-R	Per cent	£1 Level Stake
January	0-6	0.0	-6.00	January	3-11	27.3	-3.44
February	3-9	33.3	-4.07	February	6-15	40.0	-4.11
March	1-4	25.0	+0.50	March	2-10	20.0	+3.50
April	2-11	18.2	-7.55	April	7-41	17.1	-22.63
May	7-31	22.6	+0.35	May	15-99	15.2	-37.00
June	4-24	16.7	-14.54	June	17-93	18.3	-20.22
July	1-15	6.7	-11.50	July	7-42	16.7	-16.13
August	4-11	36.4	+10.38	August	5-21	23.8	+2.38
September	4-16	25.0	+11.88	September	17-78	21.8	+10.29
October	0-8	0.0	-8.00	October	11-98	11.2	-44.97
November	0-2	0.0	-2.00	November	5-32	15.6	-6.25
December	0-1	0.0	-1.00	December	2-14	14.3	-3.63

DISTANCE

2-y-o	W-R	Per cent	£1 Level Stake	3-y-o	W-R	Per cent	£1 Level Stake
5f-6f	7-45	15.6	-21.21	5f-6f	8-35	22.9	+10.33
7f-8f	11-89	12.4	-4.70	7f-8f	20-115	17.4	-43.52
9f-13f	0-1	0.0	-1.00	9f-13f	24-121	19.8	-41.19
14f+	0-0	0.0	0.00	14f+	1-10	10.0	-8.50

4-y-o	W-R	Per cent	£1 Level Stake	Totals	W-R	Per cent	£1 Level Stake
5f-6f	1-30	3.3	-25.67	5f-6f	16-110	14.5	-36.55
7f-8f	8-40	20.0	+5.49	7f-8f	39-244	16.0	-42.73
9f-13f	16-53	30.2	+1.79	9f-13f	40-175	22.9	-40.40
14f+	1-15	6.7	-13.17	14f+	2-25	8.0	-21.67

TYPE OF RACE

Non-Handicaps	W-R	Per cent	£1 Level Stake	Handicaps	W-R	Per cent	£1 Level Stake
2-y-o	16-124	12.9	-34.66	2-y-o	2-11	10.2	+7.75
3-y-o	32-150	21.3	-26.83	3-y-o	21-131	16.0	-56.04
4-y-o+	12-52	23.1	+62.00	4-y-o+	14-86	16.3	-27.04

RACECLASS / FIRST TIME OUT

RACECLASS	W-R	Per cent	£1 Level Stake	FIRST TIME OUT	W-R	Per cent	£1 Level Stake
Class 1	9-68	13.2	-18.28	2-y-o	5-59	8.5	-16.58
Class 2	13-64	20.3	+4.17	3-y-o	14-73	19.2	-4.32
Class 3	12-59	20.3	-25.25	4-y-o+	10-35	28.6	-11.42
Class 4	14-128	10.9	-71.85	Totals	29-167	17.4	-32.32
Class 5	46-206	22.3	-9.63				
Class 6	3-29	10.3	-20.50				
Class 7	0-0	0.0	0.00				

Spangled leads en route to winning at Newmarket in July before following up in a Group 3 at Doncaster on her final start

"We'll look to make her a winner before returning to stakes level and I have one eye on the Listed Daisy Warwick Stakes at Goodwood as her first major target."

Stayer could be cup powerhouse

As far as stayers are concerned, Varian is not short-handed, and in **Battersea** he hopes to have a horse capable of making a mark in all the big long-distance contests. The son of Galileo has proved slightly disappointing in recent starts but it is conceivable that sitting out a trip to Meydan will make him a little fresher for when the proper season begins.

"I thought he ran a career-best when fourth in the Ebor at York having been dropped in from a wide draw, and the form of that race has been well advertised since.

"He didn't win in Britain last year but acquitted himself well and we've gelded him over the winter. I've always held him in high regard and he'll be going down the Cup route this year as I feel he could mix it with the best in staying company. He bounces off fast ground so he won't start back until May, with

the Yorkshire Cup a potential first port of call."

Steve Rogers also has stamina in abundance and although he's possibly not quite as talented as Battersea, he is still capable of some smart form on his day.

His trainer says: "He's been a wonderful servant and a model of consistency over the past few seasons. He was narrowly denied at Ascot last summer, but we made a plan in the autumn to target the Marathon Championship on Good Friday and that's where he's heading.

"He's run three solid qualifying races, not really being suited by the long straight at Newcastle before finding the extended two miles too much of a test at Wolverhampton, but I expect Lingfield to suit him much better as a track and we've deliberately kept him fresh for the race."

More expected from smart colt

As with any major yard, there are some lightly raced sorts lurking under the radar, and one of the most exciting is **Wadigor**. The four-year-old is unbeaten from two starts

Battersea (right): failed to score in Britain last season but put up some fine efforts in defeat

and produced an impressive performance on his handicap debut to wallop a good field by seven lengths in October.

"He's two from two and we don't really know how good he is," says Varian.

"The form of his Newmarket win is really solid for the level, although the handicapper thought the same, raising him 15lb to a mark of 96. He's going to have to move into a much better class of race without much experience, but his pedigree suggests he'll be better this year. I don't see any reason why he wouldn't get 1m4f, but he'll start back over 1m2f. We're not in any rush with him, so I don't envisage running him before May."

Frankel fever was rife last season with many of his progeny starting their races at short prices and winning first time out. However, he is yet to father a regular Group winner and perhaps **Nothing But Dreams** can buck the trend.

"She's a beautifully bred filly," says Varian. "She was working nicely last year, but needed a little time as her pedigree suggested she would. We hope she can make a start in the spring. She's shown promise at home."

SUPER STATS

Varian's runners are best followed for a profit at Doncaster (27-104, 26%, +43.70pt) and Windsor (26-87, 30%, +23.88pt)

Not many trainers can turn over a level-stake profit at Ascot, but Varian has achieved that (14-91, 15%, +20.50pt)

The hint should be taken when any Varian juvenile is sent north to Beverley (4-8, 50%, +12.50pt)

On the all-weather, Varian's three-year-olds can be backed with confidence at Kempton (18-77, 23%, +17.93pt). Varian's older horses do well at Epsom (4-12, 33%, +6.48pt) and Nottingham (5-15, 33%, +3.50pt)

Three-year-olds running over distances from 7f to a mile return a healthy strike-rate and level-stake profit (101-438, 23%, +43.68pt)

With his juveniles, Varian returns decent figures in nurseries (8-44, 18%, +17.75pt), but the numbers make for even better reading in Group races (5-20, 25%, +45.00pt)

Varian's string is often best followed in September. He returned a profit for the month in 2013 (18-53, 34%, +46.85pt), 2015 (16-69, 23%, +27.18pt) and 2016 (17-78, 22%, +10.29pt)

Andrea Atzeni rode most winners for the yard last year. His record on juveniles for Varian was 12-70 (17%, +4.75pt) and 19-65 on older horses (29%, +18.66pt)

Goodwood Cup record attempt the main plan for Bell's Big Orange

MICHAEL BELL

BELL has his headline act Big Orange all dressed up for Dubai, but his season will pivot around an attempt to win the Goodwood Cup for a record-breaking third time in July, *writes David Milnes*.

The globetrotter ended last year in Australia and Hong Kong where he finished tenth in the Melbourne Cup and third in a Group 2 at Sandown.

Bell says: "Big Orange is fine and the plan is to start him off as we did last year in the Dubai Gold Cup at Meydan and then all roads lead to Goodwood for his hat-trick bid. Now the race has been promoted to a Group 1 it might be harder to win, but he's wintered well and we're looking forward to another good year with him."

Bill Gredley, who owns and bred Big Orange, is also responsible for the lightly raced **Towerlands Park**, whom Bell thinks could pay to follow this year, adding: "He goes in the 'could be anything' category. He won nicely after a long layoff at Kempton before Christmas and has an exciting profile. We could look to start him off in a handicap at the Newmarket Craven meeting."

Another four-year-old with few miles on the clock is **Batts Rock**, who hasn't run since last May.

Bell says: "Batts Rock is lightly raced and we've gelded him since last season. He has plenty of scope and is open to considerable improvement."

Of his three-year-olds Bell also points out two fillies expected to pay their way in 2017, saying: "**Ice Dancing** is an unraced Raven's Pass filly who showed us some potential last year but she had a few niggly problems.

"I also like **Glassalt**, who is owned by the Queen and ran well on her second start."

The hint should be taken when Bell sends one north to Catterick. He's had nine winners from just 18 runners at the North Yorkshire track (50%, +28.53pt)

Bell's juveniles are best followed in nurseries where he has a record of 19 winners from 90 runners (21%, +26.08pt)

Last year the booking of Ed Greatrex for the Bell yard was significant. He rode three winners from 11 runners (27%, +7.38pt)

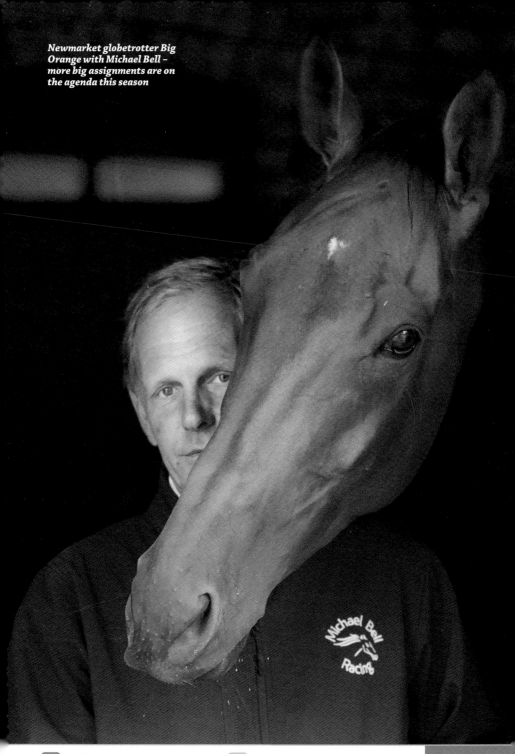

Newmarket globetrotter Big Orange with Michael Bell – more big assignments are on the agenda this season

Warren Hill in Newmarket is a hive of activity as the home of the Flat gears up for a new season

LUCA CUMANI

CUMANI may not have a star older performer to go to war with at Bedford House Stables for 2017, but he has some decent three-year-old stock to fill the void including one or two fillies who might make the Classics, *writes David Milnes.*

Although he has lost Postponed, he still has half-sister **God Given**, who it is hoped can make up into an Oaks filly after finishing third on both starts last autumn.

The daughter of Nathaniel was staying on best over a mile behind the smart Shutter Speed last time and has scope. Cumani says: "She's wintered well and we'll aim her towards a maiden over a mile and a quarter before we think about anything else."

Also well up the pecking order is **Gorgeous Noora**, who scored by six lengths at Wolverhampton in November. The trainer adds: "She won over six furlongs at Wolverhampton but the intention is to see if she'll stay a mile and train her for the 1,000 Guineas. Whether she will stay is another matter."

Of some of the darker horses in his yard, Cumani says: "**Spun Gold** is a nice horse by Exceed And Excel who had his issues last year but is fine now and had done well physically.

Another one to note is the filly **Great Court** by Mastercraftsman, who is going nicely at the moment."

Of the senior brigade Cumani is hopeful four-year-old **Banksea** can improve a few pounds to take a hand in all the top handicaps. He says: "Banksea was consistent last season and hopefully can be again. If there's a valuable mile handicap around he'll be in it."

Cumani has solid records at left-handed, flat, galloping tracks of Doncaster (19-85, 22%, 0.23pt) and Newbury (15-57, 26%, +11.13pt)

Punters should take note of top jockey bookings: Ryan Moore (6-29, 21%, +13.38pt) and William Buick (7-19, 37%, +15.50pt) catch the eye

DAVID LANIGAN

LANIGAN has returned to Newmarket in style five years after he left and is hopeful he can make a flying start from his new base at the palatial Rathmoy Stables on the Hamilton Road, *writes David Milnes*.

Flagbearer for the yard is the five-year-old **Mitchum Swagger**, whose best run last year was probably his third in the Royal Hunt Cup. The son of Paco Boy travels very well in his races and may well have some headgear fitted this season.

Lanigan says: "Mitchum Swagger has done well over winter and is looking good in his coat which he hasn't always done. Hopefully we'll have some fun with him and we'll put some cheekpieces on him as he travels well in his races but just hasn't finished off. We might start him off in the Gladness Stakes at the Curragh."

Two four-year-olds who could pay to look out for are **Wapping** and the enigmatic **Acrux**.

Lanigan adds: "Wapping is a lovely horse owned by the Lloyd-Webbers. He won as a juvenile at Bath but he wants it like a road so we could do with a dry summer for him. He's done well over the winter and could be one to go abroad with if he goes the right way."

Acrux won a maiden at Wolverhampton last year although he was tailed off after that, but Lanigan is hoping an operation over winter will help him.

The trainer says: "Acrux had some issues with a suspensory when he was a yearling and he was too immature to run at two. The way he won at Wolverhampton was the way we expected him to win first time but he then ran a disaster at Sandown. He's been gelded since and could be a nice type."

The former assistant to Sir Henry Cecil also points out two three-year-olds to follow for the coming campaign, adding: "**Kuiper Belt**, who is owned by the Niarchos family is a nice horse who should improve, while **Take A Turn** could be well treated off a mark of 62."

Lanigan has a fine record on the all-weather with his records at Kempton (18-82, 22%, +10.45pt) and Lingfield (11-60, 18%, +5.33pt) standing out

Lanigan's handicappers aged three and older provide a decent return to a level-stake (54-214, 25%, +17.66pt). The same age range is also best followed over distances ranging from 5f to 6f (9-32, 28%, +7.47pt)

Lanigan enjoys a fruitful association with George Baker who is by far the most profitable rider for the yard (35-138, 25%, +19.42pt)

THE EXPERTS WITH ALL THE ANGLES

It's all about Ballydoyle – and it's all about the Classics and Churchill

THERE is only one place to start when considering Irish-trained Classic prospects for 2017.

In becoming Aidan O'Brien's fifth winner of the Dewhurst, and a ninth Irish winner of the race since 2006, **Churchill** set the seal on an outstanding juvenile campaign. The Galileo colt progressed from a debut reverse to take in victory in the Chesham Stakes and three domestic Pattern wins, including an emphatic defeat of the now-retired July Stakes and Richmond winner Mehmas in the National Stakes, on the way to Newmarket.

Not everything went right for Ryan Moore and Churchill in the Dewhurst, but he showed authority when it mattered, staying on powerfully to beat his long-priced stablemate Lancaster Bomber. The runner-up gave the form a significant boost by taking second place in the Breeders' Cup Juvenile Turf at Santa Anita in November, and further value has been added to the form by two members of the home team.

Fourth-placed Thunder Snow captured the Group 1 Criterium International at Saint-Cloud and resumed with victory in the UAE 2,000 Guineas at Meydan in February, while fifth-placed Rivet ended the season as a Group 1 winner in the Racing Post Trophy.

Churchill is in pole position for the 2,000 Guineas. His racing style points to resources of stamina, but his pedigree will provide material for debate should he retain his winter status as ante-post favourite for the Derby after the Newmarket Classic.

There are certainly more stoutly bred sons of the 2001 Derby winner in Ballydoyle's 2017 squad. His dam Meow, a daughter of Storm Cat, raced only at two and exclusively at the minimum trip, finishing second in the Queen Mary before winning a Listed race at the Curragh. She is a half-sister to two useful performers by Galileo – Aloof, a Group 3 winner over just a bit shorter than 1m2f, and Orator, a mile Listed winner who also scored at 1m2f.

The strength of Churchill's 2,000 Guineas claim might resolve an important issue for O'Brien and the Coolmore team. In other circumstances, there would be a strong temptation to test the stamina credentials of **Caravaggio**, the stable's other outstanding juvenile colt of 2016.

A son of Scat Daddy, Caravaggio was unbeaten in four races, including a weak edition of the Group 1 Phoenix Stakes at the Curragh. He had previously given a much more meaningful performance in defeating Mehmas in the Coventry Stakes, and appeals as a champion sprinter in the making.

War Decree, who did not appear again after beating Thunder Snow in the Group 2

Vintage Stakes at Goodwood in July, may become a Group 1 contender at a mile, while the Galileo colt **Cliffs Of Moher** staked a late claim as a Classic hopeful with a wide-margin maiden win in the season's finale at Leopardstown.

Leading middle-distance prospects for Ballydoyle include Capri and Yucatan, winner and second of the Beresford Stakes.

O'Brien has won that race 16 times, and **Capri** extended his current sequence to six. Yet the stable's winners of this Group 2 event in the years since St Nicholas Abbey in 2009 have been unexceptional.

With any luck, Capri will reverse the trend, although he looked rather one-paced when third in the Criterium de Saint-Cloud on his final start, while **Yucatan** couldn't get the better of Rivet in the Racing Post Trophy on his final start when trying Group 1 company for the first time.

The twice-raced **Sir John Lavery**, a wide-margin winner of a Gowran maiden, could make a significant impression, and **Lancaster Bomber** may continue to improve having emerged from the shadow

cast by Churchill to run so well in defeat at Santa Anita. As a son of War Front, he appeals as one of the stable's more likely challengers for major transatlantic races.

The 2017 crop of three-year-old fillies at Ballydoyle has a hard act to follow after last season when a talented squad more than made up for the relatively low-key time experienced by the colts.

Rhododendron, a daughter of Galileo, is set to lead the Irish challenge for the 1,000 Guineas after victory in the Fillies' Mile in October, defeating stablemate **Hydrangea**, who was just in front of her when the pair were placed behind shock winner Intricately in the Moyglare Stud Stakes.

Having failed to make her presence felt on her two attempts at 7f, in the Debutante Stakes won by Rhododendron and in the Moyglare, Albany Stakes winner **Brave Anna** redeemed herself with a short-head victory over stablemate **Roly Poly** in the Cheveley Park, a race notable for the eclipse of the Queen Mary and Prix Morny winner Lady Aurelia.

By War Front out of a Sadler's Wells mare

Churchill (centre): big player in this season's Classics

who won over 6f at two, Brave Anna is less likely to be suited by a mile than Roly Poly whose dam Misty For Me counted the Irish 1,000 Guineas and the Pretty Polly among her three Group 1 wins

Beyond the Guineas, Rhododendron has the making of an Oaks filly, while **Promise To Be True** is another interesting middle-distance prospect. She ran her best race when second in the Prix Marcel Boussac at Chantilly before ending the season with a third place to Thunder Snow at Saint-Cloud. Her dam won at 5f but was a close relative of Oaks winner Dancing Rain.

Arc winner Found has been retired, but seven-time Group 1 winner **Minding** returns to action at four. Winner of the Oaks on her only attempt at 1m4f, she is probably at her most effective between a mile and 1m2f. She will be a formidable Group 1 competitor again.

Among the older colts **Highland Reel**, who has considerable international experience, could be a candidate for races including the Coronation Cup and King George.

Last season's Derby runner-up **US Army Ranger** is likely to be a tough competitor this season, while the transfer of the former Queen Mary winner Acapulco from Wesley Ward gives O'Brien another option for major sprints.

Ascot Gold Cup winner **Order Of St George** and Great Voltigeur winner **Idaho** will compete at the other end of the distance spectrum, and high-class fillies **Seventh Heaven** and **Alice Springs** add further substance to the team of older horses.

Zawraq a big player for Weld

Dermot Weld has to plan for 2017 without dual Derby hero Harzand and Champion Stakes winner Fascinating Rock who have been retired. One horse who could help to fill the void is the lightly raced five-year-old **Zawraq**. He was a leading Derby fancy after a Leopardstown win in the spring of 2014 and is likely to have needed the run when second in the Trigo Stakes towards the end of last season after a mammoth break of 560 days.

Weld's 2015 Ascot Gold Cup third **Forgotten Rules** needs to find top form

again after an unproductive 2016 campaign.

The Aga Khan-owned **Eziyra** is probably Weld's best Classic prospect. The Teofilo filly has won two of her four starts and signed off last season with a fine display at the Curragh in September.

Making Light, winner of two of her three races, could also take high rank. She hacked up in a Limerick maiden and was too strong for a couple of Ballydoyle-trained colts in the Group 3 Killavullan Stakes at Leopardstown.

A pair of late-season maiden winners by Dansili – the filly **Tempera** and the colt **Titus** – should also make a mark.

Dubai heads strong Bolger team

Eyrefield Stakes winner **Dubai Sand** has the makings of an Irish Derby contender for Jim Bolger, whose impressive Curragh maiden winner **Holistic Approach** was found to be coughing after his flop in the Killavullan. His Roscommon maiden winner **Zorion** and Curragh maiden scorer **Vociferous Marina** are other promising types for the Coolcullen trainer.

Only O'Brien had more individual juvenile winners last season than Ger Lyons. A good many have found new homes, but **Psychedelic Funk**, third in the Coventry and second in the Anglesey Stakes, can mature into a fine standard-bearer for the stable despite his eclipse on his only attempt at 7f in the National Stakes.

Glastonbury Song won his sole start at Dundalk in good style and can graduate to Pattern races.

Ambassadorial should do well for Mick Halford following his victory in a Listed event on the Polytrack in October. The trainer's **Rehana** captured a notable scalp when beating Rhododendron in a Curragh maiden in June and may not have been suited by softer ground in her two subsequent races.

Intricately provided Joseph O'Brien with his first Group 1 winner when upstaging his father's fillies in the Moyglare Stud Stakes and will be his first potential Classic contender.

Aneen, who stepped up from a fourth place in a strong maiden at Leopardstown to gain a handsome win at the Curragh in October, can keep veteran trainer Kevin Prendergast in the news.

Minding: the dual Classic winner is sure to prove a potent force again this season

With value elsewhere O'Brien market leaders look worth opposing

2,000 GUINEAS

Churchill has all the right credentials for 2,000 Guineas glory and might well win, but the natural instinct for punters with any adventure is to look for something at a bigger price that might emerge through the trials.

That 'something' could be **Swiss Storm**, trained by David Elsworth. Godolphin have now bought a half share in this Frankel colt, and it may prove money well spent if he can put the promise he showed last season into practice in 2017.

His career didn't start off in the way it was intended as he was a beaten odds-on favourite at Haydock. However, he made up for that at Newbury a couple of weeks later slamming Sir Michael Stoute's City Of Joy, a winner next time.

Elsworth would have loved to have got another race into him over the autumn, but a few niggles meant he wasn't able to. But the winter bulletins have been positive and the Greenham Stakes has been pencilled in for him to make his return.

At the track where he won his maiden, that option makes a lot of sense, and if he comes through that test then the Guineas will very much be on the agenda.

He is more potential than form at this stage, but at 33-1 for the opening Classic it is worth taking the chance.

1,000 GUINEAS

There is a familiar feel to the front end of the fillies' Classic too, with an Aidan O'Brien-trained daughter of Galileo in pole position. Rhododendron easily won the Fillies' Mile on her final start last season, beating stable companion Hydrangea comfortably.

That was a good performance, but it is worth highlighting that two of her rivals in that Newmarket Group 1, Sobetsu and Spatial, made no impact at all, making her task considerably easier. Throw in the fact she was beaten on her debut, and in the Moyglare too, and there are grounds for taking her on.

Wuheida is next in the ante-post market and, as an unbeaten filly who won a Group 1 on her latest start, she deserves to be taken very seriously.

Godolphin have traditionally gone missing in most Classics in recent years, but the restructure they had last season, bringing in John Ferguson, might be about to pay dividends.

Wuheida looks the part on form, having beaten Spatial on her debut at Newmarket before following up in the Prix Marcel Boussac at the expense of Promise To Be True and Dabyah.

By Dubawi out of a Singspiel mare, she could be an Oaks contender, but she is of undoubted interest for the Guineas.

EPSOM OAKS

Rhododendron and Wuheida are likely to be big players at Epsom, but we can go further afield for a value selection in Ralph Beckett's **Crimson Rock**.

Beckett has a fine record with fillies and although it's early days with this one, her illustrious breeding and the fact she won a maiden first time up, both bode well. She is by Fastnet Rock out of Maryinsky, making her closely related to the brilliant Peeping Fawn.

She made her debut at Newbury in October and did well to win having been carried right at the start of the race and having a bit of ground to make up. Runner-up Elas Ruby is exposed but has won since and the pair put a bit of distance on the third.

The rub with her is that she is always likely to appreciate a bit of cut in the ground, but when she gets that give she ought to be very useful.

EPSOM DERBY

With the Derby so far away it makes sense to have a crack at a couple of the bigger-priced contenders who could show their hand before the first Saturday in June.

Roger Charlton's **Atty Persse** fits the bill and is available at 40-1.

He has had only one race, but it was a winning one as he triumphed in a mile Sandown maiden in September, a victory that attracted the interest of Godolphin, who now own the colt.

There was a lot to like about the way he scored, and the second and fourth have since won to uphold the form. He should also stay further as his dam

Dorcas Lane is a Listed winner over 1m2f.

Crystal Ocean is another interesting type. His sire Sea The Stars won the Derby in 2009 and on the dam's side he is related to Crystal Capella, Hillstar and Crystal Zvezda.

He failed to justify favouritism on his sole start last season at Newbury, but ran a race full of promise in finishing second to Warrior's Spirit in a 7f maiden.

Conditions probably weren't ideal as there was a fair amount of cut in the ground, but he battled on well, displaying notable promise.

He had a Dewhurst entry at that stage, but he didn't run again. That means he will need to hit the ground running this spring if he is to be ready for a first-half campaign, but an early maiden win would help and he could be one for the May meeting at Chester.

ST LEGER

While the Leger is a long way off, there is one name who could be worth looking at again nearer the time.

Venice Beach, a Galileo half-brother to Danedream, made a sound debut at Leopardstown in October when second to Titus and should improve plenty for that experience. He was 16-1 that day so not much was expected of him, and for that reason he may be one for further down the line rather than the immediate future.

He appeals as a possible Queen's Vase horse for Royal Ascot which would set him up nicely for the remainder of the season.

Wuheida: makes plenty of Classic appeal

GETTING AN EDGE RICHARD BIRCH

Five names you can boldly follow to ensure banking healthy profit

HOTSHOT APPRENTICES

One of my biggest bugbears in racing involves the way certain pundits fawn over apprentices when they have ridden a few winners. At times they make it appear that every single young rider who manages to notch a handful of winners on the all-weather over the winter is destined to be the next Ryan Moore.

Of course, that's absolute nonsense, and a far more selective approach is needed when identifying apprentices to follow.

I can only use my eyes when it comes to assessing an apprentice. I have no idea whether he or she possesses the single-minded determination to progress into a top-class rider over a series of several seasons.

I know little about whether weight issues or off-track pastimes could prove detrimental to a potentially golden career.

However, what is certain is that I have seen two apprentices over the last eight months who really excite me and, all things being equal, expect them to shine on the turf and prove punters' pals in 2017.

Lewis Edmunds, the son of former jockey Jason and grandson to trainer John Balding, first began to attract attention last summer.

With his family connections, he is clearly steeped in racing, and I remember watching his first win on Gone With The Wind in a soft-ground apprentices' handicap at Ayr in July and thinking "you're good".

That was the first time I can recall seeing him, but there was something about his poise in the saddle and polish in the finish that day which promised so much.

I have followed his career since that day, and confidently predict his claim this season will represent punting gold dust.

He seems to have an uncanny knack of always being in the right place at the right time during a race, which was perfectly illustrated aboard his grandfather's Fortinbrass at Southwell in January.

Even though the sprinter clearly didn't have much in hand of his opponents at the weights, there was never one moment up the straight when I didn't think Fortinbrass was going to win.

Edmunds pushed, caressed and cajoled, and got his mount perfectly balanced throughout, before crossing the line a neck ahead of Cadeaux Pearl.

He again looked exceptional value for his claim when nursing Thello home by a neck in a blanket finish at Newcastle in February.

After hitting the front well over a furlong out, Thello had to resist a plethora of challengers up the hill, but the body language of Edmunds suggested he always had matters firmly in control.

The youngster should enjoy plenty of

Bright future: Lewis Edmunds (left) and Ben Robinson (below right) can shine this summer

opportunities in the north this season, and is emphatically one to follow.

Ben Robinson, who is attached to Brian Ellison's powerful yard, is the other apprentice who stood out in 2016.

A graduate of the British Racing School, it was his ride on 1-2 favourite Always Resolute in a 1m6f handicap at Ripon last May which lingers in the memory.

Although in theory Robinson had been awarded a straightforward winning chance on a horse who had plenty in hand at the weights, it was his sheer confidence which marked him down as one to keep bang on side.

Ripon is first and foremost a front-runner's track. Irrespective of going conditions it is famously hard to make ground from behind at a course which contains plenty of gradients and ridges in the straight.

Robinson adopted exaggerated hold-up tactics on Always Resolute, yet I always got the impression the pair were going to win easily, even when taking into account the circuit's bias against those settled way off the pace.

Produced with exquisite timing by Derbyshire-born Robinson on the outside to lead inside the final furlong, Always Resolute won by a comfortable length and a quarter from Stormin Tom, who hosed up on a return visit to Ripon next time out.

Robinson was also seen to terrific effect when partnering another hot favourite Big

Time Dancer for his boss at Hamilton last August.

At various points during that low-grade handicap, Big Time Dancer looked anything but a 4-6 favourite, but not once did Robinson panic. I thought he showed real horsemanship to keep the big, inexperienced gelding balanced and then push him clear passing the two-furlong pole.

And although Big Time Dancer clearly idled inside the final furlong, Robinson had matters in full control and got him home for odds-on backers by half a length from Galilee Chapel.

Ellison made excellent use of Megan Carberry's valuable claim over the jumps during the winter on hurdlers such as Dominada, and it will be no surprise if the master dual-purpose handler has similar plans for the immensely promising Robinson this summer.

THREE TO BACK FOR A PROFIT

Churchill, red-hot ante-post favourite for the 2,000 Guineas and Derby, is a richly talented and exciting horse who put up a striking display when thrashing rock-solid yardstick Mehmas by four and a quarter lengths in the Group 1 National Stakes at the Curragh last September.

He may not have been quite so impressive in landing the Group 1 Dewhurst Stakes the following month, but that was his sixth run at the end of his first season and he could have been close to going over the top.

There is no reason why Churchill won't develop into a brilliant three-year-old and carry all before him this year, but punters are most unlikely to get rich following him.

Here's my three to follow for 2017 who ought to produce a profit to a level stake – on the basis of backing them each time they run – headed by the Ralph Beckett-trained **Magic Circle**.

I returned home two days early from a Florida holiday last September to plan my biggest ever bet on the stayer for Newmarket's Cesarewitch.

Much to my dismay – and my wife's annoyance – three hours after we touched down at Gatwick I learnt Magic Circle hadn't even been declared for the 2m2f marathon, presumably on account of the fast ground.

Magic Circle, a highly progressive stayer who appreciates plenty of give underfoot, has the potential to win minor Pattern races this season at five when conditions are in his favour, or perhaps Beckett will lay him out for the Cesarewitch again in the hope of getting proper autumn terrain this time.

Whichever route the trainer elects to take with Magic Circle, impressive scorer of a 2m

Magic Circle could be a force over staying trips

York handicap last July, I expect him to win more races and improve his current rating of 99 by another five to 10lb.

Giant Spark, a huge shell of a horse during his early career, began to mature physically and strengthen into his considerable frame during 2016.

The result was an upward surge in form which saw him win four 6f handicaps, including a competitive Navan event off a mark of 89 on his final start in October.

Ideally suited by soft or heavy ground, Giant Spark boasts a high cruising speed in such conditions, and it was particularly pleasing to see him really knuckle down for Pat Smullen's urgings and grind out victory in Ireland, having previously appeared still babyish when put under pressure.

Paul Midgley's sprinter has the raw ability to land a major 6f handicap this season – perhaps the Ayr Gold Cup – before making a splash in minor Group company.

His trainer excels with this type of horse, and there is no reason to believe the son of Orientor isn't open to further progress. After all, his rating shot up from 58 to 95 last season, and horses with that sort of profile usually continue on an upward curve.

Annie Salts is much lower rated on official figures than either Magic Circle or Giant Spark, but that doesn't mean she will be less of a money-spinner in 2017.

I identified the Chris Dwyer-trained filly as one to follow after she had made all under Silvestre de Sousa to register a breakthrough success at Yarmouth in August off a mark of 60.

The daughter of Zebedee unleashed an explosive burst of early speed to take command of that 5f handicap and needed only to be pushed out by the former champion to beat Chip Or Pellet by a cosy length and a half.

Annie Salts failed to reproduce that level of form on her next four starts, but she bounced back on the all-weather early this year, culminating in another all-the-way success over the minimum trip at Wolverhampton.

Her trapping prowess and initial speed render it unlikely many rivals in the 65-75 bracket will be able to lead Annie Salts, and she is likely to prove even more effective on a fast, downhill track where she can really blast away in the early stages and open up a considerable advantage.

I have her firmly in mind for a touch at Brighton at some stage during the early part of the season and, if she progresses as well as I expect her to, a better-class event at somewhere like Epsom could also provide rich pickings.

Happy punting.

Tin Man heads cast nailed on to produce plenty more winners

BRITTANIC David Simcock

This three-year-old is a half-brother to five winners, but is already by some way the best of his siblings having won both his starts on the all-weather in fine style in December and January. After the second victory he was withdrawn from the Tattersalls February Sales and whether he goes somewhere privately or remains with current connections he should be followed. He is going to need to prove that turf suits as well, but it was no problem for sire Excelebration, and he could be the one who puts his top-class miler of a sire on the map. Brittanic has certainly shown the ability to quicken and connections will surely be hoping he can turn into a Group performer, even though he has no fancy entries.

MALMOOSA Brian Meehan

A return of just one win from seven starts was not great for Malmoosa as a three-year-old and it's easy enough to argue she finished the season looking exposed. However, she seemed to be simply a big baby last term and was actually getting her act together in a big way until going to the well once too often in October. A really big filly, Malmoosa started her campaign well enough when second in a maiden to the subsequently Listed-placed Shall We, but failed to make the expected improvement until the end of August when she made all in a five-runner contest at Lingfield to get off the mark. Back in much deeper company next time, she again tried to make all the running, but was gunned down by progressive Sharja Queen at Newmarket in October. However, defeat does not always represent a step backwards and according to Racing Post Ratings it was her best run. She didn't repeat the dose at Doncaster on Racing Post Trophy day, but raced too close to a hot pace and paid the price, although she may also have been over the top by then. Given her size, this really should be her year, and she's the type to pop up at a price in a Listed or Group 3 contest at some point.

MORANDO Roger Varian

This four-year-old soared through the handicap in five starts last year, winning the middle three of them and being particularly impressive at Ayr in September. That was enough to make him 5-1 favourite despite a mark of 104 for the Balmoral Handicap at Ascot on Champions Day and, while he could manage only seventh place, his performance there made him one of the horses to take out of the race. Flat to the boards with three furlongs to run, he had just started to storm home when the gaps closed and there is little doubt he'd have been right on the premises with a clearer run. One of the big handicaps could easily come his way this season off his current mark, while Group races will surely be entertained at some point, especially if there is a little cut in the ground. He may also be suited to a step up in trip to 1m2f, even though it wouldn't be hugely obvious on pedigree. He stays a stiff mile very well.

NATIONAL DEFENSE
Criquette Head-Maarek

By the sire of top-class milers Kingman, Charm Spirit and Moonlight Cloud, National Defense served notice he could be one to follow in their footsteps in three starts for Criquette Head-Maarek last season. An impressive maiden winner on his debut at Deauville in August, he didn't step up straight away when beaten in the Group 3 Prix des Chenes at Chantilly the following month, but he looked electric when sauntering home in the Group 1 Grand Criterium in October by four and a half lengths from Salouen. The runner-up would not be one of Britain or Ireland's leading lights, but he was beaten only two lengths when third to Rivet in the Racing Post Trophy at Doncaster, so the form ties in nicely with some of the best over here. Head-Maarek is no stranger to plundering Newmarket Classics, having taken four 1,000 Guineas over the years, and this one, who has a 2,000 Guineas entry, makes a fair bit more appeal than those ahead of him in the betting outside obvious hot favourite Churchill. Of course, he may be kept in France, but he's a potential star wherever he goes.

POETIQUE John Gosden

Gosden is no stranger to introducing decent horses on the all-weather at the end of the year and, with various bugs doing the rounds in Newmarket throughout the summer, he probably had his fair share of unraced ones to choose from when the turf season closed. Poetique was certainly one of his more impressive all-weather winners at Newcastle when storming home by eight lengths at odds-on in December. Admittedly you'd

struggle to say the form was anything more than ordinary as none of his victims had done anything of note by the beginning of March, but it was a promising effort for one whose future lies over middle distances.

SIGNE William Haggas

Another who only made her debut on the all-weather, but this one is a four-year-old. Signe is a half-sister to Lord Shanakill and Together Forever and she cost a massive €1.1 million in October 2014. It has to be disappointing that she did not make the racecourse until this year, but the fact connections have kept her on the go surely means she has a future, and that looked the case when she was backed as though defeat was out of the question on her belated debut in February. It's hard to claim she achieved a great deal in a half-length win at Newcastle, but she was never in any danger and was conceding chunks of weight to younger rivals. Haggas will have a gameplan mapped out and she will surely be winning races and bagging some black type.

THE TIN MAN James Fanshawe

No prizes for originality here, but The Tin Man was one of the very few horses who shone from this list a year ago, so he goes in again. As you would expect from one who made his debut only in 2015, he improved again last season when, apart from one blip at Royal Ascot – the only time yours truly had a proper bet on him by the way – he announced himself as a proper Group 1 sprinter. His final two efforts were arguably his best, with a second to Quiet Reflection in the Sprint Cup at Haydock followed by his victory in the Champions Sprint at Ascot, where he came from way off the pace and ran out a commanding winner from Growl. As long as he doesn't suffer the same fate as half-brother Deacon Blues, who was forced to retire through injury two years after running his last race at the age of four, The Tin Man is likely to be the benchmark through which other up-and-coming sprinters are measured this season.

TO BE WILD Hugo Palmer

It was a long way from being a surprise to Palmer that To Be Wild won so easily on his final start last season, with Uae Prince among his victims. Indeed, despite winning only a Ffos Las maiden on his seasonal debut and second racecourse start, To Be Wild was being seriously considered for the St Leger by Palmer, who thought better of it in the end, but might have been regretting it after his colt dotted up on Town Moor in October. To Be Wild fairly tanked through that Doncaster contest and won eased down by four lengths in the hands of Josephine Gordon. With only three starts to his name, To Be Wild, whose dam was a half-sister to Al Kazeem, has any amount of improvement in him. He looks like he's going to get a trip well, so could develop into a Cup horse, although he's pretty big and may need juice in the ground to show his best.

UAE PRINCE Roger Varian

Varian's colt had such a massive reputation last year that he was only 16-1 for the Derby before his racecourse debut at Leicester in April, where he suffered a six-and-a-half length defeat at the hands of Imperial Aviator, with Ulysses ahead of him in second. Those plans were duly shelved and Uae Prince did not reappear until September, when he ran out an easy winner of a maiden at odds of 4-7. That was far from the best race as the runner-up is now a hurdler and, while the third was rated 92 at the time, he had dropped 17lb by the end of the following month. Uae Prince then went handicapping for his final start and again disappointed, finishing only sixth to To Be Wild at Doncaster, although he was struck over the head by a rival's whip a furlong out. That's hardly the profile of a really promising sort, but Varian rarely gets things wrong and there has to be a big chance Uae Prince simply needed time. He could come into his own at four and, if his homework from last year was any guide, his handicap mark could look very reasonable.

UDONTDODOU Richard Guest

Rated by Guest as the best horse he had trained at the start of last season, he certainly looked to be living up to that when bolting up over 5f on his first two starts, and he ran to a Racing Post Rating of 94 on the second of them at Windsor. On the back of that he was sent off favourite for a £100k handicap won by Mr Lupton from subsequent Stewards' Cup winner Dancing Star, but that is where his problems began to surface as he was much too keen upped to 6f, saw too much

Ulysses bolts up at Newbury – he has always been expected to come into his own at four

daylight and faded badly. There was no improvement on any of his next five starts, but Udontdodou had begun to get the message as far as settling was concerned and a strong-finishing seventh of 21 over 5f at Doncaster was followed by a fourth of 14 on the all-weather at Newcastle back at 6f, which he seemed to get really well this time. He starts this season on a mark of 84, which is way too low based on that Windsor effort, and he can start making up for lost time.

ULYSSES Sir Michael Stoute

Few trainers are as adept at improving lightly raced older horses as Stoute, and it will be a surprise if he doesn't turn Ulysses into a Group 1 winner somewhere in the world this year. An indication of the high regard he is held in is the fact he was asked to run in and went off at just 8-1 for last year's Investec Derby after winning a poor maiden only three weeks earlier. While he made no show at Epsom, we saw more of his potential when he won the Group 3 Gordon Stakes at Glorious Goodwood. A further Group 3 assignment at Windsor resulted in a surprise short-head defeat to the enterprisingly ridden Chain Of Daisies, but Ulysses was still then sent to the Breeders' Cup, where he finished an excellent fourth to Highland Reel

in the Turf. Connections have always said he would be better as a four-year-old and, being by a Derby winner (Galileo) out of an Oaks winner (Light Shift), he certainly has the pedigree. He had a tendency to sweat up last season, but didn't do so when running so poorly in the Derby so it may actually be a sign of his wellbeing rather than a negative.

WUHEIDA Charlie Appleby

This regally bred filly could prove a major force in the 1,000 Guineas and Oaks if all goes according to plan. Winner of her maiden at Newmarket in August, Wuheida was then pitched straight into Group 1 company. Confidence was rewarded in the Prix Marcel Boussac at Longchamp, where she overcame inexperience to run out a determined winner from highly rated Promise To Be True, with the equally well touted Dabyah in third. Being by Godolphin's standout sire Dubawi and out of Hibaayeb, who won a Fillies' Mile at two, a 1m2f Grade 1 in America and the Ribblesdale at Royal Ascot, there is every chance Wuheida will be more of an Oaks than a Guineas filly. Whatever the case, she is one to side with as long as connections can keep her free of the problems that have plagued so many of their Classic contenders over the years.

RACING POST RATINGS AND TOPSPEED

Four to keep a close eye on from our speed and ratings experts

ON THE FIGURES

Angel Palanas (Karl Burke) Started handicapping on a tough mark last year but posted a good effort in defeat behind a handicap blot on his final start of the year. Boasts some decent relations and can progress from a low base.

Cape Byron (Roger Varian) Produced an impressive effort when scoring on the Rowley Mile in October, barely being touched by Andrea Atzeni en route to a smooth win. Open to loads of improvement.

Fleetfoot Jack (David O'Meara) Costly purchase who showed plenty of promise for his trainer when earning a handicap mark in three runs as a two-year-old last year. Shouldn't be hard to place.

Starshell (Sir Mark Prescott) Three runs in 29 days last year over a mile was never likely to showcase his talents. Can do better handicapping for a trainer well versed in placing improving three-year-olds.

[Simon Turner, Racing Post Ratings]

ON THE CLOCK

Coronet (John Gosden) Successful on her Leicester debut, she set a new juvenile track record when following up in a Listed race at Newmarket and the Musidora could be a stepping stone to the Oaks.

Doctor Geoff (Ger Lyons) Left his debut form well behind when an emphatic Naas winner over a mile in a decent time in September, and this promising three-year-old can win more races.

Librisa Breeze (Dean Ivory) Ascot seems to bring out the best in the Hunt Cup runner-up. He scored twice at the track, notably when sprouting wings there in October, earning a personal best on the clock.

Make Time (David Menuisier) Wide-margin wins on testing ground need to be treated cautiously, but he had time fans purring with a resounding Salisbury success in September and could exploit a favourable handicap mark.

[Dave Edwards, Topspeed]

Make Time scoots home at Salisbury with a victory that impressed clock-watchers

DARK HORSES TO GROUP WINNERS DAVE ORTON

Colt has scope to be top performer – perhaps the next Golden Horn

AKIHIRO Andre Fabre

Unbeaten in two outings as a juvenile and with a Group 3 already under his belt, this potentially top-class son of Japanese super-sire Deep Impact is a very exciting prospect for 2017. Master trainer Fabre will plot a campaign around the Epsom Derby, and he ought to have no trouble stepping up to 1m4f on breeding. A sound surface suits and his return in a Classic trial is eagerly anticipated.

AL WUKAIR Andre Fabre

Having broken his maiden at the first time of asking at Saint-Cloud on his debut in September, this colt then took a step into Listed company in his stride, winning readily at Deauville the following month. Back in fifth that day was Paul Cole's smart Medieval, who gives the form a decent look, and a crack at the 2,000 Guineas has been on the cards ever since. Indeed, he was his master trainer's sole entry over the winter for the Classic, and big things are expected from this highly promising colt, who has gone completely under the radar.

BECKY THE THATCHER Micky Hammond

A dual winner over hurdles during the winter, Hammond's filly is expected to start making up for lost time on the Flat this term. She has improved markedly for jumping and connections are eyeing an attractive handicap Flat mark of 58. She needs a decent test, goes on most ground and has a cracking attitude.

BUENA LUNA Sir Mark Prescott

A typical work in progress for Prescott, Buena Luna is one to look forward to in her three-year-old campaign. Unplaced in three outings over 6f as a juvenile, twice on the all-weather, she kicks off this year from an official perch of just 47. Stepping up markedly in trip will be a lot more suitable looking at her pedigree, and it will be a big surprise if she fails to climb the ratings.

CHAPKA Jean-Claude Rouget

A potential Stakes filly, Chapka got her career off to a perfect start in a warm backend maiden on Deauville's Polytrack surface, coming out best in a tight three-way finish over 1m1½f. She is out of a Listed winner and very much in the right hands with her top French trainer. Stepping up for a tilt at the Prix de Diane at Chantilly in June should be on her agenda. She is one to keep on side.

CRACKSMAN John Gosden

After an impressive Newmarket maiden win,

this colt immediately drew comparison with the brilliant Golden Horn. Not only does he represent the same leading connections, but Gosden's charge is also very much viewed as a Derby candidate despite not being obviously bred to want 1m4f. Golden Horn also won his sole start as a juvenile, and Gosden struggled to hide his excitement for the future with this son of Frankel going into the winter. A Classic trial, probably the Dante at York in May (a race also won by Golden Horn), should figure on his agenda and he could go to the top.

CRIMEAN TATAR Hugo Palmer

This unexposed four-year-old colt goes into 2017 unbeaten in two outings. He made a belated winning debut in style at Newmarket over 1m4f in July, gaining an RPR of 96 in the process, and was then roughed off until a Listed race at Kempton in November on the Polytrack. He came through successfully despite inexperience and showed a neat turn of foot. His trainer is targeting a Cup campaign this season – his dam is half-sister to talented stayer Mizzou – and there ought to be plenty of improvement to come.

HARRY ANGEL Clive Cox

Following on from Ribchester in 2015, Harry Angel became the second successive maiden to win the Group 2 Mill Reef over 6f at Newbury in September. It was his second outing, having narrowly failed in an Ascot maiden last May, but still he was sent off favourite and his trainer later admitted his home work had been top-drawer. Providing he matures from two to three, there is a strong chance he is a Group 1 winner in waiting, and the Commonwealth Cup at Royal Ascot is the obvious target.

GARCIA Richard Fahey

Having suffered a halt to his rapid progression in the ultra-competitive Britannia Handicap at Royal Ascot last year, Garcia was roughed off until Ayr's Gold Cup meeting. He shaped as though the mile trip that day was going to be very much a minimum for his four-year-old career, an opinion strongly backed up by his pedigree, and there could be a lot more to come once he is stepped up in trip this term. A mark of 95 is more than workable and he could well make the grade in Pattern company.

SENGA Pascal Bary

This filly improved with each of her three outings as a juvenile, and it was her final outing that really marked her down as one to follow in 2017. Having turned over a hotpot when winning a conditions event at Saint-Cloud, the daughter of US sire Blame was a huge eyecatcher when placed in the Prix Marcel Boussac on Arc day the following month. She stood no chance after being held up off a false pace and ran on promisingly to finish fourth. Her trainer knows all about handling a top miler and she must be a player against her own sex this term. Ultimately, the Breeders' Cup is an end-of-year aim.

TALAAYEB Owen Burrows

This filly was Hamdan Al Maktoum's second string when landing her maiden at Newmarket over 7f last September, and the form has yet to work out, but there is no doubt she could make the grade as a three-year-old. Out of a half-sister to 1,000 Guineas winner Ghanaati, by a sire known for middle-distance winners, she is being primed for a crack at the Newmarket Classic and is said to have strengthened up during the winter.

WALL OF FIRE Hugo Palmer

Wall Of Fire has his own way of doing things. However, the son of Canford Cliffs took his form to a new level when tried as a stayer in the long-established Melrose Stakes at York's Dante meeting and confirmed himself as going places when backing up in the Mallard – another top staying handicap – at Doncaster's St Leger meeting. His habit of dropping out early before rattling home suggests there is very likely to be more in his locker and, versatile regards going, it will be fascinating to chart how high he can climb in the Cup division.

INTERNATIONAL CHALLENGE NICHOLAS GODFREY

Class acts from across the globe who could make mark in Britain

ERTIJAAL
Ali Rashid Al Rayhi (UAE)

Champion jockey Jim Crowley described upgraded handicapper Ertijaal as an aeroplane after the six-year-old slammed his rivals to claim the Group 3 Meydan Sprint in February to record his second blistering victory over the straight 5f at this year's Dubai Carnival, where the Group 1 Al Quoz Sprint on World Cup night was due to provide his early target. He looks an improved performer this season – his Racing Post Ratings are now in the low 120s, and he broke the track record in the Meydan Sprint with a freakish burst about a furlong out – and the King's Stand Stakes has been mentioned as a possibility if he is sent on his travels in the summer. Any such European campaign would certainly represent a change of tack for Ertijaal as he hasn't been outside the UAE since leaving William Haggas's stable at the end of 2014.

Jameka stretches her legs in the sea at Mordialloc in Melbourne. The crack filly will have plenty of middle-distance options in Europe this season

FLYING ARTIE
Mick Price (Australia)

A trip to Europe was on the agenda as soon as Newgate Farm and the China Horse Club bought into this three-year-old sprinter after his impressive victory in the Coolmore Stud Stakes over 6f at Flemington in October (RPR 120 after beating Godolphin's Astern by a length and a quarter). "I would do it if I think it's right for the horse to go there and if you think you can go there as a winter three-year-old, then it certainly helps establish him as a Northern Hemisphere stallion," said trainer Mick Price at the time. However, a subsequent appearance in the Lightning Stakes must have raised some question marks: sent off favourite on his first run against older horses, he looked a real handful, missing the break and pulling for his head during the first half of the contest and then beating only two home behind the veteran Terravista. Make no mistake, though – the talent is there if it can be better harnessed.

JAMEKA
Ciaron Maher (Australia)

One of Australia's leading middle-distance performers, Jameka was on the Royal Ascot radar after she beat the Charlie Appleby-trained Scottish by three lengths in the Caulfield Cup in October. Although she benefited from racing close to the pace in a falsely run race that day, she had the best form on offer in any case and justified favouritism in style. She shaped like a non-stayer in the Melbourne Cup on her next outing before rounding into form again in the Australian autumn, where she ran an eyecatching race when a close second to Humidor in the Australian Cup over 1m2f at Flemington in March. The prestigious BMW over her favoured 1m4f trip at Randwick was due to be next up before shipping to Europe, where there should be a few options for a filly effective at 1m2f/1m4f.

LADY AURELIA
Wesley Ward (USA)

Having scorched the Royal Ascot turf in last year's extraordinary Queen Mary Stakes victory – Frankie Dettori said it was like sitting on a rocket as she won by seven lengths, on ground described as soft – the Cartier Award-winning filly is earmarked for a return visit as part of the Wesley Ward team, with the King's Stand Stakes named as the target. Part-owner George Bolton had mentioned the Giant's Causeway Stakes at Keeneland on April 15 as a likely starting point for Lady Aurelia, who won the Prix Morny after Ascot before coming third in the Cheveley Park on her final outing as a two-year-old. "I think we want to race at Keeneland and then go over to one of the races at Ascot," Bolton told the Blood-Horse. "Then I don't know what the rest of the year is like – whether she would come back over to the States to finish her year or go back over to keep running. I think what's on everyone's mind is whether she's a stretch-out filly or a five-six furlong turf sprinter. I think that will determine the rest of the year. If that's the case, I wouldn't be surprised if she went back over there for the rest of the year." Whatever she does this term, however, she left an indelible impression in 2016 with an explosive performance that must surely rank as the most staggering seen at the Royal meeting since Frankel.

MISS TEMPLE CITY
Graham Motion (USA)

Royal Ascot is beckoning again for this top-class US turf miler, a creditable fourth in the Coronation Stakes as a three-year-old before filling the same position in the Duke of Cambridge in 2016. Although her exploits at home have been overshadowed by the brilliant Tepin, Miss Temple City has compiled quite a formidable CV in her own right, stepping up a notch last term with a trio of Grade 1 successes, including a couple of victories over her male counterparts at

Keeneland, her favourite venue, in the Maker's 46 Mile and the Shadwell Turf Mile, after which she was fifth at the Breeders' Cup. Another Grade 1 win followed, in the Matriarch at Del Mar, before she was put away for a five-year-old campaign that promises to mirror last year's adventures, according to owner-breeder Bob Feld. "We're on the same plan as last year, with the race at Keeneland and Royal Ascot," he said. Stablemate Ring Weekend was also said to be a Royal Ascot possible but his form hasn't been up to much in California since the turn of the year.

SATONO DIAMOND
Yasutoshi Ikee (Japan)

After several near-misses, the entire Japanese racing community appears to regard the Prix de l'Arc de Triomphe as a holy grail – and nobody more so than trainer Yasutoshi Ikee, who saddled Orfevre to twice finish second in Europe's greatest race. He is set to return to Paris with Satono Diamond, a son of the legendary Deep Impact and named Japan's champion three-year-old of 2016 when he was placed in both the Japanese Guineas and Derby before winning the Kikuka Sho (St Leger) and the prestigious Arima Kinen, where he earned an RPR of 123 in beating Japan Cup winner Kitasan Black (also an Arc possible). After being campaigned towards the Tenno Sho (Spring) on April 30 at Kyoto racecourse, Satono Diamond is likely to be given a summer break before heading to France for a prep run in the Prix Foy. "We'll watch his condition carefully in the coming months," said Ikee. "I want him to be in the best shape for the Arc." Japan Cup winner Kitasan Black is another possible for the Arc.

SIXTIES SONG
Alfredo Gaitan (Argentina)

Now at the end of his three-year-old season in Southern Hemisphere terms, Sixties Song is set to add a new international dimension to the Royal Ascot influx this summer by becoming the first Argentine-trained horse to

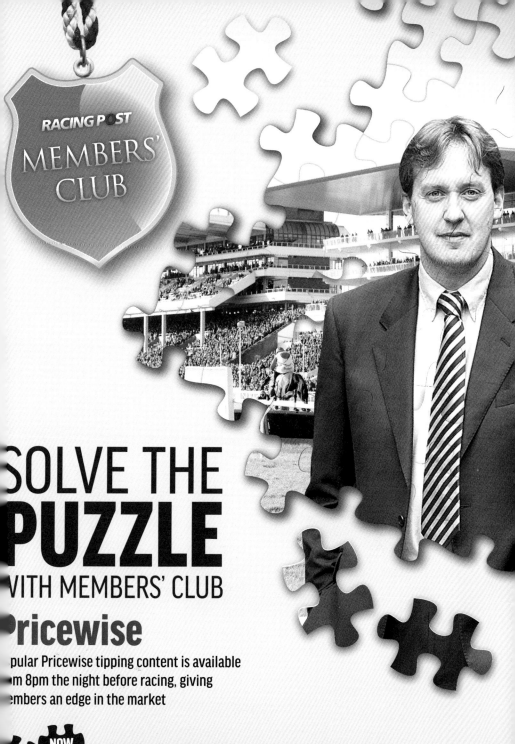

SOLVE THE
PUZZLE
WITH MEMBERS' CLUB

Pricewise

pular Pricewise tipping content is available
m 8pm the night before racing, giving
embers an edge in the market

run at the meeting, when the Hardwicke Stakes is a likely target before a crack at the King George. While the value of South American form is hard to calculate, his credentials could hardly be better as he had already won the Gran Premio Carlos Pellegrini – Argentina's top race at San Isidro in Buenos Aires in December – and the Longines-sponsored GP Latinoamericano, at $500,000 the continent's richest race at Valparaiso in Chile in March, when he had a couple of lengths in hand over an international field. Under a scheme run by Ascot and the Latin American Racing Channel, Sixties Song is now eligible for a visit to Britain, and connections are said to be keen. He was rated 116 in last year's World Rankings.

SOUNDS OF EARTH
Kenichi Fujioka (Japan)

Royal Ascot is keen to attract Japanese visitors, but Japanese visitors aren't as keen to come to Britain as they are to go to France. That said, top stayer Albert would be an intriguing Gold Cup contender, while Hong Kong Vase winner Satono Crown and Dubai Turf victor Real Steel are obvious names to conjure with, but perhaps the most likely visitor is the six-year-old Sounds Of Earth. Always a player, although usually without winning, in his nation's top middle-distance contests, he put up the best performance of his life when beaten just over two lengths into second by Kitasan Black in the Japan Cup. He was also second in the 2015 Arima Kinen, and a visit to Meydan for the Dubai Sheema Classic suggests connections are keen on clocking up the air miles this season.

SPIETH Bryce Heys (Australia)

An emerging force in the powerful Australian sprint division, New Zealand-bred Spieth featured towards the top end of the Royal Ascot hitlist after being short-headed at the

wire by Terravista in a grandstand finish to the Black Caviar Lightning Stakes (RPR 120), the nation's top five-furlong event in February at Flemington, where he had also been touched off over 6f in the Group 1 Darley Classic in the autumn. After a good start he got trapped in a tricky position on the rails when only ninth (although beaten only three and a half lengths) behind Redkirk Warrior in the prestigious Newmarket Handicap in March (sent off second favourite), but was said still to be very much on the Ascot radar. Voodoo Lad and Star Turn, second and third in the Newmarket, are also spoken of as King's Stand possibles by Ascot director of racing Nick Smith.

TEPIN Mark Casse (USA)

Although retirement cannot be far away for America's mighty mare, the setback which ruled Tepin out of her intended engagement in the Dubai Turf could make a return visit to Royal Ascot a more viable option. Although her connections had never ruled out coming back for more after her memorable victory in last year's Queen Anne Stakes, Dubai was always the primary target once the decision was taken to keep her in training as a six-year-old, with an attempt to regain her Breeders' Cup Mile crown at Del Mar at the end of the season also on the agenda. Adding Royal Ascot to that mix begins to look like a pretty arduous programme, but a bout of colic – thankfully described as minor in nature by her adoring connections – ruled her out of her comeback at Tampa Bay in February and scuppered plans to go to the Gulf. Admittedly, Casse had said previously that if there was any reason she wasn't enjoying herself this year, then there would be no hesitation in sending her to the paddocks, but at the time of writing she is still in training, raising hopes this formidable US turf performer might return to Britain in the summer. Despite surrendering her Breeders' Cup title (albeit in another valiant effort), she has still not finished worse than second in 15 starts over two years, 11 of them victories including six Group/Grade 1 contests.

Tepin (far right): last season's Queen Anne winner might be back at Royal Ascot this year

VIEW FROM FRANCE SCOTT BURTON

Wealth of talent set to dominate at home and across the Channel

FRANCE'S leading trainers have almost made an art form of sparing their most promising two-year-olds the rigorous campaigns that have produced an established pecking order in Britain and Ireland by the time the evenings draw in.

Autumn 2016 might have been an exaggerated case of hide and seek after some of the biggest yards in Chantilly were set back on their heels earlier in the season by a combination of illnesses, and it would be no surprise to see one or more of the spring Classics fall to a horse who failed to make the racecourse at all.

If that all sounds like a case of getting your excuses in early, fear not. There was enough excitement generated by those juveniles who did run to offer the hope of some genuine Group 1 contenders.

Andre Fabre suffered as much as any in 2016, finishing over €2 million behind Jean-Claude Rouget in losing his grip on the trainers' title, with Aidan O'Brien snatching second spot thanks to his historic tricast in the Arc.

But when the machine did kick into gear last September, Fabre produced an impressive 20 individual two-year-old winners in the closing two months of the season, securing a sixth win in the Group 1 Criterium de Saint-Cloud with **Waldgeist**.

The two colts who left the biggest impression among that Fabre armada both recorded stakes victories.

As a son of Dream Ahead it would be no surprise if Sheikh Joaan's **Al Wukair** was kept to trips at around the mile of his easy Listed win at Deauville in October. The turn of foot shown when dispatching his rivals in the Prix Isonomy on his second and final start left smiles all round among connections, while it later emerged Al Wukair was a rare Fabre sales selection at Tattersalls.

Freddy Head remains keen on runner-up **Gold Luck** – a Redoute's Choice half-brother to the mighty Goldikova – who arguably didn't get the run of the race.

Akihiro was awarded his maiden in the Deauville stewards' room but showed just what potential he possesses when brushing aside future Group 1 winner National Defense in the Prix des Chenes on his only subsequent start.

His sire Deep Impact already has one French Classic to his name from very limited opportunities in Europe, and Akihiro showed the kind of extended acceleration – rather than an instant turn of foot – that is likely to see him excel at middle distances.

Akihiro could emerge as a flagbearer for

Alain and Gerard Wertheimer, whose famous blue and white silks are associated with a number of promising three-year-olds in addition to Gold Luck.

Terrakova is a product of the dream union between Galileo and Goldikova, and she could hardly have made a better start to life on the track than when pulling clear of her rivals on the Chantilly all-weather under a hand ride from Maxime Guyon.

Spotify will have gone into a few notebooks when making it two from two at the same venue at the beginning of March and could be interesting if sent to a race like the Prix de Fontainebleau against rivals making their seasonal reappearance.

The Chantilly Polytrack proved no hindrance to Spotify – who is a half-brother to the talented Attendu and Impassable – although it remains to be seen if soft ground will be a necessary precondition on turf for a colt with a notable knee action.

The Wertheimers' retained jockey Guyon also has a trio of decent older horses to look forward to: Prix Vermeille heroine **Left Hand** returns, as does **Maniaco**, who was thrown into the deep end in the Juddmonte Grand Prix de Paris on only his third outing before signing off with an easy dismissal of the Hughie Morrison-trained Marmelo at Deauville in October.

And the horse who dominated the miling division in 2015, **Solow**, is back in training with Freddy Head having missed nearly all of last season. The Queen Anne at Royal Ascot will be the first big test of whether the dashing grey (now a seven-year-old) retains all of his powers.

National pride on the line

Returning to the theme of this season's Classic generation, **National Defense** is expected to fly the flag not only for trainer Criquette Head-Maarek but also owners Sun Bloodstock.

He appeared to resent being restrained by Pierre-Charles Boudot in the Chenes and proved that running all wrong when storming clear in the Prix Jean-Luc Lagardere.

The son of Invincible Spirit is likely to return in the Prix Djebel before connections make a choice between Newmarket and Deauville for his Classic assignment.

Head-Maarek's brother and near neighbour on the Avenue du General Leclerc, Freddy Head, unearthed a couple of more than promising juveniles later in the autumn, both carrying the royal blue silks of Hamdan Al Maktoum.

Musawaah was pushed out only hands and heels by Aurelien Lemaitre to account for his rivals in a soft-ground Saint-Cloud maiden and will be interesting to follow on a sounder surface given he is from the first crop of Belmont Stakes winner Union Rags.

Smart filly looks on the up

Ettisaal looked a filly of some promise when scooting clear at Maisons-Laffitte over 7½f under the same jockey and it would be no surprise to see her aimed at a Classic trial.

Indeed, it could be a big year for the assured Lemaitre, who has been nurtured by Head and will now get increased opportunities following the retirement of Thierry Jarnet.

Forty minutes before National Defense landed the Lagardere, the Prix Marcel Boussac produced a 1-2-3 for the visitors, led by Godolphin's Wuheida.

The French-trained fillies rather got in each other's way and, in that context, Frankel's **Toulifaut** might prove to be better than she was able to show.

But there is little doubting that the Niarchos family's **Senga** left the best impression among the home team, flying late to finish fourth in a manner reminiscent of Qemah 12 months earlier.

There is a fair amount of speed in Senga's immediate family but her running style suggests the daughter of Blame might be stretched out to a mile and a quarter in time, should the vastly experienced Pascal Bary choose to do so.

Talk of Bary brings us to **Monroe Bay**, one of the most intriguing once-raced fillies in France last autumn.

The daughter of Makfi should have been ineligible for the newcomers Prix de la Cascade at Chantilly but blotted her copybook by refusing to load at Deauville in July.

While still a little unruly beforehand, Monroe Bay sauntered to a three-length defeat of Turf Laurel, who gave the form a boost when finishing runner-up in what was only an ordinary edition of the Group 3 Prix des Reservoirs next time out.

With Cavale Doree and Rockfel Stakes winner Spain Burg now trained in the US (although Spain Burg has been entered in the Poule d'Essai by Christophe Clement), there is plenty of scope for less exposed fillies to emerge during the spring.

Senga's conqueror on her debut at Deauville, **La Cochere**, was restricted to a single start after picking up a minor problem but looked very smart and will be tasked with continuing Rouget's amazing conveyor belt of top class three-year-old fillies.

Rouget's riches

Stablemate **Brametot** has long been thought of as having Classic potential and, if learning to settle better, could still be Rouget's best three-year-old colt, having taken the same Bordeaux Listed prize as a certain Almanzor.

Readers will need little introduction to the headliners among Rouget's top-class four-year-old band of brothers and sisters.

Almanzor carried all before him last autumn when landing the Leopardstown and Ascot Champion Stakes double, connections having passed up the temptation of the Arc.

While the son of Wootton Bassett could be upped in trip come the first Sunday in October if he has enjoyed a fruitful season, ten furlongs will certainly be his mainstay once again, with the Prince of Wales's Stakes

back at Ascot his first major target.

Rouget won't be in a rush with his unbeaten dual Classic winner **La Cressonniere**, who missed the Arc with a setback.

Her owners have sportingly decided to race on at four with the Arc her main target but we should not expect to see her too early in the year, while any further injury problem could easily signal retirement.

Qemah ran like a filly who had done enough for the year when only third in the Matron Stakes to Alice Springs, a rival she had beaten on three previous occasions, including when taking the Group 1 Coronation Stakes at Royal Ascot.

The transition from three to four is not always an easy one for fillies but, until proven otherwise, she remains the outstanding specialist miler among her generation on the distaff side.

Zelzal earned his Group 1 stripes in the Prix Jean Prat before performing below par back at Chantilly in the Prix du Moulin.

Rouget's decision to let the son of Sea The Stars off games for the rest of the season may pay dividends in 2017 given the searing acceleration Zelzal displayed on his best days.

A similar policy might also prove fruitful with regard to Prix Hocquart winner **Mekhtaal**, who pulled away his chances in subsequent starts but remains a colt of some potential.

Taareef might have been a star in any other yard last

season but merely winning the Group 2 Prix Daniel Wildenstein put him in the second rank chez Rouget. But the master of Pau remains a fan of the Kitten's Joy four-year-old, who might be seen earlier in the year than some of his more illustrious stablemates.

Improved Zarak set to shine

Almanzor proved the rock on which **Zarak** twice had his hopes dashed last summer but an early season outing at Meydan not only gave him a first Group success but showcased a colt who appeared to have thrived physically over the winter.

The Aga Khan and trainer Alain de Royer-Dupre will be hopeful of a fruitful campaign for Zarak – who didn't always seem to have his mind on the job at the business end of his races last year – an obvious candidate for stallion duties given his parentage.

Stablemate **Vazirabad** remains France's top stayer and could be set for another successful season, while **One Foot In Heaven** looks to have a Group 1 in him over a mile and a half, judged by his third-placed effort in the Hong Kong Vase off a far from ideal preparation.

And if this really is to be a season in which a Jockey Club or a Diane winner emerges from among the unraced three-year-olds housed in Chantilly, then Royer-Dupre has more form than most in transforming April's unknowns into stars by June.

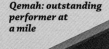

Qemah: outstanding performer at a mile

A-Z OF KEY HORSES

By Weekender
editor Dylan Hill

Abdon

4 b c Cacique - Kinnaird (Dr Devious)

Sir Michael Stoute				Al Shaqab Racing

PLACINGS: 1/28134-   RPR **113**

Starts	1st	2nd	3rd	4th	Win & Pl
6	2	1	1	1	£40,000
102	8/16	Hayd	1m2½f Cls2 83-102 Hcap gd-fm		£16,173
	8/15	Newb	1m Cls4 Mdn 2yo soft		£3,946

Didn't quite live up to big reputation last season, with sole win coming in a Haydock handicap; twice disappointed on soft ground and victory came on good to firm, although rider felt that was quicker than ideal; likely improver and should stay 1m4f.

Abingdon (USA)

4 b f Street Cry - Justlookdontouch (Galileo)

Sir Michael Stoute				Ballymacoll Stud

PLACINGS: 4/11215-   RPR **111+**

Starts	1st	2nd	3rd	4th	Win & Pl
6	3	1		1	£78,894
	8/16	York	1m4f Cls1 List gd-fm		£34,026
	6/16	Newb	1m2f Cls1 List 3yo gd-fm		£28,355
	5/16	Asct	1m2f Cls4 Mdn gd-fm		£5,175

Won three of first four races last season, culminating in an impressive win in the Galtres Stakes at York; may not have stayed when only fifth in the Park Hill next time; should progress.

Acapulco (USA)

4 ch f Scat Daddy - Global Finance (End Sweep)

Aidan O'Brien (Ir)				
		Sue Magnier, Michael Tabor & Derrick Smith		

PLACINGS: 312/116-   RPR **101**

Starts	1st	2nd	3rd	4th	Win & Pl
6	3	1	1	-	£161,802
	5/16	Chur	5f List firm		£26,857
	2/16	TurF	6f Claim 3yo fast		£8,531
	6/15	Asct	5f Cls1 Gp2 2yo gd-fm		£56,710

Towered above her rivals when winning the Queen Mary as a two-year-old in 2015; last year a bit of a write-off but due to be trained for the King's Stand by Aidan O'Brien before heading to the paddocks.

Aclaim (Ire)

4 b c Acclamation - Aris (Danroad)

Martyn Meade				Canning Downs & Partner

PLACINGS: 1/13675111-   RPR **115**

Starts	1st	2nd	3rd	4th	Win & Pl
9	5		1	-	£155,071
	10/16	NmkR	7f Cls1 Gp2 gd-fm		£92,721
	9/16	Newb	7f Cls1 List soft		£20,983
97	9/16	Asct	1m Cls2 91-102 Hcap gd-fm		£18,675
87	4/16	NmkR	6f Cls2 76-95 3yo Hcap soft		£12,938
	12/15	Kemp	6f Cls5 Mdn 2yo stand		£3,235

Went from strength to strength at the end of last

---

season after disappointing as a sprinter, winning a mile handicap at Ascot and twice over 7f, most notably the Group 2 Challenge Stakes; could be even better back on softer ground.

Across The Stars (Ire)

4 b c Sea The Stars - Victoria Cross (Mark Of Esteem)

Sir Michael Stoute				Saeed Suhail

PLACINGS: 22/13013-   RPR **113**

Starts	1st	2nd	3rd	4th	Win & Pl
7	2	2	2	-	£155,888
	6/16	Asct	1m4f Cls1 Gp2 3yo-sft		£122,210
	4/16	Ling	1m4f Cls5 Mdn 3yo stand		£2,911

Won last season's King Edward VII Stakes in good style, enjoying good to soft ground; hadn't acted at Epsom in the Derby and found good to firm quicker than ideal when third in the Great Voltigeur; may not stay beyond 1m4f.

Akihiro (Jpn)

3 b c Deep Impact - Baahama (Anabaa)

Andre Fabre (Fr)				Wertheimer & Frere

PLACINGS: 11-   RPR **113+**

Starts	1st	2nd	3rd	4th	Win & Pl
2	2	-	-	-	£38,602
	9/16	Chan	1m Gp3 2yo good		£29,412
	8/16	Deau	7½f 2yo good		£9,191

Won both starts last season, including a Group 3 at Chantilly with subsequent Lagardere winner National Defense behind; no question that rival was below par but still looks a likely contender for the French Classics.

Al Wukair (Ire)

3 b c Dream Ahead - Macheera (Machiavellian)

Andre Fabre (Fr)				Al Shaqab Racing

PLACINGS: 11-   RPR **105+**

Starts	1st	2nd	3rd	4th	Win & Pl
2	2	-	-	-	£33,823
	10/16	Deau	1m List 2yo good		£23,897
	9/16	StCl	7f 2yo good		£9,926

Unbeaten in two starts last year and made a smooth step up to Listed level at Deauville in October, travelling strongly and easily quickening clear having been slowly away; may well be a Classic contender.

....

'He went from strength to strength at the end of last season after disappointing as a sprinter and could be even better back on softer ground'

Alexios Komnenos (Ire)

3 b c Choisir - Alexiade (Montjeu)

Fozzy Stack (Ir)
Werrett Bloodstock Pty Ltd, G Britton & D S McGuinness

PLACINGS: 12-   RPR **105+**

Starts	1st	2nd	3rd	4th	Win & Pl
2	1	1	-	-	£16,522
	6/16	Curr	7f Mdn 2yo yield		£8,140

Proved his 50-1 Curragh maiden success was no fluke when running Churchill to a neck in the Tyros Stakes on his only other start, although was perhaps flattered to get so close; suffered a setback when being trained for a rematch in the National Stakes.

Algometer

4 gr c Archipenko - Albanova (Alzao)

David Simcock   Miss K Rausing

PLACINGS: 41/21716-   RPR **114**

Starts	1st	2nd	3rd	4th	Win & Pl
7	3	1	-	1	£77,538
	9/16	Newb	1m3f Cls1 Gp3 gd-sft		£34,026
	5/16	Gdwd	1m3f Cls1 List 3yo good		£22,684
	10/15	Newb	1m Cls4 Mdn 2yo gd-sft		£6,469

Finished seventh in last season's Derby before returning from a mid-season break to win the Legacy Cup at Newbury from Dartmouth; still lightly raced and open to significant improvement; shapes like a stayer.

Alice Springs (Ire)

4 ch f Galileo - Aleagueoftheirown (Danehill Dancer)

Aidan O'Brien
Sue Magnier, Michael Tabor & Derrick Smith

PLACINGS: 1253412/337318110-   RPR **118**

Starts	1st	2nd	3rd	4th	Win & Pl
16	5	2	4	1	£839,109
	10/16	NmkR	1m Cls1 Gp1 gd-fm		£141,524
	9/16	Leop	1m Gp1 yield		£151,838
	7/16	Nmkj	1m Cls1 Gp1 good		£113,420
	10/15	NmkR	7f Cls2 2yo gd-fm		£162,330
	6/15	Curr	7f Mdn 2yo good		£8,826

Filled the void left by Minding, stepping up in trip to dominate the Group 1 fillies' mile events last summer and completing a hat-trick of top-flight wins in the Sun Chariot Stakes; sure to be a force in similar races again, especially on quick ground.

Aljezeera

3 b f Frankel - Dynaforce (Dynaformer)

Luca Cumani   Al Shaqab Racing

PLACINGS: 1-   RPR **82+**

Starts	1st	2nd	3rd	4th	Win & Pl
1	1	-	-	-	£3,881
	8/16	Donc	1m Cls5 Mdn 2yo gd-fm		£3,881

Big, tall filly who did well to make a winning

debut at Doncaster in August, quickening up well; put away for the season and should show plenty of improvement, especially when stepped up to 1m2f and beyond.

Almanzor (Fr)

4 b c Wootton Bassett - Darkova (Maria's Mon)

Jean-Claude Rouget (Fr)   Ecurie Antonio Caro

PLACINGS: 1117/311111-   RPR **129+**

Starts	1st	2nd	3rd	4th	Win & Pl
10	8	-	1	-	£2,135,989
	10/16	Asct	1m2f Cls1 Gp1 good		£737,230
	9/16	Leop	1m2f Gp1 yield		£523,897
	8/16	Deau	1m2f Gp2 3yo good		£167,647
	6/16	Chan	1m2½f Gp1 3yo soft		£630,221
	5/16	Chan	1m1f Gp3 3yo gd-sft		£29,412
	10/15	Bord	1m List 2yo gd-sft		£21,318
	8/15	Claf	1m 2yo gd-sft		£11,240
	7/15	Buch	7f 2yo good		£6,202

Brilliant colt who swept all before him over 1m2f last season, most notably when running away with the Champion Stakes to add to his Irish Champion and Prix du Jockey Club wins; could step up to 1m4f this year, with the Arc the obvious aim.

Alpha Delphini

6 b g Captain Gerrard - Easy To Imagine (Cozzene)

Bryan Smart   The Alpha Delphini Partnership

PLACINGS: 0/2515/1531112-   RPR **114**

Starts	1st	2nd	3rd	4th	Win & Pl
12	5	2	1	-	£92,897
88	8/16	Bevl	5f Cls1 List good		£28,355
83	7/16	Asct	5f Cls2 85-109 Hcap gd-fm		£28,013
79	7/16	York	5f Cls3 81-94 Hcap good		£11,644
	4/16	Muss	5f Cls4 67-80 Hcap gd-fm		£5,175
	8/15	Bevl	5f Cls4 Mdn good		£5,175

Showed remarkable improvement last season given he was twice beaten in handicaps off a mark of 83; won his next three races, including the Beverley Bullet, and was just touched off by Cotai Glory in a Group 3 at Newbury; still going the right way.

Always Smile (Ire)

5 b m Cape Cross - Eastern Joy (Dubai Destination)

Saeed Bin Suroor   Godolphin

PLACINGS: 1/112/13342-   RPR **116**

Starts	1st	2nd	3rd	4th	Win & Pl
9	4	2	2	1	£156,509
105	5/16	York	1m Cls1 List 94-108 Hcap gd-fm		£28,355
89	5/15	Donc	1m Cls3 75-94 3yo Hcap gd-fm		£7,439
82	4/15	Wolv	1m½f Cls4 72-85 3yo Hcap stand		£4,690
	10/14	Kemp	6f Cls5 Mdn 2yo stand		£2,588

Not far off the best fillies over a mile last season and got close to a Group 1 win when second to Alice Springs in the Sun Chariot Stakes; had been unsuited by a quick 7f at Goodwood when a beaten favourite before that.

Alyssa
4 b f Sir Percy - Almiranta (Galileo)

Ralph Beckett   Miss K Rausing

PLACINGS: 23/311101-   RPR **102**

Starts	1st	2nd	3rd	4th	Win & Pl
8	4	1	2	-	£35,623
9/16	Asct	1m6f Cls1 List 3yo good			£20,983
85 8/16	Sals	1m6f Cls4 66-85 3yo Hcap good-fm			£5,175
75 7/16	Epsm	1m4f Cls5 56-75 Hcap good			£3,881
6/16	Wolv	1m4f Cls6 Auct Mdn 3-4yo stand			£2,264

Sharply progressive last season and won four of her last five starts, with sole flop coming in the Park Hill at Doncaster (didn't enjoy being crowded); put that behind her when narrowly winning a Listed race at Ascot; should improve.

Architecture (Ire)
4 b f Zoffany - Brigayev (Fasliyev)

Hugo Palmer   Lael Stable

PLACINGS: 31/228236-   RPR **115**

Starts	1st	2nd	3rd	4th	Win & Pl
8	1	3	2	-	£215,187
10/15	Nott	1m½f Cls5 Mdn 2yo gd-sft			£3,235

Failed to win last season but ran well in several top 1m4f races for fillies and mares, finishing second in the Oaks and Irish Oaks; blew her big chance when a below-par third in a German Group 1; should win slightly lesser Group races.

Ardad (Ire)
3 b c Kodiac - Good Clodora (Red Clubs)

John Gosden   Abdullah Saeed Al Naboodah

PLACINGS: 119719-   RPR **107**

Starts	1st	2nd	3rd	4th	Win & Pl
6	3	-	-	-	£89,722
9/16	Donc	5f Cls1 Gp2 2yo good			£39,697
6/16	Asct	5f Cls1 List 2yo soft			£45,368
6/16	Yarm	5f Cls4 2yo gd-fm			£4,658

Mixed bag last season but proved himself a very smart sprinter on his day when winning the Flying Childers, belatedly building on wide-margin Windsor Castle win; flopped twice over 6f in between and managed only ninth in the Prix de l'Abbaye.

Ardhoomey (Ire)
5 b g Dark Angel - Moy Joy (Orpen)

Ger Lyons (Ir)   Moyville Racing Syndicate

PLACINGS: /22412433/111245610-   RPR **116**

Starts	1st	2nd	3rd	4th	Win & Pl
18	5	4	2	3	£165,697
9/16	Curr	5f Gp2 yield			£108,456
5/16	Cork	5f gd-fm			£6,331
98 5/16	Navn	5f 77-100 Hcap gd-fm			£10,853
93 4/16	Dund	5f 71-100 Hcap stand			£7,235
5/15	Navn	6f Mdn gd-fm			£5,884

Proved a revelation over 5f last season, winning a hat-trick of handicaps and then adding the Group 2 Flying Five just as his progress seemed to have stalled; should be even better back on quick ground; likely to be aimed at top sprints in England.

Astronomy's Choice
3 b f Redoute's Choice - Astronomy Domine (Galileo)

John Gosden   R J H Geffen

PLACINGS: 1-   RPR **85+**

Starts	1st	2nd	3rd	4th	Win & Pl
1	1	-	-	-	£16,172
10/16	NmkR	7f Cls2 Mdn 2yo gd-fm			£16,173

Won her only start last season at Newmarket, finishing strongly having started slowly and looked green when asked to pick up; did well to win over 7f given middle-distance pedigree and could develop into an Oaks horse.

Atty Persse (Ire)
3 b c Frankel - Dorcas Lane (Norse Dancer)

Roger Charlton   Godolphin

PLACINGS: 1-   RPR **86+**

Starts	1st	2nd	3rd	4th	Win & Pl
1	1	-	-	-	£3,881
9/16	Sand	1m Cls5 Mdn 2yo good			£3,881

Beautifully bred colt who won his only start last season in a mile maiden at Sandown, coming home strongly from a next-time-out winner (pair clear); dam excelled over middle distances and should have lots more to come as he goes up in trip.

Autocratic

4 b c Dubawi - Canda (Storm Cat)

Sir Michael Stoute   Cheveley Park Stud

PLACINGS: 5/421201-   RPR **108**

Starts	1st	2nd	3rd	4th	Win & Pl
7	2	2			£41,339

96	10/16	York	1m2l/2f Cls2 96-104 Hcap good	£21,788
	6/16	Sand	1m2f Cls5 Mdn 3yo gd-fm	£3,881

Big, imposing colt who reportedly had growing issues last season but got things right on his third run in a handicap when winning over 1m2f at York, showing a good attitude; seems sure to improve again and could be a Pattern horse.

Barsanti (Ire)

5 b g Champs Elysees - Silver Star (Zafonic)

Roger Varian   Sheikh Mohammed Obaid Al Maktoum

PLACINGS: 5323/1113212-   RPR **114**

Starts	1st	2nd	3rd	4th	Win & Pl
11	4	3	3	-	£127,996

105	8/16	York	1m4f Cls2 81-105 Hcap gd-fm	£40,463
96	5/16	York	1m4f Cls2 86-108 Hcap gd-fm	£31,125
85	3/16	Kemp	1m3f Cls2 81-102 Hcap stand	£28,013
75	2/16	Chmt	1m2f Cls5 63-75 Hcap stand	£5,175

Consistent and progressive last season, winning four handicaps and finishing placed three times at Listed level; stayed 1m6f well when second on only attempt; lightly raced for his age and should have more to come; loves quick ground.

Baydar

4 b c Rock Of Gibraltar - Splashdown (Falbrav)

Hugo Palmer   V I Araci

PLACINGS: 21/811117-   RPR **111+**

Starts	1st	2nd	3rd	4th	Win & Pl
8	5	1	-	-	£97,535

99	9/16	Newb	1m2f Cls2 83-104 Hcap gd-fm	£46,688
95	8/16	Sand	1m2f Cls2 88-113 Hcap gd-sft	£31,125
90	7/16	Nmkj	1m2f Cls3 87-90 Hcap gd-fm	£9,704
82	6/16	Nmkj	1m2f Cls4 69-82 3yo Hcap gd-sft	£5,175
	11/15	Ling	1m Cls5 Mdn 2yo stand	£3,881

Completed a four-timer when winning off 99 at Newbury last September (form solid as runner-up won a more valuable contest next time); well below best when favourite for a Listed race at Newmarket but looks ready for that level.

Best Of Days

3 b c Azamour - Baisse (High Chaparral)

Hugo Palmer   Godolphin

PLACINGS: 121-   RPR **110**

Starts	1st	2nd	3rd	4th	Win & Pl
3	2	1	-	-	£78,866

	9/16	NmkR	1m Cls1 Gp2 2yo gd-fm	£56,710
	7/16	Sand	7f Cls5 Mdn 2yo gd-fm	£3,881

Snapped up by Godolphin after a six-length

maiden win and soon justified that outlay, notably when winning the Royal Lodge having been jarred up when narrowly beaten in the Acomb; has a middle-distance pedigree and looks a Derby horse.

Best Solution (Ire)

3 b c Kodiac - Al Andalyya (Kingmambo)

Saeed Bin Suroor   Godolphin

PLACINGS: 313412-48   RPR **111**

Starts	1st	2nd	3rd	4th	Win & Pl
8	2	1	2	2	£124,465

	10/16	NmkR	1m Cls1 Gp3 2yo good	£45,368
	7/16	Gdwd	6f Cls2 Mdn 2yo good	£12,938

Got better as he stepped up in trip last season, relishing the mile when winning the Autumn Stakes at Newmarket, though found 1m2f just too far when second in the Group 1 Criterium de Saint-Cloud having looked a likely winner; struggled on dirt in Dubai.

Big Orange

6 b g Duke Of Marmalade - Miss Brown To You (Fasliyev)

Michael Bell   W J & T C O Gredley

PLACINGS: 4115/471175/2311030-   RPR **119**

Starts	1st	2nd	3rd	4th	Win & Pl
21	7	2	2	3	£838,234

	7/16	Gdwd	2m Cls2 Gp2 gd-fm	£176,992
	7/16	Nmkj	1m4f Cls1 Gp2 good	£56,710
	7/15	Gdwd	2m Cls2 Gp2 good	£170,130
	7/15	Nmkj	1m4f Cls1 Gp2 good	£56,710
	10/14	Asct	1m6f Cls1 List 3yo good	£20,983
101	8/14	Ches	1m5½f Cls1 List 93-107 Hcap gd-sft	£20,983
	4/14	Ling	1m2f Cls6 Auct Mdn 3-4yo stand	£2,420

Has remarkably won the last two runnings of both the Princess of Wales's Stakes and Goodwood Cup, showing versatility from 1m4f to 2m; without a win elsewhere in last two seasons but has been second and third in top races abroad.

Blue Point (Ire)

3 b c Shamardal - Scarlett Rose (Royal Applause)

Charlie Appleby   Godolphin

PLACINGS: 112123-   RPR **116**

Starts	1st	2nd	3rd	4th	Win & Pl
6	3	2	1	-	£268,024

	8/16	York	6f Cls1 Gp2 2yo good	£124,762
	7/16	Donc	6f Cls4 2yo gd-fm	£4,528
	6/16	Nott	6f Cls5 2yo gd-fm	£3,235

Hugely impressive winner of last season's Gimcrack so slightly disappointing he was twice beaten at Newmarket later, perhaps unsuited by more undulating track and not quite seeing out 7f in the Dewhurst; could be a leading Commonwealth Cup contender.

Boynton (USA)

3 ch c More Than Ready - Baffled (Distorted Humor)

Charlie Appleby   Godolphin

PLACINGS: 113-   RPR **113**

Starts	1st	2nd	3rd	4th	Win & Pl
3	2	-	1	-	£70,122
	7/16	Nmkj	7f Cls1 Gp2 2yo gd-fm		£45,368
	6/16	Gdwd	6f Cls5 2yo good		£3,235

Claimed notable scalp of War Decree in last
season's Superlative Stakes and ran well in
defeat under a penalty in the Vintage, running on
into third having struggled to find room; missed
subsequent targets due to easy ground but was
due to return in Dubai.

Brando

5 ch g Pivotal - Argent Du Bois (Silver Hawk)

Kevin Ryan   Mrs Angie Bailey

PLACINGS: 40322/151/12212913-   RPR **119**

Starts		1st	2nd	3rd	4th	Win & Pl
16		5	5	2	1	£305,588
110	9/16	Ayr	6f Cls2 98-110 Hcap gd-sft			£124,500
	7/16	Sand	5f Cls1 Gp3 soft			£36,862
88	4/16	NmkR	5f Cls3 81-89 Hcap gd-sft			£9,057
84	9/15	Hayd	6f Cls3 80-89 Hcap soft			£8,086
	8/15	Haml	6f Cls5 Mdn good			£3,235

Tough and consistent sprinter who progressed
throughout last season, winning the Ayr Gold
Cup off a 9lb higher mark than when just beaten
in the Wokingham; won a Group 3 in between
and beaten only a length in the Champions Sprint
last time.

*Best Of Days (blue):
contender for the
Epsom Derby*

Brave Anna (USA)
3 b f War Front - Liscanna (Sadler's Wells)

Aidan O'Brien (Ir)　　　　　　　Mrs E M Stockwell

PLACINGS: 811661-　　　　　　　RPR **112**

Starts	1st	2nd	3rd	4th	Win & Pl
6	3	-	-	-	£158,326
9/16	NmkR	6f Cls1 Gp1 2yo gd-fm			£102,078
6/16	Asct	6f Cls1 Gp3 2yo gd-sft			£45,368
5/16	Curr	6f Mdn 2yo yld-sft			£7,461

Never regarded as one of O'Brien's best fillies last season but beat more fancied stablemates in the Albany (16-1) and Cheveley Park (25-1); twice disappointing over 7f in between but worth another chance over further.

Breton Rock (Ire)
7 b g Bahamian Bounty - Anna's Rock (Rock Of Gibraltar)

David Simcock　　　　　　　　John Cook

PLACINGS: 31213/773332/341510-　　RPR **116**

Starts	1st	2nd	3rd	4th	Win & Pl
26	9	4	7	1	£359,616
9/16	Donc	7f Cls1 Gp2 good			£56,710
6/16	Nmkj	7f Cls1 Gp3 heavy			£34,026
8/14	Newb	7f Cls1 Gp2 gd-sft			£56,710
5/14	Hayd	7f Cls1 List soft			£20,983
4/14	Thsk	7f Cls3 gd-sft			£9,338
97	10/13	Asct	7f Cls2 80-98 App Hcap soft		£32,345
92	9/13	Donc	7f Cls2 81-95 3yo Hcap gd-sft		£12,450
	10/12	Sals	6f Cls2 2yo gd-sft		£7,763
	8/12	Sals	6f Cls5 Mdn Auct 2yo gd-sft		£2,588

Standing dish in top 7f races for the last few seasons, winning the Park and Criterion Stakes last year to add to his 2014 Hungerford success; copes particularly well with soft ground.

Cape Cova (Ire)
4 b g Cape Cross - Sina Cova (Barathea)

John Gosden　　　　　　　　Mohamed Obaida

PLACINGS: 62311413-　　　　　　RPR **105**

Starts	1st	2nd	3rd	4th	Win & Pl
8	3	1	2		£32,859
89	10/16	Donc	1m6½f Cls3 76-95 Hcap good		£12,450
83	7/16	Donc	1m4f Cls4 72-83 3yo Hcap good		£5,175
	7/16	Ling	1m4f Cls5 Mdn 3-4yo stand		£3,235

Progressive middle-distance handicapper last season, producing his best performance when stepped up to 1m6f at Doncaster; sent off just 3-1 for the November Handicap but lacked pace of principals in a close third; should do better back over further.

Capri (Ire)
3 gr c Galileo - Dialafara (Anabaa)

Aidan O'Brien (Ir)
　　　　Derrick Smith, Sue Magnier & Michael Tabor

PLACINGS: 21113-　　　　　　　RPR **113**

Starts	1st	2nd	3rd	4th	Win & Pl
5	3	1	1	-	£107,062
9/16	Curr	1m Gp2 2yo heavy			£52,059
8/16	Tipp	7½f List 2yo yld-sft			£23,860
7/16	Gway	1m1/2f Mdn 2yo yield			£7,688

Beresford Stakes winner who was ante-post Derby favourite for much of last season, but reputation took a knock when only third at odds-on in the Group 1 Criterium de Saint-Cloud, albeit coming from further back than ideal; unproven on quick ground.

Caravaggio (USA)
3 gr c Scat Daddy - Mekko Hokte (Holy Bull)

Aidan O'Brien (Ir)
　　　　Sue Magnier, Michael Tabor & Derrick Smith

PLACINGS: 1111-　　　　　　　RPR **117**

Starts	1st	2nd	3rd	4th	Win & Pl
4	4	-	-	-	£222,204
8/16	Curr	6f Gp1 2yo gd-fm			£104,779
6/16	Asct	6f Cls1 Gp2 2yo soft			£85,065
5/16	Curr	5f List 2yo yld-sft			£26,029
4/16	Dund	5f Mdn 2yo stand			£6,331

Brilliant winner of last season's Coventry Stakes (overcame significant draw bias to thrash high-class Mehmas); sent off just 1-8 when following up in Phoenix Stakes but missed rest of season through injury; likely to be a leading sprinter but could try a mile.

Carntop
4 b g Dansili - Milford Sound (Barathea)

Ralph Beckett　　Prince Of Wales & Duchess Of Cornwall

PLACINGS: 31/256-　　　　　　　RPR **106**

Starts	1st	2nd	3rd	4th	Win & Pl
5	1	1	-	-	£33,519
10/15	NmkR	1m Cls4 Mdn 2yo gd-fm			£4,528

Failed to win last season but went close when favourite for the Lingfield Derby Trial and not beaten far when fifth in the King Edward VII; went lame when well beaten on only other start; should be a threat at Group/Listed level over 1m4f.

Certificate

6 ch g Pivotal - Graduation (Lomitas)

Roger Varian   Cheveley Park Stud

PLACINGS: /3122/06281/2261124-   RPR **114**

Starts	1st	2nd	3rd	4th	Win & Pl
17	4	6	1	1	£119,898

103	8/16	Gdwd	7f Cls2 90-108 Hcap gd-fm....................£62,250
97	8/16	Donc	7f Cls2 84-99 Hcap gd-fm.......................£15,563
90	12/15	Ling	7f Cls3 84-94 Hcap stand...........................£7,439
	6/14	Wind	1m½f Cls5 Mdn 3yo gd-fm...........................£2,911

Big horse who needed plenty of time but came good last season, winning handicaps at Doncaster and Goodwood before a half-length second at Listed level; again ran well when stepped up to a Group 2 and should do well in good 7f races.

Churchill (Ire)

3 b c Galileo - Meow (Storm Cat)

Aidan O'Brien (Ir)

Michael Tabor, Derrick Smith & Sue Magnier

PLACINGS: 311111-   RPR **121+**

Starts	1st	2nd	3rd	4th	Win & Pl
6	5		1	-	£559,193

	10/16	NmkR	7f Cls1 Gp1 2yo good.............................£283,550
	9/16	Curr	7f Gp1 2yo yield....................................£146,691
	8/16	Curr	7f Gp2 2yo yld-sft...................................£56,397
	7/16	Leop	7f Gp3 2yo gd-fm....................................£26,029
	6/16	Asct	7f Cls1 List 2yo gd-sft..............................£45,368

Progressed throughout last season, winning his last five races including twice at the top level (National Stakes and Dewhurst); favourite for next season's Classics, though looks more a miler than a middle-distance colt (dam never raced beyond 5f).

Clem Fandango (Fr)

3 b f Elzaam - Question (Coronado's Quest)

Keith Dalgleish   Middleham Park Racing LXXV

PLACINGS: 21233612-   RPR **100**

Starts	1st	2nd	3rd	4th	Win & Pl
8	2	3	2	-	£93,128

	9/16	Ayr	5f Cls1 List 2yo gd-sft...........................£28,355
	5/16	Catt	5f Cls5 Auct 2yo gd-sft.............................£2,911

Speedy filly who produced a string of good efforts last season, notably when running away with a Listed race at Ayr on good to soft (also won maiden and third in Queen Mary with cut in the ground); good second in Cornwallis despite losing her action.

Clever Cookie

9 b g Primo Valentino - Mystic Memory (Ela-Mana-Mou)

Peter Niven   P D Niven

PLACINGS: 111964/11542/221757-   RPR **115**

Starts	1st	2nd	3rd	4th	Win & Pl
17	6	3		2	£355,307

	5/16	York	1m6f Cls1 Gp2 gd-fm..............................£90,736
	5/15	York	1m6f Cls1 List good...............................£22,684
	5/15	Ches	1m5½f Cls1 Gp3 soft...............................£56,710
	5/14	York	1m6f Cls1 List gd-sft..............................£15,642
88	5/14	York	1m2½ Cls2 86-100 Hcap soft....................£16,173
	4/14	Donc	1m4f Cls5 Mdn soft..................................£2,588

Gained his biggest win in last season's Yorkshire Cup (third course-and-distance success) on good to firm ground despite trainer often stating he wants it soft; yet to win beyond 1m6f but has finished second in the Long Distance Cup and Sagaro Stakes.

Clever Cookie (left): should again prove a force over staying trips

Cliffs Of Moher (Ire)

3 b c Galileo - Wave (Dansili)

Aidan O'Brien (Ir)   Sue Magnier

PLACINGS: 51-   RPR **104**

Starts	1st	2nd	3rd	4th	Win & Pl
2	1	-	-	-	£7,593

10/16	Leop	7f Mdn 2yo yield	£7,461

Runaway winner of a 17-runner Leopardstown maiden in October, improving hugely on his debut fifth and looking a very smart colt; hard to know where he fits in Ballydoyle pecking order but well worth a crack at a 2,000 Guineas trial.

Cloth Of Stars (Ire)

4 b c Sea The Stars - Strawberry Fledge (Kingmambo)

Andre Fabre (Fr)   Godolphin

PLACINGS: 1132/1183-   RPR **114**

Starts	1st	2nd	3rd	4th	Win & Pl
8	4	1	2	-	£228,625

5/16	StCl	1m2f Gp2 3yo good	£54,485
4/16	StCl	1m2f Gp3 3yo heavy	£29,412
9/15	Lonc	1m Gp3 2yo good	£31,008
8/15	Deau	1m 2yo soft	£9,690

Sent off just 8-1 for last season's Derby after a couple of impressive wins at Saint-Cloud but raced far too keenly and faded into eighth; proved himself much better than that with a back-to-form third in the Grand Prix de Paris.

Cotai Glory

5 ch h Exceed And Excel - Continua (Elusive Quality)

Charles Hills   Kangyu Int Racing Ltd & F Ma

PLACINGS: 21U0/3501/022084910-   RPR **117**

Starts	1st	2nd	3rd	4th	Win & Pl
20	4	3	1	1	£222,638

9/16	Newb	5f Cls1 Gp3 gd-sft	£34,026
9/15	Donc	5f Cls1 List good	£22,684
7/14	Gdwd	5f Cls1 Gp3 2yo gd-fm	£28,355
7/14	Bath	5f Cls5 Mdn 2yo firm	£2,588

High-class 5f sprinter who won a Newbury Group 3 and was second in the King's Stand last season; both those performances came with cut in the ground and trainer is convinced he's better on a quick surface (rarely got those conditions last term).

Cougar Mountain (Ire)

6 b h Fastnet Rock - Descant (Nureyev)

Aidan O'Brien (Ir)

Michael Tabor, Derrick Smith, Sue Magnier & Mrs O'Brien

PLACINGS: 4034517/7285261580-2   RPR **118**

Starts	1st	2nd	3rd	4th	Win & Pl
22	3	3	1	2	£277,966

9/16	NmkR	1m Cls1 Gp2 gd-fm	£61,814
8/15	Leop	1m Gp3 gd-fm	£31,492
6/14	Naas	6f Mdn gd-fm	£5,750

Finally seems to have established himself as a miler having been highly tried from 5f to 1m2f earlier in his career; won the Joel Stakes at Newmarket last season before twice flopping in Group 1 races abroad but fascinating that connections continue to persist.

Cracksman

3 b c Frankel - Rhadegunda (Pivotal)

John Gosden   A E Oppenheimer

PLACINGS: 1-   RPR **91+**

Starts	1st	2nd	3rd	4th	Win & Pl
1	1	-	-	-	£6,469

10/16	NmkR	1m Cls4 Mdn 2yo gd-sft	£6,469

Did well to win his only start at Newmarket last season having reportedly spent the whole year growing; raced keenly early but knuckled down to win well; trainer sees him as a 1m2f horse and no surprise if he steps up in trip again for the Derby.

Crazy Horse

4 b c Sleeping Indian - Mainstay (Elmaamul)

John Gosden   Ms Rachel D S Hood

PLACINGS: 11/6122-   RPR **115**

Starts	1st	2nd	3rd	4th	Win & Pl
6	3	2	-	-	£59,163

10/16	Sals	7f Cls3 gd-sft	£9,057
10/15	Newb	7f Cls1 Gp3 2yo gd-sft	£25,520
9/15	NmkR	7f Cls4 Mdn 2yo good	£5,175

Missed much of last season due to quick ground, returning when conditions were more favourable to win at Salisbury; slightly disappointing he couldn't build on that when twice second at Saint-Cloud (favourite both times).

ON THE CLOCK

Cliffs Of Moher  Beaten on his debut but earned Pattern race speed figures when a revelation at Leopardstown in October. He could take high rank. [Dave Edwards, Topspeed]

Crimson Rock (USA)

3 b f Fastnet Rock - Maryinsky (Sadler's Wells)

Ralph Beckett   H H Sheikh Mohammed Bin Khalifa Al Thani

PLACINGS: 1-   RPR **83+**

Starts	1st	2nd	3rd	4th	Win & Pl
1	1	-	-	-	£5,175
	10/16	Newb	1m Cls4 Mdn 2yo gd-sft		£5,175

Bought for a staggering $1 million and underlined her potential when winning her only start last season in a mile maiden at Newbury; looks a likely Oaks contender for a trainer who has an exceptional record with middle-distance fillies.

Cunco (Ire)

3 b c Frankel - Chrysanthemum (Danehill Dancer)

John Gosden   Don Alberto Stable

PLACINGS: 1344327-   RPR **103**

Starts	1st	2nd	3rd	4th	Win & Pl
7	1	1	2	2	£34,466
	5/16	Newb	6f Cls4 Mdn 2yo gd-sft		£6,469

Highly tried and got better as he stepped up in trip, notably when second in the Zetland at Newmarket over 1m2f; looks an out-and-out galloper and should get further.

Custom Cut (Ire)

8 b g Notnowcato - Polished Gem (Danehill)

David O'Meara   Frank Gillespie & Pat Breslin

PLACINGS: 9243120/34834434257-   RPR **117**

Starts	1st	2nd	3rd	4th	Win & Pl
56	12	8	8	9	£564,107
	9/15	Leop	1m Gp2 yield		£93,023
	4/15	Sand	1m Cls1 Gp2 good		£53,875
	9/14	NmkR	1m Cls1 Gp2 good		£61,814
	8/14	York	1m1f Cls1 Gp3 good		£45,368
	8/14	Leop	1m Gp3 soft		£33,854
	7/14	Pont	1m Cls1 List gd-sft		£25,520
	6/14	Wind	1m½f Cls1 List gd-sft		£20,983
	4/13	Curr	7f Gp3 gd-yld		£31,707
93	7/12	Curr	7f 80-93 Hcap heavy		£10,833
86	7/12	Naas	7f 66-86 3yo Hcap heavy		£7,475
	6/12	DRoy	7f sft-hvy		£4,600
75	6/12	Cork	7f 57-80 Hcap soft		£5,750

Standing dish in mile Group races over the last couple of seasons; ran well on several occasions last season and will be helped by starting this term without the burden of a penalty.

Dabyah (Ire)

3 b f Sepoy - Samdaniya (Machiavellian)

John Gosden   Abdullah Saeed Al Naboodah

PLACINGS: 113-   RPR **111**

Starts	1st	2nd	3rd	4th	Win & Pl
3	2	-	1	-	£41,642
	9/16	Newb	7f Cls2 2yo soft		£9,960
	7/16	NmkJ	7f Cls4 Mdn 2yo gd-fm		£6,469

Sent off favourite for the Prix Marcel Boussac

after a nine-length romp at Newbury and slightly disappointing when only third having dictated a steady gallop; still ran well and worth another crack at the top level; should stay further than a mile.

Dal Harraild

4 ch g Champs Elysees - Dalvina (Grand Lodge)

William Haggas   St Albans Bloodstock Limited

PLACINGS: 4212/013131-   RPR **114**

Starts	1st	2nd	3rd	4th	Win & Pl
10	4	2	2	1	£128,411
	9/16	NmkR	1m4f Cls1 List gd-fm		£22,684
98	7/16	Gdwd	1m4f Cls2 82-100 3yo Hcap gd-fm		£46,688
87	6/16	Muss	1m4½f Cls3 69-87 3yo Hcap gd-fm		£37,350
	9/15	Hayd	1m Cls5 Mdn 2yo gd-sft		£3,235

Progressed throughout last season, winning three of last five and having excuses for both defeats at Ascot (given too much to do and then ran too quickly after a setback); finished with a Listed win at Newmarket and could go higher.

Dancing Star

4 b f Aqlaam - Strictly Dancing (Danehill Dancer)

Andrew Balding   J C Smith

PLACINGS: 417/112119-   RPR **113**

Starts	1st	2nd	3rd	4th	Win & Pl
9	5	1	-	1	£252,928
102	7/16	Gdwd	6f Cls2 97-109 Hcap gd-fm		£155,625
96	7/16	NmkJ	6f Cls2 88-101 3yo Hcap gd-fm		£62,250
80	6/16	Gdwd	6f Cls3 73-90 Hcap good		£9,704
75	5/16	Sals	6f Cls5 65-75 3yo Hcap gd-sft		£3,235
	8/15	Wind	6f Cls5 Mdn 2yo good		£3,235

Made stunning progress last season, winning four handicaps out of five including a memorable success in the Stewards' Cup; only ninth in the Sprint Cup at Haydock on soft ground but will have more chances to prove up to that level.

Dartmouth

5 b h Dubawi - Galatee (Galileo)

Sir Michael Stoute   The Queen

PLACINGS: 61/4161153/111322-   RPR **121**

Starts	1st	2nd	3rd	4th	Win & Pl
15	7	2	2	1	£534,666
	6/16	Asct	1m4f Cls1 Gp2 gd-sft		£127,598
	5/16	Ches	1m5½f Cls1 Gp3 good		£42,533
	4/16	Chmt	1m5½f Cls1 Gp3 stand		£25,520
89	8/15	Gdwd	1m4f Cls2 77-97 3yo gd-fm		£46,688
83	7/15	Asct	1m4f Cls2 82-96 3yo Hcap gd-fm		£31,125
78	5/15	Sand	1m2f Cls3 77-89 3yo Hcap gd-fm		£7,439
	9/14	Sand	1m Cls5 Mdn 2yo good		£3,881

Highly progressive in first half of last season and pipped Highland Reel by a head in the Hardwicke Stakes; came up short at the top level but was given too much to do in the King George and beaten only a length in the Canadian International.

Deauville (Ire)
4 b c Galileo - Walklikeanegyptian (Danehill)
Aidan O'Brien (Ir)
Fitri Hay, Michael Tabor, Sue Magnier & Derrick Smith

PLACINGS: 1125/2013-					RPR **117**
Starts	1st	2nd	3rd	4th	Win & Pl
8	3	2	1	-	£619,676

7/16	Belm	1m2f Gd1 3yo firm	£455,782
7/15	Leop	7f Gp3 2yo gd-fm	£30,233
5/15	List	7f Mdn 2yo heavy	£7,756

Excelled on his travels last summer, winning the Belmont Derby Invitational before a half-length third in the Arlington Million; had come up short in Europe but went close in the Dante and can win more good races at around 1m2f.

Decorated Knight

5 ch h Galileo - Pearling (Storm Cat)

Roger Charlton   Saleh Al Homaizi & Imad Al Sagar

PLACINGS: 2/21134/4121-1   RPR **112**

Starts	1st	2nd	3rd	4th	Win & Pl
11	5	3	1	2	£127,559

	2/17	Ling	1m2f Cls1 List stand	£25,520
	7/16	Leop	1m1f Gp3 gd-fm	£27,331
	5/16	Gdwd	1m2f Cls1 List good	£28,355
85	7/15	Sand	1m Cls3 80-85 3yo Hcap good	£7,439
	7/15	Hayd	1m Cls5 Mdn gd-sft	£2,983

Lightly raced for his age and maintained steady progress last season, winning Group 3 and Listed races; beaten a short head in the Diomed Stakes at Epsom despite finding good to soft ground softer than ideal; open to further improvement.

Delectation

3 b f Delegator - Chushka (Pivotal)

Andreas Wohler (Ger)   Jamie Lovett

PLACINGS: 11-   RPR **105+**

Starts	1st	2nd	3rd	4th	Win & Pl
2	2	-	-	-	£39,772

	9/16	Ayr	6f Cls1 Gp3 2yo gd-sft	£36,862
	8/16	Thsk	6f Cls5 Mdn 2yo gd-fm	£2,911

Exciting filly who maintained her unbeaten record when running away with a Group 3 at Ayr last season; was held in highest regard by former trainer Bryan Smart, who expected her to stay a mile and planned on training her for the 1,000 Guineas.

Decorated Knight (far side): puts up a fine effort in last season's Diomed Stakes at Epsom

Doha Dream (Fr)
4 b c Shamardal - Crystal Reef (King's Best)

Andre Fabre (Fr)   Al Shaqab Racing

PLACINGS: 92/1121131-   RPR **113**

Starts	1st	2nd	3rd	4th	Win & Pl
9	5	2	1	-	£169,352
10/16	Chan	1m7f Gp2 3yo good			£83,824
7/16	Vich	1m4f List 3yo good			£20,221
7/16	Nant	1m4f List 3yo gd-sft			£20,221
4/16	StCl	1m4f 3yo v soft			£12,500
3/16	Fntb	1m3f 3yo v soft			£9,191

Likely Group 1 colt who was campaigned very patiently last season, slowly climbing the ladder to win five of his seven races; stepped up to Group 2 level on last two starts, going close in the Prix Niel before winning the Prix Chaudenay.

Don't Touch
5 b g Dutch Art - Expressive (Falbrav)

Richard Fahey   Nicholas Wrigley & Kevin Hart

PLACINGS: 11111/151045-   RPR **116**

Starts	1st	2nd	3rd	4th	Win & Pl
11	7	-	-	1	£229,722
	6/16	Sals	6f Cls1 List good		£23,818
	5/16	Hayd	6f Cls2 good		£12,450
101	9/15	Ayr	6f Cls2 97-108 Hcap good		£11,050
96	8/15	Ripn	6f Cls2 91-104 Hcap soft		£43,575
91	7/15	Wolv	6f Cls3 75-94 Hcap stand		£7,763
85	5/15	Hayd	6f Cls4 74-85 3yo Hcap good		£5,499
	5/15	Newc	6f Cls5 Mdn soft		£2,911

Began last season by winning at Haydock, making it six out of six (previous wins included the Ayr Gold Cup), so slightly disappointing he won only once more in a Listed race at Salisbury; ran best race at Group level when fifth in the Champions Sprint.

Double Lady (Fr)
3 b f Stormy River - Montagne Magique (King's Best)

Andre Fabre (Fr)
                    H H Sheikh Mohammed Bin Khalifa Al Thani

PLACINGS: 215-   RPR **96+**

Starts	1st	2nd	3rd	4th	Win & Pl
3	1	1	-	-	£15,754
9/16	MsnL	6f 2yo good			£9,926

Slightly disappointing when fifth in the Oh So Sharp last season, though she had little chance from off the pace and may be telling that her master trainer brought her to Newmarket (2014 Guineas winner Miss France had won same race).

Douglas Macarthur (Ire)
3 b c Galileo - Alluring Park (Green Desert)

Aidan O'Brien (Ir)
            M J Jooste, Sue Magnier, Michael Tabor & Derrick Smith

PLACINGS: 61354-   RPR **110**

Starts	1st	2nd	3rd	4th	Win & Pl
5	1	-	1	1	£27,265
7/16	Leop	1m Mdn 2yo gd-fm			£7,461

Struggled to build on eyecatching maiden win last season but did much better when faced with a stiff stamina test, finishing fourth in the Criterium de Saint-Cloud over 1m2f (best of those ridden prominently); should continue to progress over further.

Emotionless: did well when stepped up in trip in Dubai over the winter

Dreamfield

3 b c Oasis Dream - Izzi Top (Pivotal)

John Gosden — Godolphin

PLACINGS: 11- — RPR **99+**

Starts	1st	2nd	3rd	4th	Win & Pl
2	2	-	-	-	£12,291

10/16	NmkR	7f Cls2 2yo gd-sft	£9,057
10/16	Nott	6f Cls5 Mdn 2yo gd-sft	£3,235

Eight-length winner on his debut at Newmarket last season; much less impressive over an extra furlong next time (won by a short-head at 2-5) but connections were experimenting with trip and will now stick to 6f for the Commonwealth Cup.

Dubka

4 b f Dubawi - Rosika (Sakhee)

Sir Michael Stoute — Sir Evelyn De Rothschild

PLACINGS: 611115- — RPR **102+**

Starts	1st	2nd	3rd	4th	Win & Pl
6	4	-	-	-	£39,158

91	9/16	NmkR	1m4f Cls3 79-91 Hcap good	£9,704
87	8/16	Sals	1m4f Cls2 81-95 Hcap gd-fm	£18,675
79	7/16	Donc	1m4f Cls4 79-85 Hcap soft	£6,469
	6/16	Chep	1m4f Cls5 Mdn gd-fm	£3,235

Completed four-timer when winning a Newmarket handicap but only fifth in a Listed race next time at Bath; still looks up to that level (had been a well-backed favourite and wasn't favoured by racing against rail) and possibly even better.

Duretto

5 ch g Manduro - Landinium (Lando)

Andrew Balding — Lord Blyth

PLACINGS: 21/04114/2500251- — RPR **111**

Starts	1st	2nd	3rd	4th	Win & Pl
14	4	4	-	2	£113,491

	10/16	Newb	1m4f Cls1 Gp3 gd-sft	£34,026
85	9/15	Asct	1m4f Cls2 84-102 3yo Hcap gd-sft	£40,445
78	7/15	Asct	1m4f Cls4 68-82 3yo Hcap soft	£7,763
	11/14	Kemp	1m Cls6 Auct Mdn 2yo stand	£1,941

Appeared to have reached limit last season but combination of good gallop and cut in the ground brought improvement when he won a Group 3 at Newbury at 20-1 last time; stays further and could be one for decent staying races.

Dutch Connection

5 ch h Dutch Art - Endless Love (Dubai Destination)

Charles Hills — Godolphin

PLACINGS: 32113/71225/2921560- — RPR **119**

Starts	1st	2nd	3rd	4th	Win & Pl
17	4	5	2	-	£504,843

	7/16	Gdwd	7f Cls1 Gp2 gd-fm	£170,130
	6/15	Asct	7f Cls1 Gp3 3yo gd-fm	£42,533
	8/14	York	7f Cls1 Gp3 2yo gd-fm	£45,368
	8/14	Gdwd	7f Cls2 Mdn 2yo gd-fm	£12,938

Has won good 7f races (Jersey Stakes and Lennox Stakes) in the last two seasons and come close over a mile, including when second in last year's Sandown and Summer Miles; form tailed off subsequently; best on quick ground.

Emotionless (Ire)

4 b c Shamardal - Unbridled Elaine (Unbridled's Song)

Charlie Appleby — Godolphin

PLACINGS: 117/57-62 — RPR **100**

Starts	1st	2nd	3rd	4th	Win & Pl
7	2	1	-	-	£77,129

	9/15	Donc	7f Cls1 Gp2 2yo good	£42,533
	8/15	Nmkj	7f Cls4 Mdn 2yo gd-fm	£4,528

Brilliant two-year-old in 2015 who lost his way after suffering an injury in the Dewhurst that year; showed far more promise in Dubai this winter, especially when stepped up in trip, and could be a force again over middle distances.

Endless Time (Ire)

5 b m Sea The Stars - Mamonta (Fantastic Light)

Charlie Appleby — Godolphin

PLACINGS: 51/11911/11922- — RPR **112**

Starts	1st	2nd	3rd	4th	Win & Pl
11	6	2	-	-	£226,580

	7/16	Hayd	1m4f Cls1 Gp2 soft	£52,740
	10/15	Naas	1m4f List gd-fm	£26,744
90	10/15	NmkR	1m4f Cls3 71-90 Hcap gd-fm	£9,057
82	5/15	Gdwd	1m4f Cls3 77-86 Hcap good	£9,704
76	5/15	Sals	1m4f Cls4 73-76 3yo Hcap soft	£7,763
	8/14	Kemp	1m Cls5 Mdn 2yo stand	£2,911

Sharply progressive in 2015 and stepped forward again when landing the Lancashire Oaks on her return last season; twice second when stepped up to Group 1 company in France, appearing to stay well enough in the Prix Royal-Oak.

Escobar (Ire)

3 b c Famous Name - Saying Grace (Brief Truce)

Hugo Palmer — Carmichael Jennings

PLACINGS: 117- — RPR **100+**

Starts	1st	2nd	3rd	4th	Win & Pl
3	2	-	-	-	£20,930

	8/16	Newb	7f Cls1 List 2yo gd-fm	£14,461
	7/16	Newb	7f Cls4 Mdn 2yo gd-fm	£6,469

Created a big impression when winning first two starts last season, so much so he was just 6-5 when up in grade next time at Newmarket, but scoped dirty after disappointing there; still seen as a 2,000 Guineas horse and set to start in a trial.

'He was brilliant as a two-year-old and could be a force again over middle distances'

Eternally

4 b f Dutch Art - Ardent (Pivotal)

John Gosden   Cheveley Park Stud

PLACINGS: 1/13211-   RPR **107+**

Starts	1st	2nd	3rd	4th	Win & Pl
6	4	1	1	-	£53,694
	10/16	Asct	7f Cls1 List gd-sft		£22,684
90	8/16	Ling	7½f Cls3 85-93 Hcap gd-fm		£12,602
76	6/16	Nott	1m½f Cls4 64-80 3yo Hcap gd-fm		£6,469
	11/15	Wolv	7f Cls5 Mdn 2yo stand		£2,976

Easy winner at Ascot last October when stepped up to Listed grade, proving effectiveness on good to soft having previously looked progressive on much quicker ground; should get a mile and will get chances at Pattern level.

Exemplar (Ire)

3 ro c Galileo - Miarixa (Linamix)

Aidan O'Brien (Ir)

Michael Tabor, Derrick Smith & Sue Magnier

PLACINGS: 213-   RPR **110**

Starts	1st	2nd	3rd	4th	Win & Pl
3	1	1	1	-	£18,386
	9/16	Gway	1m1/2f Mdn 2yo soft		£8,140

Half-brother to dual Classic winner Blue Bunting who followed up impressive maiden win with a close third in Beresford Stakes (only overhauled in final furlong); first two were both beaten favourites at Group 1 level but still no mean feat to push them close.

Eziyra (Ire)

3 ch f Teofilo - Eytarna (Dubai Destination)

Dermot Weld (Ir)   H H Aga Khan

PLACINGS: 2121-   RPR **108**

Starts	1st	2nd	3rd	4th	Win & Pl
4	2	2	-	-	£49,876
	9/16	Curr	7f Gp3 2yo heavy		£29,283
	7/16	Gway	7f Mdn 2yo yld-sft		£7,461

Produced big performances in two Group 3 races last season, pushing Sea Of Grace close at the Curragh and going one better back there on heavy ground; seen as a miler by her trainer and likely to be aimed at Irish 1,000 Guineas.

Fabricate

5 b g Makfi - Flight Of Fancy (Sadler's Wells)

Michael Bell   The Queen

PLACINGS: 3113/25381-   RPR **104**

Starts	1st	2nd	3rd	4th	Win & Pl
9	3	1	3	-	£46,856
97	10/16	Leic	1m4f Cls2 96-102 Hcap gd-sft		£15,753
87	5/15	Hayd	1m4f Cls3 80-92 3yo Hcap gd-sft		£12,450
	5/15	Sals	1m4f Cls5 Mdn 3yo gd-fm		£4,205

Lightly raced for his age and progressed nicely last season, signing off with victory in a 1m4f handicap at Leicester (relished good to soft ground); seems sure to stay further and a likely type for top middle-distance/staying handicaps.

Fair Eva

3 ch f Frankel - African Rose (Observatory)

Roger Charlton   K Abdullah

PLACINGS: 1132-   RPR **110+**

Starts	1st	2nd	3rd	4th	Win & Pl
4	2	1	1	-	£74,609
	7/16	Asct	6f Cls1 Gp3 2yo gd-fm		£28,355
	6/16	Hayd	6f Cls5 2yo gd-fm		£3,235

Failed to build on the rich promise of a wide-margin Princess Margaret win when twice beaten at odds-on, though did better when stepped up to 7f in the Rockfel; should progress again over further and trainer still holds her in highest regard.

Firmament

5 b g Cape Cross - Heaven Sent (Pivotal)

David O'Meara   Gallop Racing

PLACINGS: 1/26584432/12411223-   RPR **114**

Starts	1st	2nd	3rd	4th	Win & Pl
19	4	6	2	4	£160,466
96	8/16	York	1m Cls2 93-107 Hcap gd-fm		£52,913
91	8/16	Chmt	1m Cls3 82-95 Hcap stand		£9,704
85	5/16	Newc	1m Cls4 76-85 Hcap stand		£7,763
	10/14	Newb	1m Cls4 Mdn 2yo soft		£5,175

Improved throughout last season and was placed in three big autumn handicaps at Ascot, looking a shade unlucky when third in the Balmoral Handicap; surefire contender for similar races before possibly going up in class.

ON THE CLOCK

Fabricate Gained a deserved success on his final outing last season at Leicester in October. Relatively lightly raced, he could thrive in decent staying handicaps on easy ground.
[Dave Edwards, Topspeed]

Flying Officer (USA)
7 b g Dynaformer - Vignette (Diesis)

John Gosden   George Strawbridge

PLACINGS: 17/1/126/111/36-   RPR **117**

Starts	1st	2nd	3rd	4th	Win & Pl
11	6	1	1	-	£289,496

10/15	Asct	2m Cls1 Gp2 gd-sft		£195,650
9/15	NmkR	2m Cls1 List gd-sft		£22,684
9/15	Sals	1m6f Cls2 soft		£12,450
4/14	Nott	1m6f Cls1 List soft		£22,684
88	6/13	Wind	1m2f Cls3 82-88 3yo Hcap gd-fm	£7,439
9/12	Sand	1m Cls5 Mdn 2yo gd-fm		£3,881

Talented but fragile stayer; has never raced more than three times in a season; below best when sixth in the Ascot Gold Cup last year and missed the rest of the season.

Forgotten Rules (Ire)
7 b g Nayef - Utterly Heaven (Danehill)

Dermot Weld (Ir)   Moyglare Stud Farm

PLACINGS: 11/13458/272-   RPR **110**

Starts	1st	2nd	3rd	4th	Win & Pl
10	3	2	1	1	£286,984

5/15	Navn	1m6f Gp3 good	£32,752
10/14	Asct	2m Cls1 Gp2 heavy	£178,627
8/14	Gway	1m6f soft	£10,833

Has become very disappointing given he was just 5-2 for the Gold Cup in 2015 and finished third on ground much quicker than ideal; still a useful stayer, though, and twice second in Listed races last year; could yet land a big one on soft ground.

Frankuus (Ire)
3 gr c Frankel - Dookus (Linamix)

Mark Johnston   Hussain Lootah & Ahmad Al Shaikh

PLACINGS: 1534118-   RPR **107**

Starts	1st	2nd	3rd	4th	Win & Pl
7	3	-	1	1	£54,565

10/16	Chan	1m1f Gp3 2yo good	£29,412
9/16	Hayd	1m Cls1 List 2yo good	£14,461
6/16	Hayd	7f Cls4 2yo gd-fm	£3,946

Won a Listed race at Haydock on soft ground when stepped up in trip but probably better on good when following up in a 1m1f Group 3 at Chantilly; looks the type to improve at three.

Galileo Gold
4 ch c Paco Boy - Galicuix (Galileo)

Hugo Palmer   Al Shaqab Racing

PLACINGS: 21113/121285-   RPR **123**

Starts	1st	2nd	3rd	4th	Win & Pl
11	5	3	1	-	£951,470

6/16	Asct	1m Cls1 Gp1 3yo soft	£226,840
4/16	NmkR	1m Cls1 Gp1 3yo gd-fm	£283,550
7/15	Gdwd	7f Cls1 Gp2 2yo gd-sft	£113,420
7/15	Hayd	7f Cls4 2yo gd-sft	£4,528
6/15	Sals	6f Cls5 Mdn Auct 2yo gd-fm	£3,558

Proved himself a top-class miler last season when winning the 2,000 Guineas and St James's Palace Stakes and going close in the Sussex Stakes; lost his way subsequently but bodes well that connections have kept him in training, and it would be no surprise to see him shine again.

Gifted Master (Ire)
4 b g Kodiac - Shobobb (Shamardal)

Hugo Palmer   Dr Ali Ridha

PLACINGS: 142111/11393029-4   RPR **114+**

Starts	1st	2nd	3rd	4th	Win & Pl
15	6	2	2	2	£506,078

4/16	Asct	6f Cls1 Gp3 3yo gd-sft	£45,368
4/16	NmkR	6f Cls2 3yo gd-sft	£54,100
10/15	NmkR	1m Cls1 Gp3 2yo good	£45,368
10/15	NmkR	7f Cls2 2yo gd-fm	£270,550
6/15	Newc	6f Cls4 2yo gd-fm	£4,528
4/15	NmkR	5f Cls3 2yo gd-fm	£8,410

Completed a five-timer when winning at Ascot early last season; had his limitations exposed slightly afterwards but still placed three times at Group 2 level; best when dominating small fields and struggled in bigger line-ups.

Gm Hopkins
6 b g Dubawi - Varsity (Lomitas)

John Gosden   R J H Geffen

PLACINGS: 43/02187624/1803400-   RPR **116+**

Starts	1st	2nd	3rd	4th	Win & Pl
22	5	2	2	4	£229,609

4/16	Asct	1m Cls1 List gd-sft		£20,983
103	6/15	Asct	1m Cls2 97-111 Hcap gd-fm	£108,938
91	9/14	NmkR	1m1f Cls2 75-94 Hcap good	£18,675
87	9/14	Sand	1m Cls3 82-90 3yo Hcap good	£9,338
4/14	Nott	1m½f Cls5 Mdn 2yo soft		£3,881

Won a Listed race at Ascot on his reappearance last season but struggled in a higher grade and again when returned to handicaps the last twice; now back down to a lower mark than at any time since his 2015 Royal Hunt Cup victory.

Goldream
8 br g Oasis Dream - Clizia (Machiavellian)

Robert Cowell   J Sargeant & Mrs J Morley

PLACINGS: 32142/17151/7937306-   RPR **115**

Starts	1st	2nd	3rd	4th	Win & Pl
40	7	6	7	3	£553,176

10/15	Lonc	5f Gp1 good		£155,031
6/15	Asct	5f Cls1 Gp1 gd-fm		£212,663
5/15	NmkR	5f Cls1 Gp3 gd-fm		£34,026
98	8/14	Asct	5f Cls2 97-105 Hcap good	£19,672
90	9/14	NmkR	6f Cls2 80-104 Hcap gd-fm	£28,013
83	8/12	NmkJ	6f Cls4 67-85 Hcap gd-fm	£5,175
6/12	Wolv	6f Cls5 Mdn stand		£2,264

Dual Group 1 winner in 2015, landing the King's Stand Stakes and Prix de l'Abbaye; unable to hit those heights last season, with best run a half-length third in the King George Stakes; best on quick ground.

Gravity Flow (Ire)

4 ch f Exceed And Excel - Landela (Alhaarth)

William Haggas   Sheikh Juma Dalmook Al Maktoum

PLACINGS: 22/11112-   RPR **108**

Starts	1st	2nd	3rd	4th	Win & Pl
7	3	-	-	-	£41,556
90	9/16	Sals	6f Cls2 77-95 Hcap good		£13,695
84	8/16	Wind	6f Cls4 77-85 gd-fm		£6,469
77	7/16	Donc	6f Cls4 75-80 3yo Hcap gd-fm		£5,175
	6/16	Ling	6f Cls5 Mdn stand		£3,235

Completed a four-timer in a handicap at Salisbury in September and very nearly bridged the gap to Listed level at Newmarket, going down by a head to Kassia; may be better back on quick ground (has won twice on good to firm).

Grecian Light (Ire)

3 b f Shamardal - Akrivi (Tobougg)

Charlie Appleby   Godolphin

PLACINGS: 127220-   RPR **103**

Starts	1st	2nd	3rd	4th	Win & Pl
6	1	3	-	-	£36,961
	7/16	Nmkj	7f Cls5 Mdn 2yo good		£3,881

Not the most consistent last season and twice failed to beat a single rival but acquitted herself well at Pattern level in between when second in the May Hill and a Curragh Group 3; unlikely to get further than 1m2f on pedigree.

Growl

5 b g Oasis Dream - Desert Tigress (Storm Cat)

Richard Fahey   Dr Marwan Koukash

PLACINGS: 275050/444114426210-   RPR **118**

Starts	1st	2nd	3rd	4th	Win & Pl
22	4	4	-	5	£270,925
	11/16	Donc	6f Cls5 List gd-fm		£28,355
93	6/16	Wind	6f Cls2 83-102 Hcap soft		£12,450
87	6/16	Nott	6f Cls3 74-89 Hcap gd-fm		£7,470
	7/14	Asct	6f Cls2 Mdn 2yo gd-fm		£12,938

Showed remarkable improvement towards end of last season, finishing second at 50-1 in the Champions Sprint and backing that up with a Listed win at Doncaster; had been knocking on the door in big handicaps and was unlucky when fourth in the Stewards' Cup.

....

'Surprise winner of last season's St Leger who proved himself a thorough stayer having also gone close in the Queen's Vase. Should do well in Cup races'

Harbour Law

4 b c Lawman - Abunai (Pivotal)

Laura Mongan   Jackie Cornwell

PLACINGS: 211241-   RPR **116**

Starts	1st	2nd	3rd	4th	Win & Pl
6	3	2	-	1	£431,441
	9/16	Donc	1m6½f Cls1 Gp1 3yo good		£396,970
85	5/16	Sand	1m6f Cls4 66-85 3yo Hcap gd-fm		£4,690
	5/16	Sals	1m4f Cls5 Mdn 3yo gd-sft		£4,205

Surprise winner of last season's St Leger, taking advantage of favourite Idaho's stumble; proved himself a thorough stayer having also gone close in the Queen's Vase over 2m and should do well in Cup races over extreme trips.

Harlequeen

4 b f Canford Cliffs - Aurelia (Rainbow Quest)

Mick Channon   Mrs S Brandt

PLACINGS: 1/243330-   RPR **108**

Starts	1st	2nd	3rd	4th	Win & Pl
7	1	1	3	1	£135,418
	9/15	Gdwd	1m Cls5 Mdn 2yo soft		£3,235

Highly tried last season, finishing third in the Oaks and Irish Oaks; missed a good opportunity to land a first win since her maiden when only third in a Group 3 at Cork (sent off 11-10 favourite) but should be able to win at a similar level.

Harry Angel (Ire)

3 b c Dark Angel - Beatrix Potter (Cadeaux Genereux)

Clive Cox   Peter Ridgers

PLACINGS: 21-   RPR **111+**

Starts	1st	2nd	3rd	4th	Win & Pl
2	1	1	-	-	£44,842
	9/16	Newb	6f Cls1 Gp2 2yo gd-sft		£42,533

Highly regarded colt who was well backed to win the Mill Reef Stakes despite lack of experience and justified the confidence in style, though he had little to beat; seen as a sprinter by connections and a likely Commonwealth Cup type.

Hathal (USA)

5 ch h Speightstown - Sleepytime (Royal Academy)

William Haggas   Al Shaqab Racing

PLACINGS: 2/10721/18-   RPR **117**

Starts	1st	2nd	3rd	4th	Win & Pl
8	3	2	-	-	£70,675
	9/16	Hayd	1m Cls1 Gp3 good		£35,727
	9/15	Newb	7f Cls1 List soft		£20,983
	6/15	Ling	7f Cls5 Mdn 3yo gd-fm		£3,105

Out for nearly a year with niggly problems before returning last autumn but made a winning comeback in a Group 3 at Haydock; well beaten in the QEII next time but still very lightly raced for his age and could well improve again.

Hawkbill (USA)

4 ch c Kitten's Joy - Trensa (Giant's Causeway)

Charlie Appleby — Godolphin

PLACINGS: 93111/111893- — RPR **123**

Starts	1st	2nd	3rd	4th	Win & Pl
11	6	-	2	-	£394,799
	7/16	Sand	1m2f Cls1 Gp1 soft		£297,728
	6/16	Asct	1m2f Cls1 Gp3 3yo soft		£51,039
	4/16	NmkR	1m2f Cls1 List 3yo gd-sft		£22,684
	9/15	Kemp	1m Cls4 2yo std-slw		£4,528
81	8/15	Kemp	7f Cls4 71-81 2yo Hcap std-slw		£3,946
	7/15	Ling	7f Cls5 Mdn 2yo stand		£3,364

Rapid improver early last season and completed a six-timer when winning the Eclipse; possibly flattered by that win (only principal to act on soft ground) and disappointing after, though slightly better when third back in favoured conditions in Germany.

Heartbreak City (Fr)

7 b g Lando - Moscow Nights (Peintre Celebre)

Tony Martin (Ir) — Here For The Craic Partnership

PLACINGS: 59/35415/3100/1012- — RPR **118**

Starts	1st	2nd	3rd	4th	Win & Pl
15	4	1	2	1	£682,796
103	8/16	York	1m6f Cls2 98-109 Hcap good		£174,300
88	3/16	Cork	1m2f 78-103 Hcap heavy		£10,853
81	8/15	York	2m½f Cls2 81-98 Hcap gd-sft		£31,125
0	6/13	Chan	1m3f 3yo Hcap good		£12,195

Runaway winner of last season's Ebor, building on his good form over hurdles, and improved again when beaten a head in the Melbourne Cup; probably rated too high for handicaps now but may well be up to contending in top staying races.

Higher Power

5 b g Rip Van Winkle - Lady Stardust (Spinning World)

James Fanshawe — Mrs Martin Armstrong

PLACINGS: 4/62/231221- — RPR **99**

Starts	1st	2nd	3rd	4th	Win & Pl
9	2	4	1	1	£30,557
93	11/16	Kemp	2m Cls2 84-103 Hcap stand		£11,828
83	6/16	Kemp	1m3f Cls4 75-85 Hcap stand		£4,690

Won two handicaps at Kempton last year but proved just as effective on turf when a close second to Cape Cova at Doncaster having needed his first run after a break prior to that; has proved his stamina for 2m and could be one for top staying handicaps.

Highland Reel (Ire)

5 b h Galileo - Hveger (Danehill)

Aidan O'Brien (Ir) — Derrick Smith, Sue Magnier & Michael Tabor

PLACINGS: /62511531/482127212- — RPR **124**

Starts	1st	2nd	3rd	4th	Win & Pl
20	7	6	1	1	£5,283,545
	11/16	SnAt	1m4f Gd1 firm		£1,496,599
	7/16	Asct	1m4f Cls1 Gp1 gd-fm		£689,027
	12/15	ShTn	1m4f Gp1 good		£778,560
	8/15	Arlt	1m2f Gd1 3yo firm		£171,346
	7/15	Gdwd	1m4f Cls1 Gp3 3yo good		£56,710
	7/14	Gdwd	7f Cls1 Gp2 2yo gd-fm		£45,368
	7/14	Gowr	1m Mdn 2yo gd-fm		£8,338

Globetrotting flagbearer for Coolmore who has competed in a staggering 15 Group 1 races over the last two seasons, winning four of them including last year's King George and Breeders' Cup Turf; not quite as effective over 1m2f.

Highlands Queen (Fr)

4 b f Mount Nelson - Queen Of Poland (Polish Precedent)

Yohann Gourraud (Fr) — Mme N Kerjean

PLACINGS: 211D14- — RPR **111+**

Starts	1st	2nd	3rd	4th	Win & Pl
6	3	1	-	1	£111,459
	8/16	Deau	1m4½f Gp2 good		£54,485
	5/16	StCl	1m2½f Gp3 3yo gd-sft		£29,412
	4/16	StCl	1m2f 3yo heavy		£9,191

Hugely impressive winner of the Group 2 Prix de Pomone at Deauville last season (third win in four at the time with sole defeat in the Prix de Diane); only fourth in the Prix Vermeille but unsuited by being held up too far back.

Home Of The Brave (Ire)

5 ch h Starspangledbanner - Blissful Beat (Beat Hollow)

Hugo Palmer — Godolphin

PLACINGS: 213/1661d0/11220- — RPR **118**

Starts	1st	2nd	3rd	4th	Win & Pl
13	4	3	1	-	£203,425
	5/16	Hayd	7f Cls1 Gp3 good		£35,727
	4/16	Leic	7f Cls1 List gd-sft		£28,355
102	4/15	NmkR	7f Cls1 List 100-110 3yo Hcap gd-fm		£20,983
	7/14	NmkJ	6f Cls5 Auct Mdn 2yo gd-fm		£3,881

Did well over 7f last season, winning Group 3 and Listed races before finishing second in the Lennox and Hungerford Stakes; didn't get home on his only try at a mile in the 2,000 Guineas in 2015 but may be worth another chance at that trip.

ON THE CLOCK

Higher Power Won twice on the all-weather at Kempton last year and earned decent figures on three occasions. Effective at up to 2m, he has yet to win on turf but can remedy that situation this season. [Dave Edwards, Topspeed]

Horseplay

3 b f Cape Cross - Mischief Making (Lemon Drop Kid)

Andrew Balding   Cliveden Stud

PLACINGS: 41-   RPR **95+**

Starts	1st	2nd	3rd	4th	Win & Pl
2	1	-	-	1	£3,715
10/16	Nott	1m½f Cls5 Mdn 2yo soft.......................£3,235			

Bolted up by 13 lengths in a maiden at Nottingham in October, showing vast improvement on her debut third at Ascot in the summer; sure to stay middle distances, although needs to prove she's as effective on quicker ground.

Hydrangea (Ire)

3 b f Galileo - Beauty Is Truth (Pivotal)

Aidan O'Brien (Ir)
       Derrick Smith, Sue Magnier & Michael Tabor

PLACINGS: 0212220-   RPR **112**

Starts	1st	2nd	3rd	4th	Win & Pl
7	1	4	-	-	£195,825
8/16	Curr	7f 2yo gd-fm.........................£13,566			

Smart filly who was very unlucky not to add to her win in a minor race at the Curragh last season, going down narrowly in the Moyglare and Debutante Stakes, although she was put in her place by Rhododendron in the Fillies' Mile; should stay middle distances.

Ibn Malik (Ire)

4 ch g Raven's Pass - Moon's Whisper (Storm Cat)

Charles Hills   Hamdan Al Maktoum

PLACINGS: 1223/149-   RPR **112**

Starts	1st	2nd	3rd	4th	Win & Pl
7	2	2	1	1	£98,068
107	4/16	NmkR	7f Cls1 List 103-108 3yo Hcap gd-sft.............£20,983		
	6/15	NmkJ	7f Cls4 Mdn 2yo gd-fm.........................£4,528		

Held up by foot problems last season but managed to win the Free Handicap on his return and finished fourth in the Jersey Stakes; fourth time he has made the frame in a Group race and capable of winning one granted a clear run.

Icespire

3 b f Frankel - Quest To Peak (Distant View)

John Gosden   K Abdullah

PLACINGS: 1-   RPR **83+**

Starts	1st	2nd	3rd	4th	Win & Pl
1	1	-	-	-	£3,557
10/16	Sals	7f Cls5 Mdn 2yo gd-sft.........................£3,558			

Beautifully bred filly who was an impressive winner of her only start at Salisbury last season, coasting to victory by four lengths; half-sister to 1,000 Guineas winner Special Duty and could be another top miler.

Idaho (Ire)

4 b c Galileo - Hveger (Danehill)

Aidan O'Brien (Ir)
       Michael Tabor, Derrick Smith & Sue Magnier

PLACINGS: 14/23321U5-   RPR **120+**

Starts	1st	2nd	3rd	4th	Win & Pl
9	2	2	2	1	£511,232
8/16	York	1m4f Cls1 Gp2 3yo gd-fm.........................£90,736			
10/15	Curr	1m Mdn 2yo gd-fm.........................£8,826			

Flourished when stepped up to 1m4f last season, finishing third in the Derby under a forceful ride and deservedly getting closer to Harzand in a great battle in the Irish Derby; stumbled and unseated rider when odds-on for the St Leger.

Intelligence Cross (USA)

3 b c War Front - Good Vibes (Unbridled's Song)

Aidan O'Brien (Ir)
       Sue Magnier, Michael Tabor & Derrick Smith

PLACINGS: 2123149-   RPR **110**

Starts	1st	2nd	3rd	4th	Win & Pl
7	2	2	1	1	£84,398
8/16	Curr	6f Gp3 2yo good.........................£26,029			
6/16	Curr	6f Mdn 2yo gd-yld.........................£7,461			

Won a Group 3 at the Curragh in terrific fashion last season and ran well at a higher level, including when fourth in the Middle Park; should stay a mile (never a factor but stayed on well enough on only run at the trip at the Breeders' Cup).

Intimation

5 b m Dubawi - Infallible (Pivotal)

Sir Michael Stoute   Cheveley Park Stud

PLACINGS: 9/11/77331-   RPR **110+**

Starts	1st	2nd	3rd	4th	Win & Pl
8	3	-	2	-	£45,871
	10/16	Naas	1m List sft-hvy.........................£24,945		
80	7/15	Leic	1m2f Cls4 69-80 Hcap gd-sft.........................£9,452		
	5/15	Nott	1m½f Cls5 Mdn 3yo gd-sft.........................£3,881		

Initially disappointing last season but flourished on two trips to Ireland in pursuit of testing ground, especially when running away with a Listed race on soft/heavy at Naas in October; stays in training in pursuit of more black type.

....

'This beautifully bred filly was an impressive winner of her only start last season. She's a half-sister to 1,000 Guineas winner Special Duty and could be a top miler'

Intisaab
6 b g Elnadim - Katoom (Soviet Star)

David O'Meara — Stuart Graham

PLACINGS: 011956/982121222041- RPR **110**

Starts	1st	2nd	3rd	4th	Win & Pl
22	6	7	1	1	£152,903

100	10/16	York	6f Cls2 92-102 Hcap good	£62,250
86	6/16	Ayr	6f Cls3 83-95 Hcap good	£9,057
80	6/16	Ayr	6f Cls4 62-80 Hcap gd-fm	£5,175
80	4/15	Donc	7f Cls4 67-80 Am Hcap gd-fm	£4,523
77	4/15	Ripn	6f Cls4 71-85 Hcap gd-sft	£4,852
	9/14	List	6½f Mdn good	£8,050

Progressed throughout last season and showed he was still ahead of the handicapper when winning at York on his final start having climbed the handicap often without winning (unlucky in running several times); looks ready for Pattern level.

Intricately (Ire)
3 b f Fastnet Rock - Inner Realm (Galileo)

Joseph Patrick O'Brien — C C Regalado-Gonzalez

PLACINGS: 13310- RPR **113**

Starts	1st	2nd	3rd	4th	Win & Pl
5	2	-	2	-	£165,515

	9/16	Curr	7f Gp1 2yo yield	£146,691
	6/16	Gowr	7f Mdn 2yo yld-sft	£7,009

Surprise winner of last season's Moyglare but hadn't been beaten far by main rivals previously and form was boosted when second and third were one-two in the Fillies' Mile; disappointing in Breeders' Cup Juvenile Fillies Turf next time.

Jack Hobbs
5 br h Halling - Swain's Gold (Swain)

John Gosden — Godolphin & Partners

PLACINGS: 1/122113/P3- RPR **122+**

Starts	1st	2nd	3rd	4th	Win & Pl
9	4	2	2	-	£1,238,215

	9/15	Kemp	1m4f Cls1 Gp3 std-slw	£35,160
	6/15	Curr	1m4f Gp1 3yo gd-fm	£562,016
85	4/15	Sand	1m2f Cls3 76-93 3yo Hcap good	£9,338
	12/14	Wolv	1m½f Cls5 Mdn 2yo stand	£2,911

Missed nearly all of last season after suffering a pelvis injury on his comeback but finished a fine third when returning in the Champion Stakes; likely to prove best over 1m4f (won the 2015 Irish Derby) and will be fascinating in top middle-distance races.

Jallota
6 b g Rock Of Gibraltar - Lady Lahar (Fraam)

Charles Hills — Fitri Hay

PLACINGS: 56249/9771421533123- RPR **115+**

Starts	1st	2nd	3rd	4th	Win & Pl
40	5	7	5	4	£312,350

	9/16	Chan	7f Gp3 good	£29,412
	7/16	Hayd	7f Cls3 soft	£8,086
103	5/16	York	7f Cls2 96-105 Hcap good	£18,675
99	6/15	York	7f Cls2 87-105 Hcap gd-sft	£24,900
	6/13	Nmkj	6f Cls4 Mdn 2yo gd-fm	£4,528

Tough and consistent 7f specialist who won three times last season, including a Group 3 at Chantilly; came within a neck of adding a Group 1 in Italy over a mile (yet to win over that trip but has tried it only three times).

Jimmy Two Times (Fr)
4 gr c Kendargent - Steel Woman (Anabaa)

Andre Fabre (Fr) — Haras De Saint Pair

PLACINGS: 1142/201134- RPR **114**

Starts	1st	2nd	3rd	4th	Win & Pl
10	4	2	1	2	£144,921

	7/16	Deau	7f Gp3 gd-sft	£29,412
	6/16	Deau	6½f List 3yo good	£20,221
	9/15	Lonc	5f 2yo heavy	£13,178
	9/15	Cros	5½f 2yo v soft	£6,977

Won twice at Deauville last season to warrant step up to Group 1 level and more than held his own when finishing third in the Prix Maurice de Gheest and fourth in the Prix de la Foret; disappointed on only run over a mile.

Johannes Vermeer (Ire)
4 b c Galileo - Inca Princess (Holy Roman Emperor)

Aidan O'Brien (Ir) — Michael Tabor, Derrick Smith, Sue Magnier & China Horse Club

PLACINGS: 311421/3- RPR **109**

Starts	1st	2nd	3rd	4th	Win & Pl
7	3	1	2	1	£232,328

	11/15	StCl	7f Gp1 2yo v soft	£110,736
	9/15	Leop	7f Gp3 2yo yield	£46,512
	8/15	Klny	1m½f Mdn 2yo good	£7,221

High-class two-year-old in 2015, winning a Group 1 at Saint-Cloud having come second in the Racing Post Trophy; missed nearly all of last season through injury but suggested he retains all his ability when a promising third in the Darley Stakes.

Journey

5 b m Dubawi - Montare (Montjeu)

John Gosden — George Strawbridge

PLACINGS: 5/24218112/3111-   RPR **121**

Starts	1st	2nd	3rd	4th	Win & Pl
13	6	3	1	1	£590,054

10/16	Asct	1m4f Cls1 Gp1 good	£340,260
9/16	NmkR	1m4f Cls1 List gd-fm	£22,684
5/16	Hayd	1m4f Cls1 Gp3 good	£35,727
9/15	NmkR	1m4f Cls1 List good	£22,684
8/15	Sals	1m2f Cls1 List gd-fm	£23,818
6/15	Newb	1m2f Cls4 Mdn 3yo gd-fm	£5,337

Has gone from strength to strength since 33-1 Listed success in 2015, winning five of last seven (five out of six over 1m4f); better than ever when a four-length winner of the Champion Fillies & Mares Stakes and should again be a force at Group 1 level.

Just Glamorous (Ire)

4 ch g Arcano - Glamorous Air (Air Express)

Ronald Harris — Robert & Nina Bailey

PLACINGS: 2052234/23221118310-   RPR **114**

Starts	1st	2nd	3rd	4th	Win & Pl
18	4	6	3	1	£60,258

	9/16	Chan	5f Gp3 good	£29,412
83	7/16	York	5½f Cls4 65-84 3yo Hcap gd-fm	£6,469
77	7/16	Sand	5f Cls4 68-82 3yo Hcap good	£4,690
70	7/16	Hayd	5f Cls4 70-82 3yo Hcap soft	£6,469

Improved at an astonishing rate last season, sparking a hat-trick of handicap wins off 70 at Haydock and later adding a Group 3 success at Chantilly over Prix de l'Abbaye winner Marsha; beat only one home in that race next time.

Kassia (Ire)

4 b f Acclamation - Speedy Sonata (Stravinsky)

Mick Channon   Jon & Julia Aisbitt

PLACINGS: 215601/611211-   RPR **109**

Starts	1st	2nd	3rd	4th	Win & Pl
12	6	2	-	-	£77,172

	10/16	NmkR	6f Cls1 List good		£28,355
94	9/16	Pont	6f Cls2 82-95 Hcap gd-fm		£18,675
87	7/16	Bath	5¹/₂f Cls3 81-87 3yo Hcap gd-fm		£8,410
85	6/16	Bath	5f Cls4 73-85 3yo Hcap soft		£4,690
82	10/15	Pont	6f Cls4 65-84 2yo Hcap good		£4,528
	5/15	Sand	5f Cls5 Mdn 2yo gd-fm		£3,881

Out-and-out sprinter who won four of her last five races last season and successfully stepped up to Listed level when winning at Newmarket by a head in October; probably capable of better given habit of only ever doing enough.

Khairaat (Ire)

4 b c Shamardal - Mumayeza (Indian Ridge)

Sir Michael Stoute   Hamdan Al Maktoum

PLACINGS: 211-   RPR **97+**

Starts	1st	2nd	3rd	4th	Win & Pl
3	2	1	-	-	£14,277

9/16	Donc	1m2¹/₂f Cls3 good		£9,338
7/16	Pont	1m Cls5 Mdn 3-4yo gd-fm		£3,881

Progressed well in just three runs last season, winning his maiden at the second attempt and particularly impressive when making a successful handicap debut over 1m2f at Doncaster; should continue to improve and could be a Group horse.

Just Glamorous (white cap): made rapid improvement last season but has to bounce back from a disappointing run on his final start

Lady Aurelia: last season's Queen Mary winner looks likely to take in the Commonwealth Cup this year

La Cressonniere (Fr)
4 b f Le Havre - Absolute Lady (Galileo)

Jean-Claude Rouget (Fr)
Ecurie Antonio Caro & Gerard Augustin-Normand

PLACINGS: 1111/1111-   RPR **115+**

Starts	1st	2nd	3rd	4th	Win & Pl
8	8	-	-	-	£746,709

8/16	Deau	1m2f Gp2 3yo good	£54,485
6/16	Chan	1m2½f Gp1 3yo soft	£420,147
5/16	Deau	1m Gp1 3yo good	£189,066
3/16	StCl	1m List 3yo gd-sft	£20,221
11/15	Chan	7f List 2yo heavy	£21,318
10/15	Deau	1m List 2yo heavy	£21,318
9/15	Crao	1m 2yo gd-sft	£10,465
7/15	Claf	7f 2yo gd-sft	£9,690

Brilliant filly who has won all eight of her races, including a Classic double in France last season; impressed again when winning her Arc prep at Deauville only to miss the big race after a setback; hugely exciting talent.

Lady Aurelia (USA)
3 b f Scat Daddy - D'Wildcat Speed (Forest Wildcat)
Wesley Ward (US)
Stonestreet Stables, G Bolton & P Leidel

PLACINGS: 1113-					RPR **123+**
Starts	1st	2nd	3rd	4th	Win & Pl
4	3	-	1	-	£249,208

8/16	Deau	6f Gp1 2yo good	£147,051
6/16	Asct	5f Cls1 Gp2 2yo soft	£62,381
4/16	Keen	4½f 2yo fast	£20,408

Amazingly quick filly who ran away with last season's Queen Mary at Royal Ascot by seven lengths; less impressive when adding the Prix Morny and broke blood vessels when beaten in the Cheveley Park; likely to be aimed at the Commonwealth Cup.

Lancaster Bomber (USA)
3 b c War Front - Sun Shower (Indian Ridge)
Aidan O'Brien (Ir)
Michael Tabor, Derrick Smith & Sue Magnier

PLACINGS: 614522-					RPR **116**
Starts	1st	2nd	3rd	4th	Win & Pl
6	1	2		1	£239,578

8/16	Leop	7f Mdn 2yo good	£7,461

Seemed to surprise even connections with performances at end of last season having been used as a pacemaker, finishing second in the Dewhurst and Breeders' Cup Juvenile Turf; relishes quick ground and could be a very smart miler.

Landfall (Fr)

3 b g Myboycharlie - Lana Girl (Arch)

Ken Condon (Ir)
Carl Anthony Howell, Pauline Condon & R J Condon

PLACINGS: 11-   RPR **110**

Starts	1st	2nd	3rd	4th	Win & Pl
2	2	-	-	-	£50,843
9/16	Leop	1m Gp3 2yo good			£43,382
8/16	Curr	7f Mdn 2yo yld-sft			£7,461

Unbeaten in two runs last season, most notably when easily landing a Group 3 at Leopardstown having beaten Exemplar in his maiden; potentially high-class, although big-race options will be limited by already being gelded.

Larchmont Lad (Ire)

3 b c Footstepsinthesand - Fotini (King's Best)

Richard Hannon   Michael Geoghegan

PLACINGS: 131-   RPR **109**

Starts	1st	2nd	3rd	4th	Win & Pl
3	2	-	1	-	£35,464
9/16	NmkR	7f Cls1 Gp3 2yo gd-fm			£28,355
7/16	Sand	7f Cls5 Mdn 2yo gd-sft			£3,881

Won two out of three last season, suffering sole defeat when third (beaten a short-neck) in a slowly run race at Doncaster before improving on that to win a red-hot Group 3 at Newmarket; likely to start off in a 2,000 Guineas trial.

Latharnach (USA)

5 b g Iffraaj - Firth Of Lorne (Danehill)

Charlie Appleby   Godolphin

PLACINGS: 411/223/13-   RPR **116+**

Starts	1st	2nd	3rd	4th	Win & Pl
8	3	2	2	1	£143,354
10/16	Rdcr	7f Cls1 List gd-fm			£22,684
9/14	Sand	7f Cls3 2yo good			£6,469
7/14	Sand	7f Cls5 Mdn 2yo gd-fm			£3,881

Highly talented gelding (second to Gleneagles in the 2015 St James's Palace Stakes) but has had issues and was out for more than a year before a winning return in October; big horse who ought to get better again with age.

Laugh Aloud

4 ch f Dubawi - Opera Comique (Singspiel)

John Gosden   Godolphin

PLACINGS: 6/22121-   RPR **111**

Starts	1st	2nd	3rd	4th	Win & Pl
6	2	3	-	-	£30,985
9/16	NmkR	1m Cls1 List gd-fm			£22,684
7/16	Wind	1m½f Cls5 Mdn 3-4yo gd-fm			£2,911

Thrown into Listed grade at Newmarket last September despite having won only a maiden in five runs and rose to the task magnificently when

a clearcut winner; has to prove that wasn't a fluke (given an easy lead in front).

Left Hand

4 ch f Dubawi - Balladeuse (Singspiel)

Carlos Laffon-Parias (Fr)   Wertheimer & Frere

PLACINGS: 14/642110-   RPR **113+**

Starts	1st	2nd	3rd	4th	Win & Pl
8	3	1	-	2	£378,016
9/16	Chan	1m4f Gp1 good			£147,051
7/16	Deau	1m2f Gp3 3yo good			£29,412
9/15	Lonc	1m 2yo gd-sft			£9,690

Ran La Cressonniere close when second in the Prix de Diane last season and proved that was no fluke when winning next two races, including the Prix Vermeille when stepped up to 1m4f; disappointed in the Arc.

Librisa Breeze

5 gr g Mount Nelson - Bruxcalina (Linamix)

Dean Ivory   Tony Bloom

PLACINGS: 216d512d/121416-   RPR **117+**

Starts	1st	2nd	3rd	4th	Win & Pl
12	5	2	-	1	£270,221
108	10/16	Asct	7f Cls2 98-109 Hcap soft		£112,050
100	7/16	Asct	7f Cls2 87-109 Hcap gd-fm		£93,375
92	4/16	Wolv	1m½f Cls3 87-95 Hcap stand		£7,246
85	9/15	Kemp	1m Cls4 75-85 Hcap std-slw		£4,690
	3/15	Ling	1m2f Cls5 Mdn 3yo stand		£3,235

Went from strength to strength in big Ascot handicaps last season, winning two valuable pots over 7f having finished second in the Hunt Cup; needs to prove himself at Group level now and could manage only sixth in the Champions Sprint.

Lightning Spear

6 ch h Pivotal - Atlantic Destiny (Royal Academy)

David Simcock   Qatar Racing Limited

PLACINGS: 1/1/112430/36913-   RPR **122**

Starts	1st	2nd	3rd	4th	Win & Pl
13	5	1	3	1	£361,179
	8/16	Gdwd	1m Cls1 Gp2 gd-fm		£62,041
96	6/15	Sals	1m Cls2 86-100 Hcap gd-fm		£12,450
91	4/15	Ling	1m Cls3 79-93 Hcap stand		£7,246
85	10/14	Nott	1m½f Cls4 71-85 Hcap gd-sft		£5,434
	8/13	Kemp	7f Cls5 Mdn 2yo stand		£2,911

Better than ever last season when competitive in a host of top mile races, winning the Celebration Mile and third in the Queen Anne Stakes and the QEII; drawn on the wrong side that day and may yet land a Group 1 granted better fortune.

....

'Highly talented gelding who ought to get better again with age'

Limato (Ire)

5 b g Tagula - Come April (Singspiel)

Henry Candy   Paul G Jacobs

PLACINGS: 1111/12212/41216-   RPR **126+**

Starts	1st	2nd	3rd	4th	Win & Pl
14	8	4	-	1	£953,034

10/16	Chan	7f Gp1 good	£126,044
7/16	NmkJ	6f Cls1 Gp1 gd-fm	£302,690
9/15	Donc	7f Cls1 Gp2 good	£56,710
4/15	Asct	6f Cls1 Gp3 3yo gd-fm	£45,368
10/14	Rdcr	6f Cls1 List 2yo good	£117,220
7/14	Newb	6f Cls1 List 2yo gd-fm	£14,461
6/14	Kemp	6f Cls3 2yo stand	£6,225
6/14	Kemp	6f Cls5 Mdn 2yo stand	£2,588

Supremely talented and versatile performer who won Group 1 races at 6f (July Cup) and 7f (Prix de la Foret) last season as well as finishing second in the Nunthorpe and fourth in the Lockinge; loves quick ground and has never run on slower than good.

Magical Memory (Ire)

5 gr g Zebedee - Marasem (Cadeaux Genereux)

Charles Hills   Kennet Valley Thoroughbreds

PLACINGS: 62106/4313113/11470-   RPR **118+**

Starts	1st	2nd	3rd	4th	Win & Pl
18	6	1	3	2	£411,285

5/16	York	6f Cls1 Gp2 good	£68,052
4/16	NmkR	6f Cls1 Gp3 gd-sft	£34,026
102 8/15	Gdwd	6f Cls2 96-113 Hcap gd-fm	£155,625
96 7/15	NmkJ	6f Cls2 86-102 3yo Hcap gd-fm	£62,250
87 5/15	Leic	6f Cls3 80-93 3yo Hcap gd-fm	£12,450
6/14	Leic	6f Cls5 Mdn Auct 2yo gd-fm	£2,588

Stepped up on progressive 2015 form when winning the Abernant and Duke of York Stakes last season; beaten just half a length in the Diamond Jubilee and had things go against him next twice (will avoid soft ground after Sprint Cup flop).

Making Light (Ire)

3 b f Tamayuz - Instant Sparkle (Danehill)

Dermot Weld (Ir)   Moyglare Stud Farm

PLACINGS: 511-   RPR **102**

Starts	1st	2nd	3rd	4th	Win & Pl
3	2	-	-	-	£32,966

10/16	Leop	7f Gp3 2yo yield	£26,029
10/16	Limk	7f Mdn 2yo soft	£6,783

Beat colts when landing a Group 3 at Leopardstown in October, confirming the promise of eight-length maiden success; likely to reappear in a Guineas trial; out of a sister to a Ribblesdale winner but seen as a miler by her trainer.

Marsha (Ire)

4 b f Acclamation - Marlinka (Marju)

Sir Mark Prescott   Elite Racing Club

PLACINGS: 2113/2511521-   RPR **114**

Starts	1st	2nd	3rd	4th	Win & Pl
11	5	3	1	-	£244,979

10/16	Chan	5f Gp1 good	£147,051
7/16	York	5f Cls1 List good	£22,684
6/16	Ayr	5f Cls1 List gd-fm	£28,355
10/15	Dund	5f 2yo stand	£10,078
9/15	Catt	6f Cls5 Mdn 7yo good	£3,235

Big player in top sprints having won last season's Prix de l'Abbaye; sent off 16-1 there after below-par defeat last time out but no fluke about it on previous form having won twice at Listed level and been unlucky in the King George Stakes.

Massaat (Ire)

4 b c Teofilo - Madany (Acclamation)

Owen Burrows   Hamdan Al Maktoum

PLACINGS: 212/297-   RPR **117**

Starts	1st	2nd	3rd	4th	Win & Pl
6	1	2	-	-	£222,624

9/15	Leic	7f Cls4 Mdn 2yo gd-sft	£6,469

Terrific second in last season's 2,000 Guineas, splitting Galileo Gold and Ribchester, but flopped in the Derby and a distant last of seven on his only other run at Salisbury; something to prove now but still very smart on Guineas form.

Mekhtaal

4 ch c Sea The Stars - Aiglonne (Silver Hawk)

Jean-Claude Rouget (Fr)   Al Shaqab Racing

PLACINGS: 121842-   RPR **112**

Starts	1st	2nd	3rd	4th	Win & Pl
6	2	2	-	1	£105,632

5/16	Deau	1m2f Gp2 3yo good	£54,485
3/16	StCl	1m2f 3yo heavy	£9,191

Won the Prix Hocquart by six lengths last season and disappointing he couldn't build on that, although he was a fair fourth in the Grand Prix de Paris and beaten just a short-neck in a Group 3 last time; surely capable of better.

Midterm

4 b c Galileo - Midday (Oasis Dream)

Sir Michael Stoute   K Abdullah

PLACINGS: 1/15527-   RPR **117**

Starts	1st	2nd	3rd	4th	Win & Pl
5	2	1	-	-	£68,663
	4/16	Sand	1m2f Cls1 Gp3 3yo gd-sft		£36,862
	10/15	Newb	1m Cls4 Mdn 2yo gd-sft		£6,469

Winter favourite for last season's Derby and duly won the Sandown Classic Trial but missed much of the season after going wrong in the Dante; good second in the Prix Niel on his return but only seventh in the Champion Stakes.

Minding (Ire)

4 b f Galileo - Lillie Langtry (Danehill Dancer)

Aidan O'Brien (Ir)

Derrick Smith, Sue Magnier & Michael Tabor

PLACINGS: 21211/1211131-   RPR **123+**

Starts	1st	2nd	3rd	4th	Win & Pl
12	8	3	1	-	£2,261,739
	10/16	Asct	1m Cls1 Gp1 good		£656,432
	7/16	Gdwd	1m2f Cls1 Gp1 gd-fm		£340,260
	6/16	Curr	1m2f Gp1 yield		£108,640
	6/16	Epsm	1m4f Cls1 Gp1 3yo gd-sft		£269,373
	5/16	NmkR	1m Cls1 Gp1 3yo good		£297,019
	10/15	NmkR	1m Cls1 Gp1 2yo gd-sft		£302,690
	9/15	Curr	7f Gp1 2yo yield		£134,884
	6/15	Leop	6f Mdn 2yo gd-fm		£8,826

Outstanding filly who has won seven Group 1s up to 1m4f and completed a Classic double in the Oaks; probably best at a mile though and beat the boys when landing the QEII last October; won Nassau but struggled on quick ground.

Mirage Dancer

3 b c Frankel - Heat Haze (Green Desert)

Sir Michael Stoute   K Abdullah

PLACINGS: 1-   RPR **87+**

Starts	1st	2nd	3rd	4th	Win & Pl
1	1	-	-	-	£4,528
	10/16	Donc	7f Cls5 Mdn 2yo good		£4,528

Came from a long way back to make a winning debut over 7f at Doncaster last season; sure to prove better over further on that evidence, although Derby quotes may be a shade fanciful (1m2f likely to prove his limit on pedigree).

Mitchum Swagger

5 b g Paco Boy - Dont Dili Dali (Dansili)

David Lanigan   Paul Dean & The Mitchum Swagger P'Ship

PLACINGS: 1122/932205-   RPR **116**

Starts	1st	2nd	3rd	4th	Win & Pl
10	2	4	1	-	£57,716
87	9/15	Hayd	1m Cls3 77-89 Hcap soft		£8,086
	5/15	Newb	7f Cls4 Mdn 3yo good		£6,469

Without a win since his first two races in 2015

but has been beaten a head three times, including a Group 3 at Haydock last season, and looked unlucky when third in the Hunt Cup; capable of winning good races over 7f or a mile.

Mokarris (USA)

3 b c More Than Ready - Limonar (Street Cry)

Simon Crisford   Hamdan Al Maktoum

PLACINGS: 10126-   RPR **107+**

Starts	1st	2nd	3rd	4th	Win & Pl
5	2	1	-	-	£68,460
	7/16	Newb	6f Cls1 List 2yo gd-fm		£14,461
	5/16	Hayd	6f Cls4 2yo gd-sft		£4,270

Impressive winner of a Listed race at Newbury last season on favoured good to firm ground; got those conditions only once on three attempts at Group level when pulling too hard in sixth in the Middle Park; capable of better.

Mondialiste (Ire)

7 b h Galileo - Occupandiste (Kaldoun)

David O'Meara   Geoff & Sandra Turnbull

PLACINGS: 71/233011120/702140-   RPR **118**

Starts	1st	2nd	3rd	4th	Win & Pl
23	5	5	5	1	£1,186,690
	8/16	Arlt	1m2f Gd1 3yo firm		£387,755
	9/15	Wood	1m Gd1 yield		£331,492
	8/15	York	1m1f Cls1 Gp3 good		£48,204
	7/15	Pont	1m Cls1 List gd-fm		£25,520
	5/14	StCl	1m gd-sft		£11,667

Gained second international Group 1 when winning last season's Arlington Million; seems more effective over that 1m2f trip now (previous best efforts over a mile) but was much too keen on first try at 1m4f in the Breeders' Cup Turf.

Moonlight Magic

4 b c Cape Cross - Melikah (Lammtarra)

Jim Bolger (Ir)   Godolphin

PLACINGS: 11/5106363-   RPR **115**

Starts	1st	2nd	3rd	4th	Win & Pl
9	3	-	2	-	£114,328
	5/16	Leop	1m2f Gp3 3yo good		£43,382
	10/15	Leop	1m1f List 2yo gd-yld		£23,682
	10/15	Cork	7f Mdn 2yo yld-sft		£6,419

Failed to build on last season's Derrinstown Derby Trial win but produced best runs in only subsequent races back at 1m2f, finishing third in the Royal Whip and sixth in the Irish Champion on ground softer than ideal; should do better.

....

'Impressive winner of a Listed race at Newbury is capable of better'

Moonrise Landing (Ire)
6 gr m Dalakhani - Celtic Slipper (Anabaa)

Ralph Beckett   P D Savill

PLACINGS: 18/382404111/11-   RPR **110**

Starts	1st	2nd	3rd	4th	Win & Pl
13	4	1	1	2	£158,221

	5/16	York	1m6f Cls1 List good	£22,684
	3/16	Ling	2m Cls2 stand	£93,375
	12/15	Wolv	2m½f Cls2 stand	£12,602
88	11/15	Kemp	2m Cls2 84-93 Hcap stand	£12,291
83	10/15	NmkR	1m4f Cls3 75-90 Hcap soft	£8,733
	3/14	Ling	1m2f Cls5 Mdn 3yo stand	£3,409

Flourished on the all-weather last winter and stepped up again back on turf in a York Listed race, making it five in a row when beating Quest For More; missed the rest of the season but due to be back in more good staying races.

Morando (Fr)
4 gr g Kendargent - Moranda (Indian Rocket)

Roger Varian   H H Sheikh Mohammed Bin Khalifa Al Thani

PLACINGS: 41117-   RPR **109+**

Starts	1st	2nd	3rd	4th	Win & Pl
5	3	-	-	1	£31,140

96	9/16	Ayr	1m Cls2 87-101 Hcap gd-sft	£15,563
86	6/16	Ches	7½f Cls3 62-86 3yo Hcap good	£12,450
	5/16	Wind	1m½f Cls5 Mdn 3-4yo good	£2,911

Won three in a row last season and defied a 10lb rise when completing his hat-trick easily at Ayr despite being keen early; favourite to win again in the Balmoral Handicap but couldn't find room; still on a fair mark and could be a Group horse.

Mountain Bell
4 b f Mount Nelson - Shenir (Mark Of Esteem)

Ralph Beckett   Qatar Racing Limited

PLACINGS: 2/1312-   RPR **107**

Starts	1st	2nd	3rd	4th	Win & Pl
5	2	2	1	-	£43,761

	9/16	Ches	1m4½f Cls1 List gd-sft	£22,684
	4/16	Wind	1m2f Cls5 Mdn 3yo soft	£2,911

Missed much of last season after finishing third in what proved a red-hot Lingfield Oaks Trial but bounced back with two fine efforts in the autumn, winning a Listed race at Chester and a close second in a Group 3 at Newbury; should stay further.

Move Up
4 b c Dubawi - Rosinka (Soviet Star)

Saeed Bin Suroor   Godolphin

PLACINGS: 5113/1311-   RPR **116**

Starts	1st	2nd	3rd	4th	Win & Pl
8	5	-	2	-	£200,096

	10/16	Asct	1m4f Cls1 Gp3 soft	£34,026
	9/16	Veli	1m4f Gp2 good	£132,353
94	7/16	Asct	1m2f Cls3 76-95 Hcap gd-fm	£9,704
82	9/15	Ripn	1m Cls4 64-82 2yo Hcap good	£6,469
	9/15	Leic	7f Cls4 Mdn 2yo good	£5,175

Smart and progressive middle-distance performer last season; won three out of four and did particularly well to land the Cumberland Lodge Stakes at Ascot under a 5lb penalty; acts on any ground and should have more to offer.

Mr Lupton (Ire)
4 ch g Elnadim - Chiloe Wigeon (Docksider)

Richard Fahey   N D Kershaw

PLACINGS: 261323912/33150559-   RPR **115**

Starts	1st	2nd	3rd	4th	Win & Pl
17	3	3	4	-	£326,426

102	6/16	York	6f Cls2 89-102 3yo Hcap gd-sft	£62,250
	9/15	Donc	6½f Cls2 good	£147,540
	6/15	Hayd	5f Cls5 Mdn 2yo gd-fm	£2,911

Has an outstanding record in big fields and won a valuable 6f three-year-old handicap at York last season to add to fine efforts in juvenile sales races; couldn't quite break through at higher level but may do better back in handicaps.

Mrs Danvers
3 gr f Hellvelyn - Rebecca De Winter (Kyllachy)

Jonathan Portman   Turf Club 2014

PLACINGS: 11111-   RPR **106**

Starts	1st	2nd	3rd	4th	Win & Pl
5	5	-	-	-	£196,235

	10/16	NmkR	5f Cls1 Gp3 2yo gd-fm	£45,368
	8/16	Newb	5f Cls1 List 2yo gd-fm	£14,461
	7/16	Newb	5f Cls2 2yo gd-fm	£122,925
	6/16	Wind	5f Cls2 2yo soft	£10,894
	6/16	Ling	5f Cls5 Auct 2yo soft	£2,588

Unbeaten sprinter who took advantage of a low weight when landing the Super Sprint but twice proved herself at a higher level, most notably in the Cornwallis; yet to race beyond 5f but trainer believes she will get another furlong.

Mubtasim (Ire)

3 b c Arcano - Start The Music (King's Best)

William Haggas   Sheikh Rashid Dalmook Al Maktoum

PLACINGS: 11819-   RPR **102+**

Starts	1st	2nd	3rd	4th	Win & Pl
5	3	-			£156,467
	9/16	Donc	6½f Cls2 2yo good		£147,540
	8/16	Hayd	6f Cls4 2yo gd-fm		£4,270
	6/16	Yarm	6f Cls4 2yo gd-fm		£4,658

Twice well beaten when stepped up in grade but was an impressive winner of a valuable sales race at Doncaster in between; had excuses for subsequent Middle Park defeat (held up when it paid to be prominent); could get a mile.

Muntahaa (Ire)

4 gr c Dansili - Qertaas (Linamix)

John Gosden   Hamdan Al Maktoum

PLACINGS: 321314-   RPR **116**

Starts	1st	2nd	3rd	4th	Win & Pl
6	2	1	2	1	£86,469
108	8/16	Ches	1m5½f Cls1 List 94-108 Hcap good		£20,983
	6/16	Kemp	1m4f Cls5 Mdn stand		£2,911

Pulled too hard when fourth in last season's St Leger; had emerged as a leading contender for that race when winning a Listed handicap at Chester, improving on his King Edward VII Stakes; should do well in good middle-distance/staying races.

Mustashry

4 b/br c Tamayuz - Safwa (Green Desert)

Sir Michael Stoute   Hamdan Al Maktoum

PLACINGS: 4/210124-   RPR **109**

Starts	1st	2nd	3rd	4th	Win & Pl
7	2	2		2	£50,546
95	7/16	Asct	1m Cls2 80-98 3yo gd-fm		£28,013
	5/16	Thsk	1m Cls5 Mdn good		£3,235

Progressed well last season, bouncing back from a poor run at Royal Ascot (didn't like soft ground) to win at the same track and finish second of 20 at York; beaten only a length in a Listed race last time; should be able to win at that level and perhaps beyond.

Mutakayyef

6 ch g Sea The Stars - Infallible (Pivotal)

William Haggas   Hamdan Al Maktoum

PLACINGS: 2/221223/223/1133-   RPR **122**

Starts	1st	2nd	3rd	4th	Win & Pl
14	3	7	4	-	£333,570
	7/16	Asct	1m Cls2 Gp2 gd-fm		£68,052
	6/16	York	1m Cls1 List gd-fm		£22,684
	5/14	Sand	1m2f Cls5 Mdn 3-4yo soft		£3,881

Had been slightly frustrating in 2015 but fulfilled

obvious potential last season, gaining his biggest win in the Summer Mile at Ascot; also proved stamina for 1m2f when unlucky third in the Juddmonte International and ran Tepin close in the Woodbine Mile.

Muthmir (Ire)

7 b g Invincible Spirit - Fairy Of The Night (Danehill)

William Haggas   Hamdan Al Maktoum

PLACINGS: 2151/5139163/358363-   RPR **113**

Starts	1st	2nd	3rd	4th	Win & Pl
21	5	2	5	1	£423,356
	7/15	Gdwd	5f Cls1 Gp2 gd-fm		£170,130
	5/15	Chan	5f Gp2 gd-sft		£57,442
100	9/14	Donc	5½f Cls2 93-103 Hcap good		£37,350
93	7/14	York	6f Cls2 87-104 Hcap gd-fm		£31,125
	7/13	Donc	6f Cls5 Mdn gd-fm		£2,588

Among the very best sprinters in 2015 when winning a couple of Group 2 races and finishing third in the King's Stand and Prix de l'Abbaye; disappointing last season but still went close when favourite for a couple of Listed races.

My Dream Boat (Ire)

5 b h Lord Shanakill - Betty Burke (Choisir)

Clive Cox   Paul & Clare Rooney

PLACINGS: 224/14291011/151554-   RPR **122**

Starts	1st	2nd	3rd	4th	Win & Pl
17	6	3	-	3	£664,958
	6/16	Asct	1m2f Cls1 Gp1 soft		£425,325
	4/16	Sand	1m2f Cls1 Gp3 gd-sft		£36,862
	11/15	StCl	1m Gp3 v soft		£31,008
	10/15	Chan	1m List soft		£20,155
92	8/15	York	1m Cls2 84-99 3yo Hcap gd-sft		£31,125
76	5/15	Donc	7f Cls4 71-83 3yo Hcap gd-fm		£4,690

Surprise winner of last season's Prince of Wales's Stakes; flattered by that victory (rivals well below par) but produced other good efforts to win the Gordon Richards Stakes and come fourth in the Champion Stakes; likely to step up in trip.

Nathra (Ire)

4 b f Iffraaj - Rada (Danehill)

John Gosden   Abdullah Saeed Al Naboodah

PLACINGS: 112/15293-   RPR **111+**

Starts	1st	2nd	3rd	4th	Win & Pl
8	3	2	1	-	£267,315
	4/16	NmkR	7f Cls1 Gp3 3yo gd-sft		£34,026
	9/15	Newb	7f Cls2 2yo soft		£9,960
	9/15	Sals	7f Cls3 Mdn 2yo soft		£7,116

Proved herself a smart filly early last season, winning the Nell Gwyn and beating all bar La Cressonniere in the French Guineas; disappointing on both subsequent runs, including when running on good to firm ground for only time.

National Defense

3 b c Invincible Spirit - Angel Falls (Kingmambo)

Mme C Head-Maarek				Sun Bloodstock Sarl

PLACINGS: 131-				RPR **119+**

Starts	1st	2nd	3rd	4th	Win & Pl
3	1	-	1	-	£165,066
	10/16	Chan		1m Gp1 2yo good	£147,051
	8/16	Deau		1m 2yo good	£9,191

Well backed when running away with the Prix Jean-Luc Lagardere last season; no doubt that was a soft Group 1 but clearly a smart colt and genuine Classic contender; half-brother to a 1m4f winner and should get middle distances.

Nathra: smart filly who finished second in last year's French 2,000 Guineas

Nezwaah

4 b f Dubawi - Ferdoos (Dansili)

Roger Varian				Sheikh Ahmed Al Maktoum

PLACINGS: 1131527-				RPR **111** RPR

Starts	1st	2nd	3rd	4th	Win & Pl
7	3	1	1	-	£54,276
73	6/16	Newc	1m2f Cls1 List stand	£22,684
	2/16	Wolv	1m½f Cls5 68-75 3yo Hcap stand	£3,235
	1/16	Chmt	1m Cls4 Mdn stand	£6,469

Began on the all-weather early in 2016 and progressed quickly to land a Listed race on Tapeta at Newcastle; proved equally effective on turf when second to So Mi Dar at Yarmouth and may well be up to Pattern level; should stay 1m4f.

Opal Tiara (Ire)

4 b f Thousand Words - Zarafa (Fraam)

Mick Channon			The Filly Folly & Sweet Partnership

PLACINGS: 12744239/2017117-21				RPR **109**

Starts	1st	2nd	3rd	4th	Win & Pl
17	5	4	1	2	£252,327
	2/17	Meyd	1m1f Gp2 good	£97,561
95	8/16	Gdwd	7f Cls1 Gp3 good	£34,026
	8/16	York	7f Cls2 75-97 Hcap gd-fm	£37,350
	6/16	Carl	7f Cls1 List 3yo gd-fm	£22,684
	5/15	Wolv	5f Cls5 Mdn 2yo stand	£3,235

Very smart filly who took more than a year to add to her winning debut in May 2015 but has thrived since last summer; peaked last season with a Group 3 success at Goodwood (third win in four starts) and progressed again in Dubai this winter.

Order Of St George (Ire)

5 b h Galileo - Another Storm (Gone West)

Aidan O'Brien (Ir)
Michael Tabor, Derrick Smith, Sue Magnier & L J Williams

PLACINGS: 42152/2111/111234-				RPR **122**

Starts	1st	2nd	3rd	4th	Win & Pl
15	7	4	1	2	£997,527
	8/16	Curr	1m6f Gp3 good	£27,353
	6/16	Asct	2m4f Cls1 Gp1 soft	£226,840
	6/16	Leop	1m6f List gd-fm	£21,257
	9/15	Curr	1m6f Gp1 good	£157,364
	8/15	Curr	1m6f Gp3 soft	£30,233
	7/15	DRoy	1m5f gd-fm	£10,078
	8/14	Leop	1m Mdn 2yo soft	£9,488

Leading stayer of last season by some margin, as he proved when running away with the Ascot Gold Cup, and even showed the speed to be competitive in top middle-distance races when third in the Arc; twice beaten at odds-on, though.

Orion's Bow

6 ch g Pivotal - Heavenly Ray (Rahy)

David Nicholls   T J Swiers

PLACINGS: 6405210/70811111280-   RPR **111**

Starts	1st	2nd	3rd	4th	Win & Pl
29	7	4	-	2	£109,063

97	7/16	Haml	6f Cls2 87-100 Hcap soft £21,165
91	6/16	Newc	5f Cls2 86-99 Hcap stand £18,675
85	6/16	Thsk	6f Cls4 66-85 Hcap good £4,852
75	5/16	Catt	6f Cls5 63-75 Hcap good £3,235
69	5/16	Newc	6f Cls5 62-70 Hcap stand £4,528
71	9/15	Haml	6f Cls5 55-73 Hcap gd-fm £3,235
74	7/14	Ling	7f Cls5 60-74 3yo Hcap stand £2,588

Showed remarkable improvement last season, with winning sequence (having begun off mark of 69) ended at five when a fine second in the Stewards' Cup; may have been over the top when twice beaten after and remains interesting.

Outback Traveller (Ire)

6 b g Bushranger - Blue Holly (Blues Traveller)

Robert Cowell   Lordship Stud & Mrs J Morley

PLACINGS: 1351/2053040/701950-   RPR **112+**

Starts	1st	2nd	3rd	4th	Win & Pl
23	6	2	2	2	£158,743

100	6/16	Asct	6f Cls2 100-109 Hcap gd-sft....£108,938
93	10/14	Asct	7f Cls3 80-94 3yo Hcap good £8,410
89	8/14	NmkJ	7f Cls3 71-90 3yo Hcap firm £12,938
84	6/14	NmkJ	7f Cls4 70-86 3yo Hcap gd-fm £6,469
75	10/13	Ling	6f Cls4 66-85 2yo Hcap stand £3,752
	9/13	Ling	6f Cls5 Mdn 2yo gd-fm......................£2,727

Won last season's Wokingham by a head from Brando and form looks red-hot with runner-up adding the Ayr Gold Cup; failed to build on that but had excuses every time (trip/ground) and already back on a good mark.

Pallasator

8 b g Motivator - Ela Athena (Ezzoud)

Sir Mark Prescott   Qatar Racing Limited

PLACINGS: 214713/84414/104228-   RPR **116**

Starts	1st	2nd	3rd	4th	Win & Pl
23	7	3	2	6	£373,962

	5/16	Sand	2m½f Cls1 Gp3 gd-fm.....................£36,862
	9/15	Donc	2m2f Cls1 Gp2 good.......................£56,710
	9/14	NmkR	2m Cls1 List good...........................£22,684
103	7/14	Asct	1m4f Cls2 89-103 Hcap gd-fm £18,675
91	9/12	Hayd	1m6f Cls3 81-91 3yo Hcap heavy £6,663
85	9/12	Kemp	1m4f Cls4 75-86 3yo Hcap stand £4,075
	7/12	Leic	1m2f Cls6 Auct Mdn 3-4yo good £1,941

Dual Group winner who added last season's

Henry II Stakes at Sandown to the 2015 Doncaster Cup; went on to finish second in the Goodwood and Lonsdale Cups; should continue to run well in top staying races.

Peace Envoy (Fr)

3 b c Power - Hoh My Darling (Dansili)

Aidan O'Brien (Ir)

Sue Magnier, Michael Tabor & Derrick Smith

PLACINGS: 12142138-   RPR **112**

Starts	1st	2nd	3rd	4th	Win & Pl
8	3	2	1	1	£117,514

	7/16	Curr	6½f Gp3 2yo gd-yld.......................£28,199
	5/16	Naas	6f List 2yo good.............................£28,199
	4/16	Dund	5f Mdn Auct 2yo stand £6,783

Progressive juvenile sprinter last season, producing his best effort when a length third to Lady Aurelia in the Prix Morny having won a good Group 3 at the Curragh previously; reportedly lost his action in the Middle Park on only subsequent run.

Persuasive (Ire)

4 gr f Dark Angel - Choose Me (Choisir)

John Gosden   Cheveley Park Stud

PLACINGS: 1/111112-   RPR **113+**

Starts	1st	2nd	3rd	4th	Win & Pl
6	5	1	-	-	£154,235

	8/16	Sand	1m Cls1 Gp3 gd-sft.........................£36,862
95	6/16	Asct	1m Cls1 List 93-107 3yo Hcap soft ...£45,368
87	6/16	Chmt	1m Cls2 82-95 Hcap stand £12,938
80	5/16	Gdwd	1m Cls4 67-80 3yo Hcap good £6,225
	11/15	Kemp	1m Cls4 Mdn 2yo std-slw...................£3,946

Beaten only once in her six races when second to Alice Springs in the Group 1 Matron Stakes; winning run had included the Sandringham at Royal Ascot and a Group 3 at Sandown; sure to try again in Group 1 mile races.

Platitude

4 b g Dansili - Modesta (Sadler's Wells)

Sir Michael Stoute   K Abdullah

PLACINGS: 1235/422813-   RPR **110+**

Starts	1st	2nd	3rd	4th	Win & Pl
10	2	3	2	1	£88,476

	8/16	Gdwd	1m6f Cls1 List gd-fm......................£28,355
	6/15	Donc	7f Cls5 Mdn 2yo gd-fm......................£3,235

Flourished as he stepped up in trip last season

ON THE CLOCK

Platitude Finished third at Royal Ascot and was an emphatic winner of Goodwood's March Stakes in August. He could develop into a big player in the top middle-distance contests this summer. [Dave Edwards, Topspeed]

and won a Listed race at Goodwood over 1m6f by five lengths having come second in the King George V Handicap and Bahrain Trophy; only third when 6-4 to follow up at Ascot but worth another chance.

Poet's Vanity

3 b f Poet's Voice - Vanity (Thatching)

Andrew Balding   Mrs M E Wates

PLACINGS: 411-   RPR **105**

Starts	1st	2nd	3rd	4th	Win & Pl
3	2	-	-	1	£53,467
10/16	NmkR	7f Cls1 Gp3 2yo gd-fm			£45,368
9/16	Sals	7f Cls3 Mdn 2yo gd-fm			£7,763

Ten-length Salisbury maiden winner who took a big rise in class in her stride when adding the Oh So Sharp Stakes at Newmarket (market principals below par); likely to return for 1,000 Guineas but not certain to get a mile on pedigree.

Poet's Word (Ire)

4 b c Poet's Voice - Whirly Bird (Nashwan)

Sir Michael Stoute   Saeed Suhail

PLACINGS: 4/31412-   RPR **111**

Starts	1st	2nd	3rd	4th	Win & Pl
6	2	1	1	2	£23,421
88	7/16	Gdwd	1m3f Cls3 76-88 3yo Hcap gd-fm		£12,450
5/16	Nott	1m2f Cls5 Mdn 3yo gd-fm			£3,068

Favourite for three good handicaps last season and did well to win despite finding trouble at Glorious Goodwood having struggled to handle Epsom; improved again when second at Doncaster on final start; should have more to come over 1m4f.

Portage (Ire)

5 b h Teofilo - Galley (Zamindar)

Mick Halford (Ir)   Godolphin

PLACINGS: 21/00125/112-   RPR **115**

Starts	1st	2nd	3rd	4th	Win & Pl
10	4	3			£196,285
105	6/16	Asct	1m Cls2 97-112 Hcap soft		£108,938
	6/16	Curr	1m2f List gd-fm		£20,390
90	7/15	Asct	1m Cls2 79-99 3yo Hcap soft		£28,013
	9/14	Curr	7f Mdn 2yo gd-fm		£9,488

Won last season's Royal Hunt Cup under a penalty for winning at Listed level earlier in the month; long thought capable of better (was favourite for the 2015 Cambridgeshire) but beaten at odds-on in a Group 3 at Leopardstown next time.

Pallasator: proven performer should continue to do well in leading staying contests

Postponed (Ire)

6 b h Dubawi - Ever Rigg (Dubai Destination)

Roger Varian   Sheikh Mohammed Obaid Al Maktoum

PLACINGS: 2/34311/23311/11115-   RPR **126**

Starts	1st	2nd	3rd	4th	Win & Pl
18	9	2	4	1	£4,467,523

8/16	York	1m2½f Cls1 Gp1 gd-fm £546,543
6/16	Epsm	1m4f Cls1 Gp1 gd-sft £226,840
3/16	Meyd	1m4f Gp1 good £2,448,980
3/16	Meyd	1m4f Gp2 good £102,041
9/15	Lonc	1m4f Gp2 v soft £57,442
7/15	Asct	1m4f Cls1 Gp1 soft £689,027
8/14	York	1m4f Cls1 Gp2 3yo gd-fm £85,065
7/14	Haml	1m3f Cls1 List 3yo gd-fm £22,684
8/13	Yarm	7f Cls5 Mdn 2yo gd-fm £2,911

Patiently handled by Luca Cumani in younger days and approach bore fruit for Roger Varian last season with three Group 1 wins on the spin from 1m2f to 1m4f; better than he showed when fifth in the Arc and should be a force in all top middle-distance races.

Priceless

4 b f Exceed And Excel - Molly Brown (Rudimentary)

Clive Cox   A D Spence

PLACINGS: 135/952241-   RPR **107+**

Starts	1st	2nd	3rd	4th	Win & Pl
9	2	2	1	1	£65,623

9/16	Donc	5f Cls1 List gd-sft £22,684
9/15	Hayd	6f Cls5 Mdn 2yo gd-sft £3,235

Lost her way after initial promise at two but bounced back in second half of last season with two big runs in competitive handicaps and did well to win a Listed race at Doncaster on good to soft (previous best form on good to firm).

Prize Money

4 b g Authorized - Dresden Doll (Elusive Quality)

Saeed Bin Suroor   Godolphin

PLACINGS: 1/222851-21   RPR **117**

Starts	1st	2nd	3rd	4th	Win & Pl
9	3	4	-	-	£196,300

114	2/17	Meyd	1m4f 98-114 Hcap good £78,049
107	11/16	Donc	1m4f Cls2 87-107 Hcap gd-fm £49,800
	10/15	NmkR	1m Cls4 Mdn 2yo gd-fm £6,469

Hugely progressive since being gelded midway through last season and won the November Handicap on his return at Doncaster off 107; took another step forward in Dubai over the winter and could be a Group horse at around 1m4f.

Profitable (Ire)

5 b h Invincible Spirit - Dani Ridge (Indian Ridge)

Clive Cox   Godolphin

PLACINGS: 12225/512505/111467-   RPR **120**

Starts	1st	2nd	3rd	4th	Win & Pl
18	5	5	-	1	£414,653

6/16	Asct	5f Cls1 Gp1 soft £226,840
5/16	Hayd	5f Cls1 Gp2 gd-sft £56,710
4/16	NmkR	5f Cls1 Gp3 gd-sft £34,026
5/15	York	5f Cls1 List 3yo good £22,684
7/14	Sand	5f Cls5 Mdn 2yo gd-fm £3,881

Dominant 5f sprinter in first half of last season, completing a rare Palace House/Temple/King's Stand treble with victory at Royal Ascot; perhaps lucky to get cut in the ground every time, although ran well over 6f on good to firm when fourth in the July Cup.

Projection

4 b g Acclamation - Spotlight (Dr Fong)

Roger Charlton   The Royal Ascot Racing Club

PLACINGS: 81741/453-   RPR **110**

Starts	1st	2nd	3rd	4th	Win & Pl
8	2	-	1	2	£44,891

9/15	Sals	6f Cls2 2yo gd-sft £9,704
8/15	Wind	6f Cls5 Mdn 2yo gd-fm £2,911

Ran well in three good sprint handicaps last season and particularly caught the eye when an unlucky fifth in the Stewards' Cup consolation race; beaten two short heads when well backed at Newmarket next time; still ahead of his handicap mark.

Promise To Be True (Ire)

3 b f Galileo - Sumora (Danehill)

Aidan O'Brien (Ir)

Sue Magnier, Michael Tabor & Derrick Smith

PLACINGS: 11523-   RPR **111**

Starts	1st	2nd	3rd	4th	Win & Pl
5	2	1	1	-	£108,944

7/16	Leop	7f Gp3 2yo gd-fm £26,029
6/16	Tipp	7½f Mdn 2yo yield £6,331

Slightly disappointing she couldn't win a Group 1 last season having been Aidan O'Brien's first string for the Moyglare over Rhododendron and Hydrangea; did best when staying on well over a mile into second in the Prix Marcel Boussac and should get middle distances.

ON THE CLOCK

Projection A luckless fifth in the Stewards' Cup consolation race, he was beaten subsequently at Newmarket, but a big pot like the Wokingham could come his way.
[Dave Edwards, Topspeed]

Qemah (Ire)

4 b f Danehill Dancer - Kartica (Rainbow Quest)

Jean-Claude Rouget (Fr)   Al Shaqab Racing

PLACINGS: 213/13113-   RPR **117+**

Starts	1st	2nd	3rd	4th	Win & Pl
8	4	1	3	-	£486,913
	7/16	Deau	1m Gp1 good		£126,044
	6/16	Asct	1m Cls1 Gp1 3yo gd-sft		£226,840
	4/16	Chan	1m Gp3 3yo soft		£29,412
	9/15	Lonc	1m½f 2yo gd-sft		£13,178

Dual Group 1 winner last season, adding the Prix Rothschild to her Coronation Stakes success; well beaten by Alice Springs in the Matron Stakes but much better than she showed there (slowly away and raced too keenly).

Queen Kindly

3 ch f Frankel - Lady Of The Desert (Rahy)

Richard Fahey   Jaber Abdullah

PLACINGS: 13114-   RPR **112**

Starts	1st	2nd	3rd	4th	Win & Pl
5	3		1	1	£138,145
	8/16	York	6f Cls1 Gp2 2yo gd-fm		£113,420
	7/16	Catt	5f Cls5 2yo gd-fm		£3,235
	6/16	Catt	5f Cls5 2yo gd-fm		£3,235

Impressive winner of last season's Lowther Stakes at York having looked the best filly in the Albany (close third on unsuitably soft ground); well below that form when only fourth in the Cheveley Park; not certain to stay a mile on dam's side.

Queen's Trust

4 b f Dansili - Queen's Best (King's Best)

Sir Michael Stoute   Cheveley Park Stud

PLACINGS: 15/442331-   RPR **115**

Starts	1st	2nd	3rd	4th	Win & Pl
8	2	1	2	2	£1,002,107
	11/16	SnAt	1m2f Gd1 firm		£748,299
	9/15	Kemp	7f Cls4 Mdn 2yo std-slw		£4,270

Steady improver throughout last season and justified connections' lofty ambitions when winning the Breeders' Cup Filly & Mare Turf; likely to prove equally effective over 1m4f having been unlucky on her last run over that trip at Ascot.

Quest For More (Ire)

7 b g Teofilo - No Quest (Rainbow Quest)

Roger Charlton   H R H Sultan Ahmad Shah

PLACINGS: 2201/211209/2361212-   RPR **117+**

Starts	1st	2nd	3rd	4th	Win & Pl
27	8	7	4	2	£628,488
	10/16	Chan	2m4½f Gp1 good		£126,044
	8/16	York	2m½f Cls1 Gp2 gd-fm		£113,420
104	6/15	Newc	2m Cls2 90-104 Hcap good		£86,226
96	5/15	Gdwd	1m6f Cls3 82-97 Hcap good		£19,407
87	10/14	Asct	2m Cls3 76-87 Hcap good		£8,410
80	7/14	Donc	1m4f Cls4 72-86 Hcap good		£5,175
72	9/13	Leic	1m4f Cls5 62-73 Hcap gd-fm		£2,588
68	7/13	Wind	1m½f Cls5 63-75 Hcap gd-fm		£2,588

Took time to find his form last season but bounced back with victory in the Lonsdale Cup and later added the Prix du Cadran in

Quest For More (right): Cup races sure to be on the agenda again this season

between close seconds in the Doncaster and Long Distance Cups; sure to be a threat again in similar races.

Quiet Reflection

4 b f Showcasing - My Delirium (Haafhd)

Karl Burke			Ontoawinner, Strecker & Burke	
PLACINGS: 1511/111317-				RPR **120**

Starts	1st	2nd	3rd	4th	Win & Pl
10	7	-	1	-	£626,696
	9/16	Hayd	6f Cls1 Gp1 soft		£162,191
	6/16	Asct	6f Cls1 Gp1 3yo gd-sft		£243,853
	5/16	Hayd	6f Cls1 Gp2 3yo good		£51,039
	4/16	Chan	6f Gp3 3yo heavy		£29,412
	10/15	NmkR	5f Cls1 Gp3 2yo gd-sft		£45,368
	9/15	Ayr	5f Cls1 List 2yo good		£28,355
	7/15	Haml	5f Cls5 Mdn 2yo gd-sft		£3,409

Best sprinter of her generation last season, impressively landing the Commonwealth Cup, and added a Group 1 success against her elders in the Sprint Cup; ideally suited by soft ground that day but also third on good to firm in the July Cup.

Racing History (Ire)

5 b h Pivotal - Gonbarda (Lando)

Saeed Bin Suroor				Godolphin
PLACINGS: 0/1114/62-				RPR **117**

Starts	1st	2nd	3rd	4th	Win & Pl
7	3	1	-	1	£162,959
	8/15	Wind	1m2f Cls1 Gp3 gd-sft		£34,026
91	7/15	Ches	1m2½f Cls3 79-91 Hcap good		£13,585
	5/15	Hayd	1m Cls5 Mdn gd-sft		£2,911

Missed nearly all of last season, returning when sixth in the Champion Stakes on his first run since coming fourth in the same race in 2015; second in a Group 1 in Germany next time; open to further improvement after only seven runs.

Raheen House (Ire)

3 b c Sea The Stars - Jumooh (Monsun)

Brian Meehan				J L Day
PLACINGS: 2214-				RPR **111**

Starts	1st	2nd	3rd	4th	Win & Pl
4	1	2	-	1	£22,639
	10/16	York	1m Cls3 Mdn Auct 2yo good		£7,763

Improved steadily before winning at York and coped well with a sharp rise in class when fourth in the Racing Post Trophy; pedigree suggests he should be a stayer, perhaps even a St Leger type.

'High-class juvenile in 2015 and connections have long targeted a four-year-old campaign'

Really Special

3 b f Shamardal - Rumh (Monsun)

Saeed Bin Suroor				Godolphin
PLACINGS: 11-153				RPR **100+**

Starts	1st	2nd	3rd	4th	Win & Pl
5	3		1	-	£87,967
	1/17	Meyd	7f 3yo fast		£48,780
	10/16	NmkR	1m Cls1 List 2yo gd-fm		£17,013
	10/16	Chmt	6f Cls5 Mdn 2yo stand		£3,881

Looked a potential star when running away with a Listed race at Newmarket last season; Godolphin's leading Classic hope in Dubai after that, although she flopped at 1-2 in the UAE 1,000 Guineas.

Recorder

4 ch c Galileo - Memory (Danehill Dancer)

William Haggas				The Queen
PLACINGS: 311/				

Starts	1st	2nd	3rd	4th	Win & Pl
3	2	-	1	-	£53,693
	8/15	York	7f Cls1 Gp3 2yo gd-sft		£48,204
	7/15	Nmkj	7f Cls4 Mdn 2yo soft		£4,528

High-class juvenile in 2015, stepping up on a fine maiden win at Newmarket to land the Acomb Stakes at York in good style; suffered an injury that ruled out the entire 2016 campaign but connections have long targeted a four-year-old campaign.

Red Verdon (USA)

4 ch c Lemon Drop Kid - Porto Marmay (Choisir)

Ed Dunlop				The Hon R J Arculli
PLACINGS: 21/211642-				RPR **114**

Starts	1st	2nd	3rd	4th	Win & Pl
8	3	3	-	1	£190,862
88	5/16	Hayd	1m4f Cls3 77-88 3yo Hcap gd-sft		£9,338
80	5/16	Ches	1m4½f Cls3 73-87 3yo Hcap good		£9,960
	12/15	Wolv	1m½f Cls5 Mdn 2yo stand		£3,235

Highly tried after waving goodbye to handicaps with a runaway win at Haydock last May; finished sixth in the Derby before getting closer to Harzand at the Curragh and coming second in the Grand Prix de Paris; missed the St Leger after a setback.

Remarkable

4 b g Pivotal - Irresistible (Cadeaux Genereux)

John Gosden				Cheveley Park Stud
PLACINGS: 8/112502-				RPR **110**

Starts	1st	2nd	3rd	4th	Win & Pl
7	2	2	-	-	£75,068
76	4/16	Donc	6f Cls3 76-89 3yo Hcap gd-sft		£7,763
	3/16	Sthl	7f Cls5 Mdn stand		£3,235

Showed plenty of promise early last season, including when fifth in the Jersey Stakes, and ran another cracker to finish second in the Balmoral

Handicap on his second run after a break; still lightly raced and should continue to improve.

Rhododendron (Ire)
3 b f Galileo - Halfway To Heaven (Pivotal)
Aidan O'Brien (Ir)
Sue Magnier, Michael Tabor & Derrick Smith
PLACINGS: 21131-   RPR **117**

Starts	1st	2nd	3rd	4th	Win & Pl
5	3	1	1	-	£394,218
10/16	NmkR	1m Cls1 Gp1 2yo gd-fm			£302,690
8/16	Curr	7f Gp2 2yo yld-sft			£49,890
7/16	Gdwd	7f Cls2 Mdn 2yo gd-fm			£16,173

Relished the step up to a mile and quicker ground when an impressive winner of last season's Fillies' Mile having managed only third in the Moyglare; worthy Guineas favourite on that evidence and seems sure to stay further.

Ribchester (Ire)
4 b c Iffraaj - Mujarah (Marju)
Richard Fahey   Godolphin
PLACINGS: 221/2d31312-   RPR **124**

Starts	1st	2nd	3rd	4th	Win & Pl
9	3	3	2	-	£848,346
8/16	Deau	1m Gp1 good			£294,103
6/16	Asct	7f Cls1 Gp3 3yo soft			£51,039
9/15	Newb	6f Cls1 Gp2 2yo gd-sft			£42,533

Progressed throughout last season, getting closer to the best three-year-old milers before winning the Prix Jacques le Marois and then chasing home Minding in the QEII; already top-class with the potential to carry on improving.

Rich Legacy (Ire)
3 b f Holy Roman Emperor - Borghesa (Galileo)
Ralph Beckett   Qatar Racing Limited
PLACINGS: 14140-   RPR **105**

Starts	1st	2nd	3rd	4th	Win & Pl
5	2	-	-	2	£74,396
9/16	Donc	1m Cls1 Gp2 2yo good			£39,697
8/16	NmkJ	7f Cls4 Auct Mdn 2yo gd-fm			£3,946

Relished stepping up to a mile when winning last season's May Hill; blotted her copybook subsequently (too keen in front in Fillies' Mile and never a factor when dropped out in a French Group 1) but still a good middle-distance prospect.

Richard Pankhurst
5 ch h Raven's Pass - Mainstay (Elmaamul)
John Gosden   Godolphin
PLACINGS: 41/17/50156-   RPR **117**

Starts	1st	2nd	3rd	4th	Win & Pl
9	3	-	-	1	£138,873
8/16	Newb	7f Cls1 Gp2 gd-fm			£85,065
9/15	Hayd	7f Cls3 gd-sft			£11,321
6/14	Asct	7f Cls1 List 2yo gd-fm			£34,026

Beset by injury problems since a runaway winner of the Chesham in 2014 but showed that ability again when landing last season's Hungerford Stakes; largely disappointing otherwise but still one to watch over 7f when getting quick ground.

Rivet (Ire)
3 b c Fastnet Rock - Starship (Galileo)
William Haggas   The Starship Partnership
PLACINGS: 21151-   RPR **116**

Starts	1st	2nd	3rd	4th	Win & Pl
5	3	1	-	-	£210,480
10/16	Donc	1m Cls1 Gp1 2yo good			£113,420
9/16	Donc	7f Cls1 Gp2 good			£42,533
8/16	York	7f Cls2 Mdn 2yo good			£37,350

Won last season's Racing Post Trophy at Doncaster, putting behind him a poor effort in the Dewhurst (unsuited by undulating track) albeit in a weaker race for the top level; out of a Galileo mare so should stay further, perhaps even 1m4f.

Rodaini (USA)
3 ch c Exchange Rate - Blessings Count (Pulpit)
Simon Crisford   Abdullah Saeed Al Naboodah
PLACINGS: 111190-   RPR **104**

Starts	1st	2nd	3rd	4th	Win & Pl
6	4	-	-	-	£32,126
9/16	Donc	7f Cls1 List 2yo good			£17,013
84	8/16	NmkJ	7f Cls3 82-84 2yo Hcap gd-fm		£6,469
8/16	Ling	7f Cls5 2yo gd-fm			£3,881
8/16	Leic	7f Cls4 Mdn 2yo gd-fm			£4,528

Won first four starts last season and did particularly well to land a strong Listed race at Doncaster (third won in higher grade next time); failed to act on the track when well beaten at Newmarket and forced very wide when never a factor at Breeders' Cup.

ON THE FIGURES

Rhododendron Didn't quite hit the heights of stablemate Minding but was still very impressive when winning the Fillies' Mile last year. Doesn't need to improve on that form to have a great chance in the 1,000 Guineas and promises to stay beyond a mile. [Simon Turner, Racing Post Ratings]

Roly Poly (USA)
3 b f War Front - Misty For Me (Galileo)

Aidan O'Brien (Ir)

Michael Tabor, Derrick Smith & Sue Magnier

PLACINGS: 14811229-				RPR 112
Starts	1st	2nd	3rd	4th	Win & Pl
8	3	2	-	1	£164,275

	7/16	Nmkj	6f Cls1 Gp2 2yo gd-fm	£45,368
	6/16	Curr	6f Gp3 2yo yield	£28,199
	4/16	Naas	5f Mdn 2yo good	£7,009

Standing dish in top 6f races last season and a close second in Cheveley Park and Lowther Stakes; out of a 1m2f Group 1 winner and seems sure to get at least a mile (ridden too close to a furious gallop when ninth on only attempt at the Breeders' Cup).

Royal Artillery (USA)
4 b/br c War Front - Masseuse (Dynaformer)

John Gosden

Sue Magnier, Michael Tabor & Derrick Smith

PLACINGS: 1/4513-				RPR 117
Starts	1st	2nd	3rd	4th	Win & Pl
5	2	-	1	1	£74,248

	8/16	Hayd	1m2½f Cls1 Gp3 gd-fm	£35,727
	10/15	Donc	7f Cls5 Mdn 2yo gd-sft	£3,235

Took time to find his feet last season but impressed when winning the Rose of Lancaster at Haydock and again ran well when third behind Almanzor at Deauville; big, scopey horse who should improve again as a four-year-old.

Salsabeel
3 b c Exceed And Excel - Tokyo Rose (Jade Robbery)

Charlie Appleby

Godolphin

PLACINGS: 12-				RPR 104
Starts	1st	2nd	3rd	4th	Win & Pl
2	1	1	-	-	£11,108

	8/16	Yar	7f Cls4 2yo gd-fm	£4,657

Ran a cracker to split Rodaini and Larchmont Lad when losing his unbeaten record at Doncaster last season; still green and raw so seems sure to improve and trainer reckons he has three-year-old written all over him.

Sans Equivoque (Ger)
3 gr f Stormy River - Suissesse (Malibu Moon)

Didier Guillemin (Fr)

Sun Bloodstock Sarl

PLACINGS: 3123111-				RPR 108
Starts	1st	2nd	3rd	4th	Win & Pl
7	4	1	2	-	£153,823

	10/16	MsnL	6f Gp2 2yo gd-sft	£79,632
	9/16	MsnL	6f Gp3 2yo gd-sft	£29,412
	8/16	Deau	5f List 2yo good	£20,221
	5/16	Bord	5f 2yo good	£5,882

Finished last season on a roll, completing a hat-trick with victory in the Group 2 Criterium de Maisons-Laffitte; has a middle-distance pedigree on paper so bodes well that she's achieved so much over shorter trips.

Scottish (Ire)
5 b g Teofilo - Zeiting (Zieten)

Charlie Appleby

Godolphin

PLACINGS: 0/212251/31212-				RPR 119
Starts	1st	2nd	3rd	4th	Win & Pl
12	4	5	1	-	£386,283

	8/16	York	1m1f Cls1 List gd good	£48,204
	7/16	Newb	1m2f Cls1 List gd-fm	£20,983
	9/15	Ayr	1m2f Cls1 List good	£36,862
	5/15	Newb	1m2f Cls4 Mdn 3yo good	£6,469

Did well after joining Godolphin from Andrew Balding last season and gained his biggest win in the Strensall Stakes at York over 1m1f; just as effective all the way up to 1m4f and ran a cracker when second in the Caulfield Cup in Australia.

Sea Of Grace (Ire)
3 ch f Born To Sea - Lady Dettoria (Vettori)

John Oxx (Ir)

Sunderland Holding Inc

PLACINGS: 311-				RPR 104+
Starts	1st	2nd	3rd	4th	Win & Pl
3	2	-	1	-	£42,128

	8/16	Curr	1m Gp3 2yo good	£34,706
	7/16	Tipp	7½f Mdn 2yo yield	£6,331

Twice beat Listed winner Eziyra last season, most notably in the Flame of Tara at the Curragh; reportedly found good ground quicker than ideal and may prove even better with some cut; should prove best over middle distances.

ON THE CLOCK

Sea Of Grace Provided John Oxx with his first Group winner for almost three years when successful at the Curragh in August and her time stacked up well compared to a couple of other races over a mile. She looks on the up. [Dave Edwards, Topspeed]

Seamour (Ire)

6 b g Azamour - Chifney Rush (Grand Lodge)

Brian Ellison — P J Martin

PLACINGS: 21/616160/629522- — RPR **110**

Starts	1st	2nd	3rd	4th	Win & Pl
14	3	4	-	-	£89,132

93	7/15	Asct	2m Cls2 82-98 Hcap soft £18,675
85	5/15	Hayd	2m Cls2 81-100 Hcap good £12,938
	9/14	Kemp	1m4f Cls5 Mdn stand £2,588

Hard to know how he failed to win last season having been mugged close to home in the Northumberland Plate and Mallard Stakes before rider just overdid waiting tactics in a Listed race at Newmarket; capable of winning good races.

Senga (USA)

3 b f Blame - Beta Leo (A.P. Indy)

Pascal Bary (Fr) — Flaxman Stables Ireland Ltd

PLACINGS: 214- — RPR **109+**

Starts	1st	2nd	3rd	4th	Win & Pl
3	1	1	-	1	£31,477

	9/16	StCl	1m 2yo good £15,206

Largely unconsidered at 16-1 for last season's Prix Marcel Boussac having won only an ordinary conditions race but ran a cracker in fourth, doing much the best of those held up; saw out the mile well despite a speedy pedigree.

Seven Heavens

3 b c Frankel - Heaven Sent (Pivotal)

John Gosden — K Abdullah

PLACINGS: 117- — RPR **105**

Starts	1st	2nd	3rd	4th	Win & Pl
3	1	-	-	-	£24,619

	8/16	Gdwd	7f Cls2 2yo good £15,563
	7/16	Asct	6f Cls3 Mdn 2yo gd-fm.........£9,049

Made an impressive start last season when winning a maiden at Ascot and easily following up at Goodwood, albeit in a match; fluffed his lines when up in class for the Dewhurst (raced too keenly) but likely to prove much better than that.

Seventh Heaven (Ire)

4 b f Galileo - La Traviata (Johannesburg)

Aidan O'Brien (Ir) — Derrick Smith, Sue Magnier & Michael Tabor

PLACINGS: 74/1161154- — RPR **121**

Starts	1st	2nd	3rd	4th	Win & Pl
9	4	-	-	2	£493,686

	8/16	York	1m4f Cls1 Gp1 gd-fm...............£207,417
	7/16	Curr	1m4f Gp1 3yo good...............£167,647
	5/16	Ling	1m3½f Cls1 List 3yo good...............£22,684
	4/16	Dund	1m Mdn 3yo stand...............£4,974

Very smart middle-distance filly last season, winning the Irish and Yorkshire Oaks when

benefiting from quicker ground and flatter tracks than when flopping at Epsom; not quite as effective over 1m2f when fourth at Breeders' Cup.

Sheikhzayedroad

8 b g Dubawi - Royal Secrets (Highest Honor)

David Simcock — Mohammed Jaber

PLACINGS: 16/25448633/183311-3 — RPR **117**

Starts	1st	2nd	3rd	4th	Win & Pl
37	11	4	9	3	£999,172

	10/16	Asct	2m Cls1 Gp2 good...............£198,485
	9/16	Donc	2m2f Cls1 Gp2 good...............£56,710
	3/16	Meyd	1m6f Gp3 good...............£81,633
	9/14	Wood	1m4f Gd1 good...............£102,273
	7/14	York	1m2½f Cls1 Gp2 gd-fm...............£56,710
	6/14	Nmkj	1m4f Cls1 List gd-sft...............£20,983
106	1/14	Meyd	1m2f 100-109 Hcap good...............£43,373
92	6/13	Epsm	1m4f Cls2 76-92 Hcap good...............£15,563
84	4/13	Donc	1m2½f Cls3 82-89 Hcap good...............£7,763
76	7/12	Brig	1m2f Cls4 66-79 Hcap gd-sft...............£4,075
	5/12	Haml	1m1½f Cls5 Mdn 3-5yo gd-sft...............£3,235

Transformed by step up to staying trips last season having begun to look exposed over middle distances in 2015; gutsy winner over Quest For More in the Doncaster and Long Distance Cups and proved stamina for further when third in the Gold Cup.

Shraaoh (Ire)

4 b c Sea The Stars - Jumooh (Monsun)

Sir Michael Stoute — Al Shaqab Racing

PLACINGS: 631025- — RPR **99**

Starts	1st	2nd	3rd	4th	Win & Pl
6	1	1	1	-	£20,941

	5/16	Newc	1m2f Cls5 Mdn 3yo stand...............£4,528

Disappointing favourite for the King George V Handicap at Royal Ascot and the Melrose at York last season but showed true colours in between when running Dal Harraild to a short-head at Goodwood; likely to progress well beyond his mark.

Signs Of Blessing (Ire)

6 b g Invincible Spirit - Sun Bittern (Seeking The Gold)

Francois Rohaut (Fr) — Isabelle Corbani

PLACINGS: 112319/7050/1153145- — RPR **119**

Starts	1st	2nd	3rd	4th	Win & Pl
21	8	2	2	1	£479,515

	8/16	Deau	6½f Gp1 good...............£159,656
	3/16	Fntb	5½f List v soft...............£19,118
	3/16	Chan	5½f List good...............£18,382
	8/14	Badn	6f Gp3 soft...............£26,667
	4/14	Chan	6f List 3yo good...............£22,917
	3/14	Fntb	5½f List 3yo good...............£15,417
	10/13	Lonc	5f List 2yo v soft...............£22,358
	9/13	Nime	6f 2yo...............£6,911

Won last season's Prix Maurice de Gheest at Deauville, proving his 25-1 third in the Diamond

Jubilee Stakes was no fluke; fourth and fifth in other Group 1 races at Ascot and Sha Tin and should again do well in top sprints.

Simple Verse (Ire)

5 b m Duke Of Marmalade - Guantanamera (Sadler's Wells)

Ralph Beckett

QRL, Sheikh Suhaim Al Thani & M Al Kubaisi

PLACINGS: 63121111/24713-   RPR **115**

Starts		1st	2nd	3rd	4th	Win & Pl
13		6	2	2	1	£930,140
	9/16	Donc	1m6½f Cls1 Gp2 good			£51,039
	10/15	Asct	1m4f Cls1 Gp1 gd-sft			£327,858
	9/15	Donc	1m6½f Cls1 Gp1 3yo good			£393,738
	7/15	Gdwd	1m6f Cls1 Gp3 good			£56,710
82	6/15	Sals	1m4f Cls3 71-90 3yo Hcap gd-fm			£13,695
	4/15	Ling	1m4f Cls5 Mdn 3yo stand			£2,911

Dual Group 1 winner in 2015, including the St Leger; struggled over 1m4f last season but did much better back over staying trips, winning the Park Hill and finishing third in the Long Distance Cup; leading player in top staying races.

Sir Dancealot (Ire)

3 b c Sir Prancealot - Majesty's Dancer (Danehill Dancer)

David Elsworth

C Benham, D Whitford, L Quinn & K Quinn

PLACINGS: 911316-   RPR **107+**

Starts		1st	2nd	3rd	4th	Win & Pl
6		3	-	1	-	£44,327
	10/16	York	6f Cls1 List 2yo good			£28,355
	9/16	Kemp	7f Cls4 2yo std-slw			£3,946
	8/16	Kemp	7f Cls4 Mdn Auct 2yo std-slw			£3,946

Excellent winner of a 6f Listed race at York last October, coming from last to first despite initially struggling with drop in trip (had won twice over 7f); stepped up to a mile in the Racing Post Trophy but didn't get home after travelling strongly.

Sir John Lavery (Ire)

3 b c Galileo - Race For The Stars (Fusaichi Pegasus)

Aidan O'Brien (Ir)   Michael Tabor

PLACINGS: 31-   RPR **95+**

Starts		1st	2nd	3rd	4th	Win & Pl
2		1	-	1	-	£8,101
	10/16	Gowr	1m Mdn 2yo sft-hvy			£7,009

Impressive winner of a mile maiden at Gowran Park on his second run last season; coped well with soft to heavy ground but should be equally effective on quicker after an eyecatching debut third on good ground; likely to get his chance in a Derby trial.

Simple Verse (gold cap): the 2015 Leger winner looks sure to be a force in the big staying races this season

So Mi Dar

4 b f Dubawi - Dar Re Mi (Singspiel)

John Gosden   Lord Lloyd-Webber

PLACINGS: 1/11113-   RPR **118+**

Starts		1st	2nd	3rd	4th	Win & Pl
5		4	-	1	-	£147,304
	9/16	Yarm	1m2f Cls1 List gd-fm			£22,488
	5/16	York	1m2½f Cls1 Gp3 3yo good			£56,710
	4/16	Epsm	1m2f Cls2 3yo soft			£31,125
	10/15	Wind	1m½f Cls5 Mdn 2yo good			£3,364

Hugely impressive winner of last season's Musidora but missed next four months through injury; won well again on her return at Yarmouth and slightly unlucky when third in the Prix de l'Opera; surefire contender for Group 1 honours.

Sobetsu

3 b f Dubawi - Lake Toya (Darshaan)

Charlie Appleby   Godolphin

PLACINGS: 315-   RPR **99+**

Starts		1st	2nd	3rd	4th	Win & Pl
3		1	-	1	-	£19,559
	9/16	NmkR	1m Cls4 Mdn 2yo good			£4,528

Stunning ten-length winner of a Newmarket maiden last season and sent off joint-favourite for the Fillies' Mile as a result; blotted her copybook there with a distant fifth on quicker ground but still a fine prospect over middle distances.

Solow

7 gr g Singspiel - High Maintenance (Highest Honor)

Freddy Head   Wertheimer & Frere

PLACINGS: 241/116111/111111/1-   RPR **120+**aw

Starts		1st	2nd	3rd	4th	Win & Pl
18		13	2	1	1	£4,049,721
	3/16	Chan	1m stand			£18,382
	10/15	Asct	1m Cls1 Gp1 gd-sft			£623,810
	7/15	Gdwd	1m Cls1 Gp1 good			£560,200
	6/15	Asct	1m Cls1 Gp1 good			£212,663
	5/15	Lonc	1m1f Gp1 good			£110,736
	3/15	Meyd	1m1f Gp1 good			£2,307,692
	3/15	Chan	1m stand			£19,380
	10/14	Lonc	1m Gp2 good			£95,000
	8/14	Deau	1m Gp3 v soft			£33,333
	8/14	Claf	1m1f heavy			£18,750
	5/14	StCl	1m2½f soft			£13,750
	4/14	Lonc	1m2f 4yo good			£11,667
	6/13	Lonc	1m4f 3yo gd-sft			£9,756

Missed most of last season through injury but has won his last ten starts since dropped to a mile, including five successive Group 1 races in 2015; suspicion he was dominating a modest division that year but should be a force in similar races.

Somehow (Ire)

4 b f Fastnet Rock - Alexandrova (Sadler's Wells)

Aidan O'Brien (Ir)

Michael Tabor, Derrick Smith & Sue Magnier

PLACINGS: 3/114521- RPR **114**

Starts	1st	2nd	3rd	4th	Win & Pl
7	3	1	1	1	£111,723
	8/16	Curr	1m1f Gp3 good		.....£28,199
	5/16	Ches	1m3½f Cls1 List 3yo good		.....£34,026
	4/16	Leop	1m2f Mdn 3yo heavy		.....£6,783

Came up well short against leading middle-distance fillies after winning last season's Cheshire Oaks but blossomed when dropped to 1m1f, showing remarkable speed for her pedigree to land a Curragh Group 3 by seven lengths.

South Seas (Ire)

3 ch c Lope De Vega - Let It Be Me (Mizzen Mast)

Andrew Balding Qatar Racing Limited

PLACINGS: 11162- RPR **108**

Starts	1st	2nd	3rd	4th	Win & Pl
5	3	1	-	-	£81,472
	8/16	Sand	7f Cls1 Gp3 2yo gd-sft		.....£25,520
	7/16	Hayd	6f Cls4 2yo soft		.....£4,270
	6/16	Wind	6f Cls5 Mdn 2yo soft		.....£2,911

Hugely impressive winner of the Solario Stakes last season on good to soft with several useful rivals behind; didn't quite live up to that promise in two subsequent runs at Group 1 level, although quicker ground a possible excuse in the Dewhurst.

Spangled

5 ch m Starspangledbanner - Zykina (Pivotal)

Roger Varian Cheveley Park Stud

PLACINGS: 71147/10511- RPR **111**

Starts	1st	2nd	3rd	4th	Win & Pl
10	5			1	£76,489
99	9/16	Donc	7f Cls1 Gp3 good		.....£34,026
	7/16	Nmkj	7f Cls2 81-99 Hcap gd-fm		.....£12,938
87	5/16	Leic	7f Cls3 gd-fm		.....£7,561
	7/15	Nmkj	7f Cls2 77-96 3yo Hcap gd-fm		.....£15,563
	6/15	Ling	7f Cls6 Auct Mdn 3-4yo gd-fm		.....£2,458

Big mare who belatedly lived up to her good home reputation towards the end of last season, winning twice over 7f including a Group 3 at Doncaster; loves quick ground; looks the type to improve again with age.

Spark Plug (Ire)

6 b g Dylan Thomas - Kournikova (Sportsworld)

Brian Meehan J L Day

PLACINGS: 625/21F8765/6502541- RPR **115**

Starts	1st	2nd	3rd	4th	Win & Pl
19	4	3	-	1	£169,162
104	9/16	NmkR	1m1f Cls2 89-112 Hcap gd-fm		.....£99,600
102	5/15	Newb	1m Cls2 87-105 Hcap good		.....£24,900
86	5/14	Donc	1m Cls3 75-89 3yo Hcap good		.....£8,410
	9/13	Bath	1m Cls4 Mdn 2yo good		.....£3,752

Clearcut winner of last season's Cambridgeshire, deservedly landing a big prize after several hard-luck stories; raised 8lb for that but had already gone close to winning a Listed race at Sandown and looks to have improved again since.

Spatial

3 b f New Approach - Spacious (Nayef)

Sir Michael Stoute   Cheveley Park Stud

PLACINGS: 216-   RPR **86+**

Starts	1st	2nd	3rd	4th	Win & Pl
3	1	-	-	-	£13,081
	8/16	NmkJ	7f Cls4 Mdn 2yo gd-fm		£4,528

Ran well in two strong 7f maidens at Newmarket last season, winning at the second attempt (Sobetsu third) having chased home Group 1 winner Wuheida on her debut; only sixth in the Fillies' Mile but likely to prove much better than that.

Spiritual Lady

3 b f Pastoral Pursuits - Rouge Dancer (Elusive City)

Philip McBride   PM Racing

PLACINGS: 1511-   RPR **103**

Starts	1st	2nd	3rd	4th	Win & Pl
4	3	-	-	-	£37,835
	10/16	NmkR	6f Cls1 List 2yo good		£17,013
78	8/16	Chmt	6f Cls4 70-78 2yo Hcap stand		£6,469
	6/16	NmkJ	6f Cls4 2yo soft		£4,528

Beaten only once last season when fifth in the Super Sprint and proved that running all wrong when running away with a nursery and a Listed race subsequently; has the scope to progress again and likely to start in a Guineas trial.

St Michel

4 b c Sea The Stars - Miss Provence (Hernando)

Sir Mark Prescott   J L C Pearce

PLACINGS: 374/4212121130-   RPR **113**

Starts	1st	2nd	3rd	4th	Win & Pl
13	4	3	2	2	£65,137
93	8/16	Gdwd	2m Cls2 84-103 Hcap good		£12,938
86	8/16	NmkJ	2m Cls3 72-86 Hcap gd-fm		£9,704
76	7/16	Bevl	2m Cls4 73-85 Hcap good		£6,225
70	6/16	Chmt	1m6f Cls4 66-75 3yo Hcap stand		£8,086

Big improver last season, winning four handicaps out of six (second in other two) before fine third in the Doncaster Cup; travelled well for a long way in the Cesarewitch; weighted out of handicaps now but likely Cup contender.

St Michel: progressive stayer won four times last season

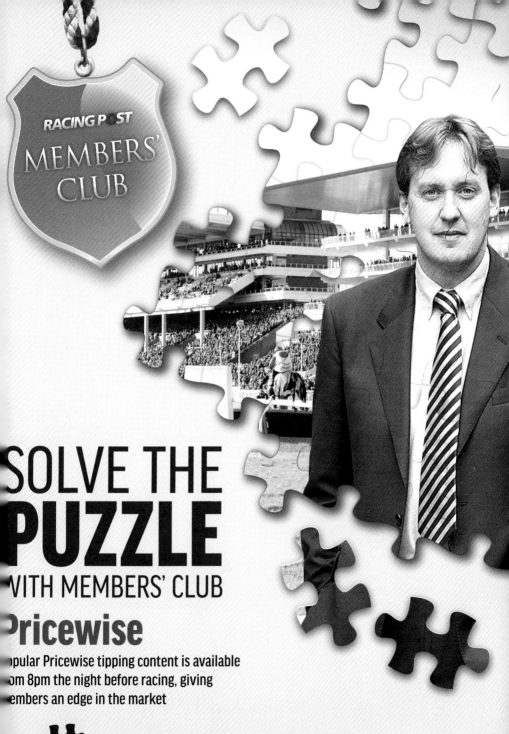

SOLVE THE
PUZZLE
WITH MEMBERS' CLUB

Pricewise

popular Pricewise tipping content is available
from 8pm the night before racing, giving
members an edge in the market

 RACING POST.com/membersclub

Stargazer (Ire)

4 b c Canford Cliffs - Star Ruby (Rock Of Gibraltar)

Sir Michael Stoute   Michael Tabor

PLACINGS: 432/135-   RPR **104+**

Starts	1st	2nd	3rd	4th	Win & Pl
6	1	1	2	1	£18,733
87	4/16	Sand	1m2f Cls3 81-93 3yo Hcap gd-sft		......£9,338

Won an informative Sandown handicap first time out last season and twice looked unlucky in running when favourite to follow up at Goodwood and Ascot; still on a very workable mark of 100 and could even progress into a Group horse.

Stellar Mass (Ire)

4 b c Sea The Stars - Juno Marlowe (Danehill)

Jim Bolger (Ir)   June Judd

PLACINGS: 2343/2451131157-   RPR **114+**

Starts	1st	2nd	3rd	4th	Win & Pl
14	4	2	3	2	£208,212
	8/16	Leop	1m4f Gp3 good		......£27,353
	7/16	DRoy	1m6f List good		......£21,691
92	6/16	DRoy	1m4½f 76-98 3yo Hcap good		......£43,382
	6/16	Curr	1m4f Mdn gd-fm		......£5,653

Needed eight runs to win his maiden but went from strength to strength once off the mark, winning four out of five with sole defeat being a 33-1 third in the Irish Derby; well below that form on last two runs in the autumn.

Stormy Antarctic

4 ch c Stormy Atlantic - Bea Remembered (Doyen)

Ed Walker   P K Siu

PLACINGS: 33112/10276-   RPR **116**

Starts	1st	2nd	3rd	4th	Win & Pl
10	3	2	2	-	£176,811
	4/16	NmkR	1m Cls1 Gp3 3yo gd-sft		......£34,026
	9/15	Newb	1m Cls2 2yo soft		......£9,960
	8/15	Sand	7f Cls5 Mdn 2yo gd-sft		......£3,881

Won last season's Craven Stakes in impressive fashion but came up short in four runs at Group 1 level, although he was second in the Prix Jean Prat and not beaten far in the Prix Jacques le Marois; should benefit from having sights lowered.

Success Days (Ire)

5 gr h Jeremy - Malaica (Roi Gironde)

Ken Condon (Ir)   Robert Ng

PLACINGS: 715/11107/22310-   RPR **116+**

Starts	1st	2nd	3rd	4th	Win & Pl
13	5	2	1	-	£155,426
	8/16	Curr	1m2f Gp3 yield		......£28,199
	5/15	Leop	1m2f Gp3 3yo heavy		......£46,512
	4/15	Leop	1m2f Gp3 3yo sft-hvy		......£30,233
	4/15	Cork	1m½f 3yo heavy		......£8,558
	8/14	Gowr	7f Mdn 2yo gd-yld		......£8,338

Suffered sore shins after running in the Derby in 2015 but bounced back to form last season and won a Group 3 at the Curragh from Fascinating Rock (not at his best) having run well behind that horse and Found previously; needs soft ground.

Suedois (Fr)

6 b g Le Havre - Cup Cake (Singspiel)

David O'Meara   George Turner

PLACINGS: 141/1132818/2252433-   RPR **118**

Starts	1st	2nd	3rd	4th	Win & Pl
25	6	8	4	2	£384,904
	8/15	Deau	6f Gp3 v soft		......£31,008
	4/15	MsnL	6f List good		......£20,155
	3/15	Chan	6½f stand		......£19,380
	12/14	Deau	6½f 3yo stand		......£12,083
	10/14	Chan	7f 3yo stand		......£10,000
	2/14	Chan	6½f 3yo stand		......£10,000

Failed to win last season after joining David O'Meara from France but ran well in a string of top sprints, notably when second in the July Cup; third or fourth three more times at Group 1 level after that and should continue to threaten in similar races.

Swiss Storm

3 b c Frankel - Swiss Lake (Indian Ridge)

David Elsworth   Godolphin & Lordship Stud

PLACINGS: 71-   RPR **86+**

Starts	1st	2nd	3rd	4th	Win & Pl
2	1	-	-	-	£5,175
	9/16	Newb	7f Cls4 Mdn 2yo gd-sft		......£5,175

Big colt who looked clueless on his debut at Haydock but made rapid progress to win well at Newbury soon after, making all over 7f despite

further greenness; seems sure to make a better three-year-old and should get at least a mile.

Syphax (USA)
3 b c Arch - Much Obliged (Kingmambo)

Kevin Ryan   Godolphin

PLACINGS: 11-   RPR **109**

Starts	1st	2nd	3rd	4th	Win & Pl
2	2	-	-	-	£51,438
8/16	York	7f Cls1 Gp3 2yo gd-fm			£48,204
7/16	Muss	7f Cls5 Mdn 2yo good			£3,235

Overcame obvious greenness to win both starts last season, most notably when coming from last to first to nail Best Of Days on the line in the Acomb; subsequently bought by Godolphin and seems likely to get better with experience.

Tabarrak (Ire)
4 b g Acclamation - Bahati (Intikhab)

Richard Hannon   Hamdan Al Maktoum

PLACINGS: 212/21-   RPR **108**

Starts	1st	2nd	3rd	4th	Win & Pl
5	2	3	-	-	£30,780
97	5/16	Asct	7f Cls2 89-105 3yo Hcap gd-fm		£18,675
	9/15	Newb	7f Cls4 Mdn 2yo gd-sft		£5,175

Looked set for a big season when winning a 7f handicap at Ascot in May but missed the rest of the campaign; trainer reports him to be over those niggling problems and has also been gelded subsequently; should have plenty more to offer.

Take Cover
10 b g Singspiel - Enchanted (Magic Ring)

David C Griffiths   Norcroft Park Stud

PLACINGS: 46/0602301/25101360- RPR **117**

Starts	1st	2nd	3rd	4th	Win & Pl
33	10	5	2	1	£487,040
	7/16	Gdwd	5f Cls1 Gp2 gd-fm		£176,992
	5/16	Hayd	5f Cls1 List gd-fm		£20,983
	10/15	Dund	5f List stand		£22,674
	8/14	Gdwd	5f Cls1 Gp2 gd-fm		£56,710
	7/14	York	5f Cls1 List gd-fm		£22,684
92	10/13	York	5f Cls3 87-95 Hcap good		£12,291
79	9/12	Hayd	6f Cls3 74-87 Hcap heavy		£8,410
71	11/11	Sthl	6f Cls6 60-71 Hcap stand		£1,704
65	11/11	Sthl	6f Cls6 51-65 Hcap stand		£1,704
	10/11	Sthl	7f Cls5 Mdn stand		£2,704

Remarkably durable sprinter who was better than ever last season and gained his second win in the King George Stakes at Goodwood; has also finished 1121 on last four runs below Group level; best when faced with a fast 5f on quick ground.

....

'Overcame greenness to win both starts and looks likely to improve with experience'

Talaayeb
3 b f Dansili - Rumoush (Rahy)

Owen Burrows   Hamdan Al Maktoum

PLACINGS: 1-   RPR **90+**

Starts	1st	2nd	3rd	4th	Win & Pl
1	1	-	-	-	£5,175
	9/16	NmkR	7f Cls4 Mdn 2yo gd-fm		£5,175

Hugely impressive when winning her only start at Newmarket last season, travelling strongly to win going away; could even be a Guineas filly on that evidence and could get further than a mile (dam was third in the Oaks).

Tartini (USA)
3 ch c Giant's Causeway - Vignette (Diesis)

John Gosden   George Strawbridge

PLACINGS: 1-   RPR **84**

Starts	1st	2nd	3rd	4th	Win & Pl
1	1	-	-	-	£5,175
	10/16	Nott	1m½f Cls4 Mdn 2yo good		£5,175

Did remarkably well to win his only start at Nottingham last season, coming from a long way back and overcoming obvious greenness to land a decent maiden; seems sure to progress and could follow a similar route to half-brother/Leger winner Lucarno.

The Anvil (Ire)
3 b c Galileo - Brightest (Rainbow Quest)

Aidan O'Brien (Ir)   Derrick Smith, Sue Magnier, Michael Tabor & Annemarie O'Brien

PLACINGS: 23230-   RPR **109**

Starts	1st	2nd	3rd	4th	Win & Pl
5	-	2	2	-	£34,065

Failed to win last season but showed plenty of potential when getting closest to Best Of Days in the Royal Lodge, running on strongly having briefly lost his action in the Dip; form tailed off subsequently but capable of bouncing back in good races.

The Black Princess (Fr)
4 b f Iffraaj - Larceny (Cape Cross)

John Gosden   R J H Geffen

PLACINGS: 1/2231-   RPR **103+**

Starts	1st	2nd	3rd	4th	Win & Pl
5	2	2	1	-	£55,649
	11/16	StCl	1m2f List 3yo v soft		£20,221
	11/15	Kemp	1m Cls4 Mdn 2yo std-slw		£3,946

Made light of a five-month absence when winning a Listed race at Saint-Cloud last November; had run well in good races earlier in the season, notably when third in the Ribblesdale; likely improver after just five races.

The Juliet Rose (Fr)
4 b/br f Monsun - Dubai Rose (Dubai Destination)
Nicolas Clement (Fr)
Mayfair Speculators Sarl & Equifrance Holdings

PLACINGS: 1/2110231-   RPR **113+**

Starts	1st	2nd	3rd	4th	Win & Pl
8	4	2	1	-	£217,046
10/16	Chan	1m4f Gp2 good			£104,779
6/16	Chan	1m4f Gp3 3yo soft			£29,412
5/16	Chan	1m3f List 3yo gd-sft			£20,221
11/15	StCl	1m 2yo heavy			£9,690

Smart middle-distance filly who progressed throughout last season; finished with a comfortable Group 2 success in the Prix de Royallieu (made all) having not been beaten far by Left Hand in the Prix Vermeille.

The Tin Man
5 b g Equiano - Persario (Bishop Of Cashel)
James Fanshawe   Fred Archer Racing - Ormonde

PLACINGS: 611814/18121-   RPR **121**

Starts	1st	2nd	3rd	4th	Win & Pl
11	6	1	-	1	£516,937
	10/16	Asct	6f Cls1 Gp1 good		£340,260
	7/16	Newb	6f Cls1 Gp3 gd-fm		£34,026
	5/16	Wind	6f Cls1 List good		£20,983
91	10/15	Asct	6f Cls2 84-103 3yo Hcap good		£18,675
79	7/15	Donc	6f Cls4 68-80 3yo Hcap gd-fm		£4,690
	6/15	Donc	6f Cls5 Mdn gd-fm		£2,911

Top-class sprinter on quick ground and won all three races on good or quicker last season, including the Champions Sprint at Ascot when perhaps favoured by the draw; not as effective on soft but still managed second in the Sprint Cup.

Thunder Snow (blue): Group 1 winner is likely to do well over middle distances

Thikriyaat (Ire)

4 b g Azamour - Malaspina (Whipper)

Sir Michael Stoute   Hamdan Al Maktoum

PLACINGS: 1/11215-   RPR **109+**

Starts	1st	2nd	3rd	4th	Win & Pl
6	4	1	-	-	£112,988
7/16	Gdwd	1m Cls1 Gp3 3yo gd-fm			£56,710
5/16	NmkR	7f Cls1 List 3yo gd-fm			£20,983
4/16	NmkR	7f Cls3 3yo gd-sft			£9,057
10/15	Chmt	1m Cls4 Mdn 2yo stand			£3,946

Won four of first five races, suffering only defeat to Ribchester in the Jersey Stakes before getting back to winning ways in a Group 3 at Goodwood; much better than he showed when a beaten favourite back there in the Celebration Mile.

Thunder Snow (Ire)

3 b c Helmet - Eastern Joy (Dubai Destination)

Saeed Bin Suroor   Godolphin

PLACINGS: 162241-1   RPR **119**

Starts	1st	2nd	3rd	4th	Win & Pl
7	3	2	-	1	£319,466
2/17	Meyd	1m Gp3 3yo fast			£121,951
10/16	StCl	7f Gp1 2yo soft			£105,037
5/16	Leic	6f Cls4 Mdn 2yo gd-fm			£4,528

Capped a busy campaign by easily winning the Group 1 Criterium International at Saint-Cloud; possibly flattered by that given he'd been beaten in four previous runs at Group level but successfully stepped up in trip in Dubai and should get middle distances.

Tis Marvellous

3 b c Harbour Watch - Mythicism (Oasis Dream)

Clive Cox   Miss J Deadman & S Barrow

PLACINGS: 21159-   RPR **111**

Starts	1st	2nd	3rd	4th	Win & Pl
5	2	1	-	-	£66,620
	7/16	MsnL	5½f Gp2 2yo good		£54,485
	7/16	Wind	6f Cls5 Mdn 2yo gd-fm		£3,235

Brilliant winner of last season's Prix Robert Papin but disappointed twice subsequently when last of five in Prix Morny and ninth when favourite for the Flying Childers (trainer reported two trips abroad had taken toll); could be a very smart sprinter.

Titus

3 b c Dansili - Mirror Lake (Dubai Destination)

Dermot Weld (Ir)   K Abdullah

PLACINGS: 1-   RPR **89+**

Starts	1st	2nd	3rd	4th	Win & Pl
1	1	-	-	-	£7,461
	10/16	Leop	1m Mdn 2yo yield		£7,461

Won what looked a strong maiden at Leopardstown on his only run last season and should step up to Pattern level, with trainer mentioning a Classic trial; could start at a mile but seems likely to stay middle distances.

To Be Wild (Ire)
4 br c Big Bad Bob - Fire Up (Motivator)

Hugo Palmer   Carmichael Jennings

PLACINGS: 5/11-   RPR **106+**

Starts	1st	2nd	3rd	4th	Win & Pl
3	2	-	-	-	£19,407
93	10/16	Donc	1m4f Cls2 87-99 Hcap good		£16,173
	7/16	Ffos	1m4f Cls5 Mdn gd-sft		£3,235

Big colt who had injury issues last season but won both his races, returning from a long absence (had pulled muscles after maiden win) to hack up in a Doncaster handicap by four lengths; seems sure to improve after only three runs.

To Eternity
4 b f Galileo - All's Forgotten (Darshaan)

John Gosden   Lady Bamford

PLACINGS: 2212-   RPR **104**

Starts	1st	2nd	3rd	4th	Win & Pl
4	1	3	-	-	£18,155
	8/16	Wolv	1m4f Cls5 Mdn stand		£3,235

Made rapid progress last summer, finishing second in the Galtres Stakes two weeks after winning her maiden; very lightly raced and should have more to come as a full sister to 2,000 Guineas third Gan Amhras plus Group 3 and Listed winners.

Toscanini (Ire)
5 b g Shamardal - Tuzla (Panoramic)

Richard Fahey   Godolphin

PLACINGS: 12/13512244/5031310-   RPR **114**

Starts	1st	2nd	3rd	4th	Win & Pl
21	5	6	4	2	£193,300
	8/16	Curr	6f Gp3 gd-fm		£26,029
	6/16	Curr	6f List gd-yld		£20,607
	7/15	Naas	6f 3yo gd-fm		£8,023
	5/15	Navn	6f 3yo good		£8,023
	8/14	Dund	6f Mdn 2yo stand		£7,188

Ex-Irish sprinter who has never quite fulfilled early potential but won Group 3 and Listed races over 6f at the Curragh last season; has since moved to Richard Fahey and should find more opportunities on preferred quick ground.

To Be Wild powers home at Doncaster and looks on the up

Toulifaut (Ire)

3 b f Frankel - Cassydora (Darshaan)

Jean-Claude Rouget (Fr) — Andrew-James Smith

PLACINGS: 1118- — RPR **104+**

Starts	1st	2nd	3rd	4th	Win & Pl
4	3	-	-	-	£51,102
	9/16 Chan	1m Gp3 2yo good			£29,412
	8/16 Deau	7½f 2yo stand			£12,500
	7/16 Claf	7f 2yo good			£9,191

Won her first three starts last season, including a Group 3 at Chantilly; given too much to do and got no run when well beaten in the Prix Marcel Boussac but sent off just 7-2 that day and remains an exciting prospect.

Tribal Beat (Ire)

4 b c Street Cry - Tashelka (Mujahid)

Jim Bolger (Ir) — Godolphin

PLACINGS: 47212/17- — RPR **114+**

Starts	1st	2nd	3rd	4th	Win & Pl
7	2	2	-	1	£46,706
	8/16 Leop	1m Gp3 gd-fm			£27,114
	10/15 Naas	6f Mdn 2yo gd-fm			£8,291

Ran only twice last season but made an instant impression on his belated return in August when winning the Desmond Stakes at Leopardstown; flopped next time but remains lightly raced and open to plenty of improvement.

Trip To Paris (Ire)

6 b g Champs Elysees - La Grande Zoa (Fantastic Light)

Ed Dunlop — La Grange Partnership

PLACINGS: 004/41112135240/343- — RPR **108**

Starts	1st	2nd	3rd	4th	Win & Pl
24	6	3	3	4	£802,976
	6/15 Asct	2m4f Cls1 Gp1 gd-fm			£229,854
	95 5/15 Ches	2m2½f Cls2 91-106 Hcap gd-fm			£74,700
	92 4/15 Ripn	2m Cls2 78-94 Hcap gd-fm			£25,876
	88 4/15 Ling	1m4f Cls2 84-103 Hcap stand			£11,972
	84 7/14 Asct	1m4f Cls4 74-84 3yo Hcap good			£7,763
	7/13 Ling	7f Cls6 Mdn Auct 2yo stand			£2,045

Won the Gold Cup in 2015 but picked up an injury later that year in Japan and missed his title defence; showed some promise on first two runs back last summer before running below par on unsuitably soft ground in the Irish St Leger.

Twilight Payment (Ire)

4 b c Teofilo - Dream On Buddy (Oasis Dream)

Jim Bolger (Ir) — Godolphin

PLACINGS: 423121- — RPR **109**

Starts	1st	2nd	3rd	4th	Win & Pl
6	2	2	1	1	£46,439
	9/16 Curr	2m List heavy			£20,390
	7/16 Curr	1m4f Mdn good			£5,653

Finished last season with a 2m Listed win at the Curragh having finished third over that trip in the Queen's Vase; described by his trainer as very backward and should be much better as a four-year-old, with the Ascot Gold Cup probably on his agenda.

Uae Prince (Ire)

4 b c Sea The Stars - By Request (Giant's Causeway)

Roger Varian — Sheikh Mohammed Obaid Al Maktoum

PLACINGS: 316- — RPR **95+**

Starts	1st	2nd	3rd	4th	Win & Pl
3	1	-	1	-	£4,314
	9/16 Leic	1m4f Cls5 Mdn gd-sft			£3,881

Mentioned in Derby terms at the start of last season but immediately had his bubble burst when well beaten at Leicester on his debut; won at the same track in September but only sixth on his handicap debut; seems sure to prove much better.

Ulysses (Ire)

4 ch c Galileo - Light Shift (Kingmambo)

Sir Michael Stoute — Flaxman Stables Ireland Ltd

PLACINGS: 6/210124- — RPR **118**

Starts	1st	2nd	3rd	4th	Win & Pl
7	2	2	-	1	£212,999
	7/16 Gdwd	1m4f Cls1 Gp3 3yo gd-fm			£56,710
	5/16 Newb	1m2f Cls4 Mdn 3yo gd-sft			£6,469

Won last season's Gordon Stakes and bodes well that his master trainer stepped him up in class for the Derby and Breeders' Cup Turf either side of that (fair fourth in the latter); no surprise to see him make his mark in top 1m4f events.

US Army Ranger (Ire)

4 b c Galileo - Moonstone (Dalakhani)

Aidan O'Brien (Ir) — Sue Magnier, Michael Tabor & Derrick Smith

PLACINGS: 112428- — RPR **122+**

Starts	1st	2nd	3rd	4th	Win & Pl
6	2	2	-	1	£397,372
	5/16 Ches	1m4½f Cls1 Gp3 3yo good			£42,533
	4/16 Curr	1m2f Mdn 3yo heavy			£6,783

Made his debut only last April and made rapid progress to finish second in the Derby just two months later; failed to build on that and twice beaten at short prices later in the year but looked in need of further than 1m2f.

....

'She won her first three starts last season and is an exciting prospect'

Usherette (Ire)

5 b m Shamardal - Monday Show (Maria's Mon)

Andre Fabre (Fr)   Godolphin SNC

PLACINGS: 117/11116-					RPR **119+**
Starts	**1st**	**2nd**	**3rd**	**4th**	**Win & Pl**
8	6	-	-	-	£196,338
	6/16	Asct	1m Cls1 Gp2 soft		£99,243
	5/16	NmkR	1m1f Cls1 Gp2 good		£51,039
	4/16	Chan	7f stand		£12,132
	3/16	Deau	7½f stand		£10,294
	6/15	Chan	1m 3yo gd-sft		£11,240
	3/15	Chan	1m1½f 3yo stand		£9,690

Emerged as a top-class filly in first half of last season and completed a four-timer when winning the Duke of Cambridge Stakes at Royal Ascot; didn't run again after a disappointing effort when favourite for the Falmouth Stakes.

Vazirabad (Fr)

5 gr g Manduro - Visorama (Linamix)

Alain De Royer-Dupre (Fr)   H H Aga Khan

PLACINGS: 6211111/117121-2					RPR **120+**
Starts	**1st**	**2nd**	**3rd**	**4th**	**Win & Pl**
14	9	3	-	-	£1,018,562
	10/16	StCl	1m7½f Gp1 soft		£147,051
	9/16	Chan	1m7f Gp3 good		£29,412
	5/16	StCl	1m7½f Gp2 soft		£54,485
	3/16	Meyd	2m Gp2 good		£408,163
	10/15	StCl	1m7½f Gp1 3yo soft		£155,031
	10/15	Lonc	1m7f Gp2 3yo good		£88,372
	9/15	Lonc	1m7f Gp3 3yo good		£31,008
	8/15	Deau	1m5½f 3yo good		£11,240
	7/15	Diep	1m7f 3yo v soft		£7,752

Top-class French stayer who has won nine of his last 12 races, including successive runnings of the Group 1 Prix Royal-Oak; also beaten a short-neck in last season's Prix du Cadran, with only disappointing run when dropped to 1m4f.

Volta (Fr)

4 b f Siyouni - Persian Belle (Machiavellian)

Francis-Henri Graffard (Fr)   Ecurie Salabi

PLACINGS: 523/111327-					RPR **113**
Starts	**1st**	**2nd**	**3rd**	**4th**	**Win & Pl**
9	3	2	2	-	£224,724
	6/16	Chan	1m Gp2 3yo soft		£54,485
	5/16	Chan	1m List 3yo good		£20,221
	3/16	StCl	1m 3yo good		£9,191

Won first three races last season, including

a Group 2 at Chantilly; couldn't quite break through at Group 1 level in three attempts but was placed in the Prix de Diane and Prix Rothschild.

Waady (Ire)

5 b g Approve - Anne Bonney (Jade Robbery)

John Gosden   Hamdan Al Maktoum

PLACINGS: 51/114110/3350-					RPR **113+**
Starts	**1st**	**2nd**	**3rd**	**4th**	**Win & Pl**
12	5		2	1	£111,078
	7/15	Sand	5f Cls1 Gp3 gd-fm		£36,862
	6/15	Sand	5f Cls1 List 3yo gd-fm		£20,983
90	4/15	Sand	5f Cls2 81-98 3yo Hcap gd-fm		£12,450
83	4/15	Nott	5f Cls4 72-83 3yo Hcap soft		£5,175
	9/14	Sand	5f Cls5 Mdn 2yo good		£3,881

Three-time winner over 5f at Sandown in 2015 (up to Group 3 level), all on good to firm; ran well on ground much softer than ideal early last season before going wrong in the July Cup; leading contender for top sprints on quick going.

Waldgeist

3 ch c Galileo - Waldlerche (Monsun)

Andre Fabre (Fr)   Derrick Smith

PLACINGS: 131-					RPR **113**
Starts	**1st**	**2nd**	**3rd**	**4th**	**Win & Pl**
3	2	-	1	-	£123,786
	10/16	StCl	1m2f Gp1 2yo soft		£105,037
	9/16	Chan	1m2f 2yo good		£9,926

Won last season's Group 1 Criterium de Saint-Cloud over 1m2f, relishing an extreme test of stamina having been a beaten favourite in a Chantilly Group 3 previously; likely to stay further and holds a Derby entry.

Wall Of Fire (Ire)

4 b c Canford Cliffs - Bright Sapphire (Galileo)

Hugo Palmer   Carmichael Jennings

PLACINGS: 15/701011-					RPR **110+**
Starts	**1st**	**2nd**	**3rd**	**4th**	**Win & Pl**
8	4	-	-	-	£104,902
102	9/16	Donc	1m6½f Cls2 94-109 Hcap good		£25,876
94	8/16	York	1m6f Cls2 80-95 3yo Hcap good		£52,913
88	7/16	Hayd	1m2½f Cls3 86-92 3yo Hcap soft		£12,938
	7/15	Asct	6f Cls2 Mdn 2yo gd-sft		£12,450

Hugely progressive when stepped up to staying/

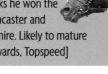

ON THE CLOCK

Wall Of Fire In the space of three weeks he won the Melrose at York and the Mallard at Doncaster and bettered standard time on the Knavesmire. Likely to mature into a Cup horse this season. [Dave Edwards, Topspeed]

middle-distance trips last season, winning three of his last four; hugely impressive when winning the Melrose at York and followed up in good style at Doncaster, both over 1m6f; should get further.

War Decree (USA)
3 b c War Front - Royal Decree (Street Cry)

Aidan O'Brien (Ir)   Andrew Rosen, Sue Magnier,
     Michael Tabor & Derrick Smith

PLACINGS: 121-   RPR **113**

Starts	1st	2nd	3rd	4th	Win & Pl
3	2	1	-	-	£138,081
7/16	Gdwd	7f Cls1 Gp2 2yo gd-fm			£113,420
6/16	Leop	7f Mdn 2yo gd-fm			£7,461

Proved himself a very smart colt when running away with a strong Vintage Stakes at Goodwood, reversing Superlative form with Boynton (had been green that day); not seen since but remains a leading 2,000 Guineas contender.

Washington DC (Ire)
4 b c Zoffany - How's She Cuttin' (Shinko Forest)

Aidan O'Brien (Ir)
     Sue Magnier, Michael Tabor & Derrick Smith

PLACINGS: 21212/17123520227-   RPR **115**

Starts	1st	2nd	3rd	4th	Win & Pl
16	4	7	1	-	£366,263
5/16	Navn	6f List 3yo gd-fm			£20,607
4/16	Dund	7f List 3yo stand			£19,522
6/15	Asct	5f Cls1 List 2yo gd-fm			£34,026
4/15	Tipp	5f Mdn 2yo good			£7,221

High-class and consistent sprinter who flourished when dropped to 5f last season, finishing second in the King George Stakes, Flying Five and Prix de l'Abbaye; seems sure to be a contender for top sprints and deserves to win one.

Whitecliffsofdover (USA)
3 b c War Front - Orate (A.P. Indy)

Aidan O'Brien (Ir)
     Michael Tabor, Derrick Smith & Sue Magnier

PLACINGS: 4123-   RPR **108**

Starts	1st	2nd	3rd	4th	Win & Pl
4	1	1	1	1	£47,659
8/16	Naas	7f Mdn 2yo good			£7,009

Twice ran well when stepped up in class after maiden win at Naas last season, finishing second to Larchmont Lad in a strong Group 3 at Newmarket and third in the Prix Jean-Luc Lagardere; still babyish according to his trainer and should do better.

....

'This very smart colt remains a leading Guineas contender'

Wicklow Brave
8 b g Beat Hollow - Moraine (Rainbow Quest)

Willie Mullins (Ir)   Wicklow Bloodstock (Ireland) Ltd

PLACINGS: 114233/264310-   RPR **115**

Starts	1st	2nd	3rd	4th	Win & Pl
12	3	2	3	2	£353,491
9/16	Curr	1m6f Gp1 yield			£167,647
5/15	List	1m6f heavy			£6,953
5/15	Gowr	2m Mdn heavy			£5,884

Former hurdler now best known for his Irish St Leger victory over Order Of St George, benefiting from a masterful front-running ride; probably flattered by that but had also made the frame in the Goodwood and Lonsdale Cups.

Wings Of Desire
4 ch c Pivotal - Gull Wing (In The Wings)

John Gosden   Lady Bamford

PLACINGS: 311429-   RPR **119**

Starts	1st	2nd	3rd	4th	Win & Pl
6	2	1	1	1	£438,825
5/16	York	1m2½f Cls1 Gp2 3yo gd-fm			£90,736
4/16	Wolv	1m4f Cls5 Mdn stand			£3,235

Won last season's Dante within a month of making his debut; came up short when fourth in the Derby but improved again to finish second in the King George before disappointing in the Juddmonte; should have more to come.

Wuheida
3 ch f Dubawi - Hibaayeb (Singspiel)

Charlie Appleby   Godolphin

PLACINGS: 11-   RPR **113**

Starts	1st	2nd	3rd	4th	Win & Pl
2	2	-	-	-	£130,572
10/16	Chan	1m Gp1 2yo good			£126,044
8/16	Nmkj	7f Cls4 Mdn 2yo gd-fm			£4,520

Did remarkably well to win last season's Prix Marcel Boussac on only her second start having impressed on her debut at Newmarket; likely to prove best over middle distances (out of a Singspiel mare who won over 1m4f).

Yalta (Ire)
3 b c Exceed And Excel - Lacily (Elusive Quality)

Mark Johnston
     Sheikh Hamdan Bin Mohammed Al Maktoum

PLACINGS: 11881006-   RPR **111**

Starts	1st	2nd	3rd	4th	Win & Pl
8	2	-	-	-	£61,237
7/16	Gdwd	5f Cls1 Gp3 2yo good			£42,533
5/16	Pont	6f Cls2 2yo good			£12,450
5/16	Gdwd	6f Cls4 2yo good			£5,175

Highly regarded early last season and fulfilled his potential when running away with the Molecomb

Stakes on first run over 5f; that smacks of a fluke after three subsequent flops but time was exceptional and could be a top sprinter if coaxed back to form.

Yucatan (Ire)
3 b c Galileo - Six Perfections (Celtic Swing)

Aidan O'Brien (Ir)			Flaxman Stables, Sue Magnier, Michael Tabor & Derrick Smith

PLACINGS: 7122-   RPR **112**

Starts	1st	2nd	3rd	4th	Win & Pl
4	1	2	-	-	£67,226
	8/16	Curr	1m Mdn 2yo good		...........£7,461

Second in last season's Racing Post Trophy when unable to justify favouritism having chased home Capri in the Beresford; unlikely to be top of the Ballydoyle pecking order on that evidence but a good middle-distance prospect.

Zainhom (USA)
3 ch c Street Cry - Kaseema (Storm Cat)

Sir Michael Stoute			Hamdan Al Maktoum

PLACINGS: 312-   RPR **106+**

Starts	1st	2nd	3rd	4th	Win & Pl
3	1	1	1	-	£25,277
	9/16	York	7f Cls4 Mdn 2yo gd-sft		...........£7,116

Shaped with great promise when second in last season's Autumn Stakes despite looking green; described as a big baby by connections and looks just the type to continue to improve as the year goes on; likely to be best at a mile.

Zarak (Fr)
4 b c Dubawi - Zarkava (Zamindar)

A De Royer-Dupre (Fr)			H H Aga Khan

PLACINGS: 1/152243-1   RPR **116+**

Starts	1st	2nd	3rd	4th	Win & Pl
8	3	2	1	1	£482,489
	2/17	Meyd	1m2f Gp3 good		...........£97,561
	4/16	MsnL	1m 3yo soft		...........£12,500
	10/15	Deau	1m 2yo heavy		...........£9,690

First foal of Zarkava who didn't quite live up to expectations last season having been sent off just 2-1 for the French Guineas (fifth); proved better over 1m2f and unlucky to bump into Almanzor, twice finishing second to that horse.

Zelzal (Fr)
4 b c Sea The Stars - Olga Prekrasa (Kingmambo)

Jean-Claude Rouget (Fr)			Al Shaqab Racing

PLACINGS: 110113-   RPR **122+**

Starts	1st	2nd	3rd	4th	Win & Pl
6	4	-	1	-	£256,981
	7/16	Chan	1m Gp1 3yo good		...........£168,059
	6/16	Chan	1m Gp3 3yo good		...........£29,412
	4/16	Chan	1m 3yo stand		...........£12,500
	3/16	Deau	7½f 3yo stand		...........£9,191

Redeemed his reputation after a disappointing effort in the French Guineas when winning the Prix Jean Prat in impressive fashion; only third when favourite for the Prix du Moulin next time; by Sea The Stars and may well get further.

Zhukova (Ire)
5 b m Fastnet Rock - Nightime (Galileo)

Dermot Weld (Ir)			Mrs C C Regalado-Gonzalez

PLACINGS: 4141/1117-   RPR **117**

Starts	1st	2nd	3rd	4th	Win & Pl
8	5	-	-	2	£135,497
	9/16	Leop	1m4f Gp3 good		...........£43,382
	5/16	Naas	1m2f Gp3 yld-sft		...........£34,706
	4/16	Curr	1m2f List heavy		...........£20,390
	9/15	Gway	1m4f List yield		...........£27,713
	6/15	Navn	1m2f Mdn gd-fm		...........£7,221

Won Group 3 races over 1m2f and 1m4f last season, gaining a notable scalp in US Army Ranger when completing a four-timer at Leopardstown in September; disappointed on step up to Group 1 company but worth another chance.

Zonderland
4 ch c Dutch Art - Barynya (Pivotal)

Clive Cox			Cheveley Park Stud

PLACINGS: 145/61812-   RPR **114**

Starts	1st	2nd	3rd	4th	Win & Pl
8	3	1	-	1	£101,622
	8/16	Sals	1m Cls1 Gp3 gd-fm		...........£42,533
	5/16	Sand	1m Cls1 List 3yo gd-fm		...........£20,983
	9/15	Kemp	7f Cls4 2yo std-slw		...........£3,946

Progressed well at a more realistic level after finishing sixth in last season's 2,000 Guineas; won two of next three before a good second to Lightning Spear in the Celebration Mile; could soon be running in Group 1 races again.

THIS SEASON'S KEY HORSES LISTED BY TRAINER

Charlie Appleby
Blue Point
Boynton
Emotionless
Endless Time
Grecian Light
Hawkbill
Latharnach
Salsabeel
Scottish
Sobetsu
Wuheida
Andrew Balding
Dancing Star
Duretto
Horseplay
Poet's Vanity
South Seas
Pascal Bary
Senga
Ralph Beckett
Alyssa
Carntop
Crimson Rock
Moonrise Landing
Mountain Bell
Rich Legacy
Simple Verse
Michael Bell
Big Orange
Fabricate
Jim Bolger
Moonlight Magic
Stellar Mass
Tribal Beat
Twilight Payment
Karl Burke
Quiet Reflection
Owen Burrows
Massaat
Talaayeb
Henry Candy
Limato
Mick Channon
Harlequeen
Kassia
Opal Tiara
Roger Charlton
Atty Persse
Decorated Knight
Fair Eva
Projection
Quest For More
Nicolas Clement
The Juliet Rose
Ken Condon
Landfall
Success Days
Robert Cowell
Goldream
Outback Traveller
Clive Cox
Harry Angel
My Dream Boat
Priceless

Profitable
Tis Marvellous
Zonderland
Simon Crisford
Mokarris
Rodaini
Luca Cumani
Aljezeera
Keith Dalgleish
Clem Fandango
Alain de Royer-Dupre
Vazirabad
Zarak
Ed Dunlop
Red Verdon
Trip To Paris
Brian Ellison
Seamour
David Elsworth
Sir Dancealot
Swiss Storm
Andre Fabre
Akihiro
Al Wukair
Cloth Of Stars
Doha Dream
Double Lady
Jimmy Two Times
Usherette
Waldgeist
Richard Fahey
Don't Touch
Growl
Mr Lupton
Queen Kindly
Ribchester
Toscanini
James Fanshawe
Higher Power
The Tin Man
John Gosden
Ardad
Astronomy's Choice
Cape Cova
Cracksman
Crazy Horse
Cunco
Dabyah
Dreamfield
Eternally
Flying Officer
Gm Hopkins
Icespire
Jack Hobbs
Journey
Laugh Aloud
Muntahaa
Nathra
Persuasive
Remarkable
Richard Pankhurst
Royal Artillery
Seven Heavens
So Mi Dar
Tartini

The Black Princess
To Eternity
Waady
Wings Of Desire
Y Gourraud
Highlands Queen
F Graffard
Volta
David Griffiths
Take Cover
Didier Guillemin
Sans Equivoque
William Haggas
Dal Harraild
Gravity Flow
Hathal
Mubtasim
Mutakayyef
Muthmir
Recorder
Rivet
Mick Halford
Portage
Richard Hannon
Larchmont Lad
Tabarrak
Ron Harris
Just Glamorous
Freddy Head
Solow
C Head-Maarek
National Defense
Charlie Hills
Cotai Glory
Dutch Connection
Ibn Malik
Jallota
Magical Memory
Dean Ivory
Librisa Breeze
Mark Johnston
Frankuus
Yalta
Carlos Laffon-Parias
Left Hand
David Lanigan
Mitchum Swagger
Ger Lyons
Ardhoomey
Tony Martin
Heartbreak City
Philip McBride
Spiritual Lady
Martyn Meade
Aclaim
Brian Meehan
Raheen House
Spark Plug
Laura Mongan
Harbour Law
Willie Mullins
Wicklow Brave

David Nicholls
Orion's Bow
Peter Niven
Clever Cookie
Aidan O'Brien
Alice Springs
Brave Anna
Capri
Caravaggio
Churchill
Cliffs Of Moher
Cougar Mountain
Deauville
Douglas Macarthur
Exemplar
Highland Reel
Hydrangea
Idaho
Intelligence Cross
Johannes Vermeer
Lancaster Bomber
Minding
Order Of St George
Peace Envoy
Promise To Be True
Rhododendron
Roly Poly
Seventh Heaven
Sir John Lavery
Somehow
The Anvil
US Army Ranger
War Decree
Washington DC
Whitecliffsofdover
Yucatan
Joseph O'Brien
Intricately
David O'Meara
Custom Cut
Firmament
Intisaab
Mondialiste
Suedois
John Oxx
Sea Of Grace
Hugo Palmer
Architecture
Baydar
Best Of Days
Galileo Gold
Gifted Master
Home Of The Brave
To Be Wild
Wall Of Fire
Jonathan Portman
Mrs Danvers
Sir Mark Prescott
Marsha
Pallasator
St Michel
Francois Rohaut
Signs Of Blessing
Jean-Claude Rouget
Almanzor

La Cressonniere
Mekhtaal
Qemah
Toulifaut
Zelzal
Kevin Ryan
Brando
Syphax
David Simcock
Algometer
Breton Rock
Lightning Spear
Sheikhzayedroad
Bryan Smart
Alpha Delphini
Delectation
Tommy Stack
Alexios Komnenos
Sir Michael Stoute
Abdon
Abingdon
Across The Stars
Autocratic
Dartmouth
Dubka
Intimation
Khairaat
Midterm
Mirage Dancer
Mustashry
Platitude
Poet's Word
Queen's Trust
Shraaoh
Spatial
Stargazer
Thikriyaat
Ulysses
Zainhom
Saeed Bin Suroor
Always Smile
Best Solution
Move Up
Prize Money
Racing History
Really Special
Thunder Snow
Roger Varian
Barsanti
Certificate
Morando
Nezwaah
Postponed
Spangled
Uae Prince
Ed Walker
Stormy Antarctic
Wesley Ward
Acapulco
Lady Aurelia
Dermot Weld
Eziyra
Forgotten Rules
Making Light
Titus
Zhukova

LEADING FLAT TRAINERS IN BRITAIN 2016

Trainer	Wins-runs	Wins (%)	2nd	3rd	4th	Win prize	Total prize	Profit/loss (£)
Aidan O'Brien	28–133	21%	28	16	17	£5,059,170	£8,130,756	+22.67
John Gosden	141–613	23%	107	78	64	£1,957,729	£3,462,784	+2.14
Richard Fahey	198–1739	11%	195	225	217	£1,555,030	£3,162,108	-397.84
Richard Hannon	173–1357	13%	185	166	173	£1,602,588	£2,847,607	-203.92
Mark Johnston	195–1413	14%	206	176	169	£1,553,728	£2,724,681	-316.95
Sir Michael Stoute	111–505	22%	93	67	49	£1,491,548	£2,525,774	-25.48
Roger Varian	97–554	18%	73	66	61	£1,788,832	£2,393,915	-141.34
William Haggas	137–596	23%	107	89	48	£1,423,781	£2,126,782	-83.29
Hugo Palmer	71–344	21%	54	50	36	£1,277,308	£2,091,598	+13.28
Charlie Appleby	70–331	21%	62	44	36	£1,307,474	£1,979,286	-15.97
David O'Meara	103–975	11%	124	115	105	£767,372	£1,679,545	-336.62
Andrew Balding	107–731	15%	103	96	91	£1,038,999	£1,672,624	-102.74
David Simcock	85–457	19%	61	76	65	£955,353	£1,646,019	-29.73
Clive Cox	65–435	15%	54	52	43	£1,175,717	£1,524,464	-51.45
Kevin Ryan	94–733	13%	91	93	75	£769,403	£1,457,569	-106.12
Saeed bin Suroor	68–319	21%	62	33	36	£720,144	£1,385,648	-38.64
Ralph Beckett	101–506	20%	70	56	60	£834,320	£1,300,689	+7.83
Karl Burke	68–587	12%	54	59	69	£883,227	£1,196,416	-16.74
Charlie Hills	76–543	14%	74	74	58	£670,583	£1,172,073	-192.65
Roger Charlton	48–250	19%	38	27	36	£683,191	£1,137,712	-49.31
Mick Channon	71–625	11%	79	65	85	£695,033	£1,133,050	-139.15
Jean-Claude Rouget	2–5	40%	0	2	0	£964,070	£1,071,670	+4.38
Henry Candy	22–225	10%	21	29	31	£786,789	£1,020,717	-64.88
James Fanshawe	43–243	18%	35	32	35	£640,458	£974,381	-36.02
Marco Botti	51–397	13%	55	51	48	£580,516	£895,727	-126.45
Dermot Weld	1–8	13%	0	1	0	£876,170	£889,715	-0.50
Tom Dascombe	75–569	13%	62	58	62	£505,921	£796,517	+14.80
Tim Easterby	76–807	9%	82	84	81	£472,566	£781,669	-213.08
Michael Dods	50–487	10%	57	58	49	£525,112	£764,312	-148.88
Keith Dalgleish	81–664	12%	88	60	81	£496,197	£742,517	-103.56
Michael Bell	37–323	11%	51	56	33	£518,422	£684,699	-134.77
Sir Mark Prescott	55–278	20%	45	23	23	£367,258	£655,882	-60.61
Ed Dunlop	51–385	13%	49	39	34	£366,753	£636,239	-111.01
Michael Appleby	70–787	9%	63	70	94	£376,253	£634,622	-200.78
Hughie Morrison	43–351	12%	47	31	36	£432,904	£627,943	-80.88
David Evans	70–720	10%	94	99	86	£287,452	£621,355	-241.98
Dean Ivory	35–318	11%	34	26	22	£440,727	£619,456	-111.63
Michael Easterby	61–476	13%	52	55	47	£426,954	£618,295	-6.29
Stuart Williams	51–369	14%	32	38	40	£423,098	£581,206	-50.01
Luca Cumani	38–255	15%	36	38	31	£252,606	£574,486	-82.38
David Barron	38–354	11%	42	32	27	£383,017	£559,051	-57.03
James Tate	54–302	18%	39	51	39	£286,630	£511,161	-33.10
Eve Johnson Houghton	41–329	12%	32	42	51	£354,124	£502,560	+9.19
Laura Mongan	13–120	11%	9	12	9	£439,698	£479,838	+13.75
Robert Cowell	34–340	10%	29	46	35	£342,506	£477,043	-114.42
Brian Ellison	60–471	13%	51	54	50	£278,091	£462,550	-88.70
Jamie Osborne	48–376	13%	60	44	52	£319,979	£457,385	-57.83
Jeremy Noseda	19–109	17%	20	11	13	£240,116	£445,246	-47.85
David Nicholls	24–241	10%	38	26	21	£195,947	£427,541	-59.42
David Elsworth	27–189	14%	18	26	16	£272,155	£416,209	-18.79

LEADING FLAT TRAINERS IN IRELAND 2016

Trainer	Wins-runs	Wins (%)	2nd	3rd	4th	Win prize	Total prize	Profit/loss (£)
Aidan O'Brien	121–632	19%	110	95	68	€2,965,213	€5,230,561	-169.60
Dermot Weld	90–465	19%	68	58	38	€2,345,100	€2,919,963	-120.21
Jim Bolger	67–555	12%	75	60	60	€919,490	€1,814,488	-123.61
Ger Lyons	57–353	16%	63	38	39	€863,813	€1,375,178	-66.06
Mick Halford	53–446	12%	45	60	39	€648,628	€1,038,648	-165.32
Willie McCreery	29–270	11%	23	26	30	€543,688	€780,435	-79.31
Jean-Claude Rouget	1–2	50%	0	1	0	€725,000	€760,000	+6.00
Kevin Prendergast	22–167	13%	15	18	19	€564,500	€704,784	+40.94
Joseph O'Brien	23–186	12%	13	20	20	€430,688	€577,163	-0.65
Johnny Murtagh	35–248	14%	26	26	27	€370,700	€566,033	-7.25
Jessica Harrington	22–283	8%	24	28	32	€280,325	€562,021	-66.33
Andrew Slattery	18–139	13%	14	15	14	€361,250	€483,485	-5.17
Michael O'Callaghan	19–201	9%	21	26	20	€191,625	€460,388	-106.15
Tony Martin	11–99	11%	10	3	6	€280,625	€386,488	-13.67
Ken Condon	14–162	9%	20	22	13	€200,250	€382,750	-57.33
Adrian Keatley	10–159	6%	6	9	17	€315,500	€371,825	-71.75
Willie Mullins	7–20	35%	1	0	3	€357,625	€365,600	+28.98
John Oxx	12–121	10%	19	12	14	€187,500	€336,450	-70.95
Joseph Murphy	13–147	9%	13	22	15	€208,975	€323,913	-30.63
Edward Lynam	18–178	10%	13	11	15	€198,313	€309,195	-76.34
John Feane	28–203	14%	17	14	25	€193,238	€292,608	-41.50
Tommy Stack	16–154	10%	18	9	23	€163,750	€285,560	-1.07
Brian Ellison	2–13	15%	1	2	1	€210,000	€256,600	+10.00
Paul Deegan	7–153	5%	10	19	9	€137,500	€241,370	-58.00
Patrick Prendergast	11–131	8%	12	15	17	€136,500	€229,795	-24.00
David Wachman	9–118	8%	11	17	13	€90,938	€225,298	-34.45
John Joseph Murphy	15–236	6%	14	23	21	€97,500	€205,303	+8.50
Johnny Levins	16–220	7%	15	20	23	€109,925	€201,553	-80.60
Adrian McGuinness	14–184	8%	14	22	29	€112,700	€196,518	-70.50
Mick Channon	2–7	29%	1	2	2	€109,800	€191,050	+21.00
Charles O'Brien	11–115	10%	13	15	9	€80,925	€184,308	-56.92
Hugo Palmer	0–7	—	2	1	1	€0	€173,250	-7.00
Harry Rogers	9–143	6%	17	14	10	€74,688	€162,388	-71.38
Gavin Cromwell	4–95	4%	7	6	8	€86,825	€160,804	-55.50
Andy Oliver	10–190	5%	16	14	11	€74,350	€155,753	-97.50
Denis Hogan	12–132	9%	6	14	10	€114,350	€155,153	-47.50
Sheila Lavery	9–129	7%	10	12	17	€77,500	€152,513	-68.58
Damian English	14–95	15%	4	7	4	€112,763	€150,898	+42.00
David Barron	1–4	25%	1	0	0	€90,000	€150,000	+19.00
Ed Dunlop	0–4	—	1	1	1	€0	€135,000	-4.00
Tom Hogan	4–69	6%	8	3	4	€94,500	€132,400	-31.13
David Marnane	7–163	4%	8	10	20	€59,375	€131,658	-114.25
John Kiely	6–25	24%	5	3	3	€78,400	€124,250	+1.75
Patrick Flynn	10–119	8%	13	11	6	€60,288	€122,975	-24.88
Edward O'Grady	8–45	18%	4	4	8	€85,344	€113,131	-5.00
Tracey Collins	7–110	6%	9	8	9	€69,450	€111,395	-66.20
Donal Kinsella	3–43	7%	0	2	1	€102,813	€108,475	-6.50
Patrick Martin	7–141	5%	6	22	16	€57,388	€105,878	-91.75
Robert Cowell	2–5	40%	0	1	0	€61,500	€87,400	+10.25
David Nicholls	1–4	25%	3	0	0	€28,200	€82,200	-1.13

LEADING FLAT JOCKEYS IN BRITAIN 2016

Jockey	Wins-runs	Wins (%)	2nd	3rd	4th	Win prize	Total prize	Profit/loss (£)
Jim Crowley	189–1017	19%	137	113	103	£1,267,082	£1,920,275	-46.53
Silvestre de Sousa	165–928	18%	125	108	108	£1,285,813	£2,091,201	-116.95
Luke Morris	159–1391	11%	194	186	146	£1,005,430	£1,576,248	-509.69
Adam Kirby	152–932	16%	102	112	117	£1,886,587	£2,467,603	-118.48
Joe Fanning	129–1025	13%	129	118	129	£864,958	£1,330,176	-311.14
Pat Cosgrave	120–734	16%	113	105	63	£981,163	£1,361,277	+21.80
Andrea Atzeni	116–618	19%	99	68	61	£2,452,894	£3,538,446	-49.72
Oisin Murphy	114–869	13%	101	112	105	£984,010	£1,962,569	-101.61
George Baker	114–683	17%	91	79	90	£1,067,563	£1,702,706	-124.04
Richard Kingscote	113–703	16%	80	77	70	£729,072	£1,084,308	+97.79
Paul Mulrennan	106–932	11%	101	96	99	£836,546	£1,196,999	-308.14
Ryan Moore	103–462	22%	72	60	53	£5,849,891	£8,085,004	-113.21
James Doyle	99–541	18%	95	66	64	£1,075,672	£2,244,190	-70.11
Jamie Spencer	96–597	16%	72	86	72	£1,206,614	£1,958,964	-74.20
Graham Gibbons	93–657	14%	90	79	47	£677,621	£962,008	-33.42
Daniel Tudhope	90–595	15%	90	79	72	£603,185	£1,088,235	-46.59
Tony Hamilton	89–753	12%	78	92	87	£500,616	£802,199	-120.09
Josephine Gordon	87–834	10%	103	109	103	£467,565	£728,496	-250.39
Frankie Dettori	85–391	22%	65	44	45	£2,625,038	£4,132,945	-0.85
Robert Havlin	81–557	15%	77	65	63	£688,116	£1,138,190	+15.88
PJ McDonald	79–812	10%	78	102	94	£469,208	£725,722	-103.30
William Buick	79–421	19%	60	57	41	£1,466,638	£2,711,325	-27.87
Martin Harley	76–602	13%	64	73	77	£795,652	£1,288,836	-133.46
Ben Curtis	74–620	12%	75	59	68	£332,769	£538,250	-132.14
Franny Norton	74–504	15%	83	64	59	£496,832	£832,372	-64.89
Paul Hanagan	73–510	14%	72	60	45	£586,225	£1,423,142	-146.96
Tom Eaves	71–837	8%	73	88	75	£536,490	£880,987	-148.16
Sean Levey	67–519	13%	73	73	67	£692,780	£1,080,861	-128.59
Tom Marquand	63–663	10%	57	76	57	£371,588	£604,244	-161.60
Phillip Makin	63–476	13%	63	57	60	£402,548	£703,565	-81.08
Robert Winston	63–475	13%	51	56	43	£567,173	£793,399	-14.79
Connor Beasley	61–603	10%	70	72	56	£427,736	£626,949	-183.25
David Allan	61–533	11%	63	57	58	£520,366	£802,686	-77.33
John Egan	60–629	10%	83	66	82	£270,072	£508,206	-211.08
David Probert	60–468	13%	59	49	54	£498,929	£734,321	-71.45
Shane Kelly	59–671	9%	74	75	91	£312,048	£546,011	-318.16
Harry Bentley	59–344	17%	36	44	43	£678,614	£965,541	-5.27
Andrew Mullen	57–671	8%	58	62	73	£391,480	£614,533	-103.42
James Sullivan	57–655	9%	63	58	80	£262,007	£417,194	-186.52
Martin Dwyer	54–483	11%	42	54	37	£356,274	£587,257	-42.64
Graham Lee	53–644	8%	78	63	74	£386,740	£828,647	-281.35
Adam McNamara	53–424	13%	54	52	54	£406,361	£569,366	-126.37
Tom Queally	49–536	9%	44	46	43	£641,732	£851,744	-176.92
Nathan Evans	49–451	11%	46	59	46	£338,189	£523,965	-93.90
Liam Keniry	47–552	9%	53	53	46	£182,142	£294,242	-175.42
William Carson	46–665	7%	59	68	85	£289,129	£450,229	-279.47
Ted Durcan	46–354	13%	49	31	45	£400,745	£563,280	-88.34
Kieran O'Neill	43–607	7%	57	59	73	£207,981	£411,592	-248.93
Frederik Tylicki	42–405	10%	45	44	54	£256,170	£641,576	-183.32
Fran Berry	42–357	12%	41	39	43	£288,524	£533,496	-50.22

LEADING FLAT JOCKEYS IN IRELAND 2016

Jockey	Wins-runs	Wins (%)	2nd	3rd	4th	Win prize	Total prize	Profit/loss (£)
Pat Smullen	129–685	19%	97	88	64	€2,843,438	€3,771,773	-158.81
Colin Keane	90–620	15%	89	63	71	€1,161,563	€1,906,835	-80.31
Kevin Manning	67–560	12%	70	62	63	€919,840	€1,642,095	-169.69
Seamie Heffernan	59–422	14%	47	47	47	€1,325,400	€1,769,884	-159.34
Shane Foley	57–604	9%	64	72	59	€915,975	€1,459,800	-265.73
Billy Lee	57–466	12%	47	39	56	€902,706	€1,281,271	-91.40
Declan McDonogh	55–487	11%	64	56	49	€690,700	€1,192,410	-74.56
Donnacha O'Brien	55–347	16%	58	48	49	€701,963	€1,172,043	-113.08
Wayne Lordan	50–603	8%	52	47	65	€509,940	€956,073	-238.89
Chris Hayes	40–529	8%	49	47	57	€1,031,063	€1,462,354	-172.81
Gary Halpin	36–330	11%	24	25	35	€314,038	€490,228	-61.38
Ronan Whelan	32–422	8%	35	38	40	€282,838	€691,011	-143.48
Gary Carroll	30–351	9%	16	32	32	€357,338	€512,754	-54.45
Colm O'Donoghue	28–331	8%	27	34	41	€453,438	€836,291	-40.67
Killian Leonard	26–443	6%	29	25	45	€260,669	€430,726	-166.75
Ryan Moore	23–77	30%	17	12	5	€1,150,875	€2,089,063	-14.51
Leigh Roche	21–402	5%	32	35	28	€276,825	€513,353	-142.89
Conor Hoban	21–340	6%	21	34	21	€229,965	€391,275	-99.88
Oisin Orr	21–186	11%	18	13	16	€234,313	€343,165	-1.38
Rory Cleary	20–390	5%	15	20	16	€203,965	€313,333	-108.50
Robbie Downey	19–238	8%	14	18	10	€142,675	€225,400	-42.67
Ana O'Brien	19–237	8%	18	24	13	€180,188	€280,843	-86.92
Donagh O'Connor	17–219	8%	11	26	24	€111,338	€190,278	-89.75
Connor King	14–259	5%	24	22	26	€114,963	€247,898	-181.39
Niall McCullagh	13–286	5%	11	22	24	€110,000	€237,948	-136.88
Tom Madden	12–247	5%	15	15	21	€71,925	€152,130	-123.00
Denis Linehan	10–114	9%	9	16	5	€72,375	€119,563	-45.50
Michael Hussey	9–207	4%	8	9	12	€84,100	€204,315	-77.25
Kieren Fallon	9–115	8%	7	9	11	€101,000	€199,700	-66.68
Conor McGovern	9–104	9%	7	6	12	€57,000	€92,608	-44.75
Ross Coakley	8–208	4%	14	10	18	€57,188	€122,389	-101.50
Shane B Kelly	6–78	8%	4	4	5	€40,625	€63,538	-24.75
Fran Berry	6–23	26%	2	2	1	€84,500	€95,193	+13.54
Sean Davis	5–118	4%	10	5	7	€118,750	€163,063	-51.50
Daniel Redmond	5–113	4%	17	5	8	€33,725	€98,665	-78.50
Danny Sheehy	5–81	6%	2	9	1	€40,625	€60,438	-41.50
Andrew Breslin	4–92	4%	4	5	4	€31,250	€52,698	-30.67
Nina Carberry	4–15	27%	2	0	0	€37,500	€41,975	+4.75
Danny Grant	3–127	2%	8	7	5	€17,788	€86,760	-107.88
Dylan Hogan	3–56	5%	4	3	4	€20,000	€35,288	-28.00
Caroline Murtagh	3–24	13%	2	2	1	€22,075	€30,528	-5.50
William Buick	3–15	20%	2	2	1	€65,500	€109,850	+9.00
Emmet McNamara	2–98	2%	3	6	6	€19,063	€56,918	-77.50
Keith Moriarty	2–80	3%	5	4	5	€11,225	€29,898	-42.00
Julie Burke	2–60	3%	2	3	1	€11,563	€21,075	-26.00
Evan Daly	2–48	4%	3	3	1	€15,938	€26,538	-17.50
Robbie Dolan	2–48	4%	3	1	3	€11,875	€22,088	-16.50
Robert Smithers	2–24	8%	1	0	3	€16,875	€25,738	-7.50
DM Simmonson	2–22	9%	2	3	3	€25,938	€38,738	-10.50
Keith Quinn	2–20	10%	1	0	1	€11,225	€13,775	+5.00

RACING POST RATINGS: LAST SEASON'S LEADING TWO-YEAR-OLDS

KEY: Horse name, best RPR figure, finishing position when earning figure, (details of race where figure was earned)

Afandem (IRE) 107 2 (5f, York, Gd, Aug 20)
Al Hamdany (IRE) 100 2 (1m 4y, Pont, Sft, Oct 17)
Al Johrah 98 2 (5f, Asco, Sft, Jun 15)
Alexios Komnenos (IRE) 105 2 (7f, Leop, GF, Jul 21)
Alicante Dawn 101 1 (6f, Ripo, GS, Aug 29)
Ambassadorial (USA) 105 1 (7f, Dunw, SD, Oct 7)
Apex King (IRE) 97 4 (7f 16y, Sand, GS, Aug 20)
Arcada (IRE) 107 3 (1m, Newm, GF, Sep 24)
Ardad (IRE) 107 1 (5f, Donc, Gd, Sep 9)
Asidious Alexander (IRE) 94 7 (6f, Newj, GF, Jul 8)
Bahamas (IRE) 94 5 (7f, Asco, GF, Jul 23)
Barrington (IRE) 98 6 (6f, Newj, GF, Jul 7)
Battaash (IRE) 101 3 (5f, Newm, GF, Oct 7)
Bay Of Poets (IRE) 101 8 (1m, Donc, Gd, Oct 22)
Bear Valley (IRE) 97 1 (7f, Good, GF, Jul 28)
Best Of Days 110 1 (1m, Newm, GF, Sep 24)
Best Solution (IRE) 111 1 (1m, Newm, Gd, Oct 8)
Big Time Baby (IRE) 105 1 (5f, York, Gd, Aug 20)
Bletchley 103 2 (6f, Asco, GS, Jun 17)
Blue Point (IRE) 116 2 (6f, Newm, GF, Sep 24)
Born To Be (IRE) 97 2 (6f, Fair, Hvy, Sep 27)
Bound (IRE) 96 2 (1m, Curr, Gd, Oct 9)
Boyfriend Brian (IRE) 98 2 (7f 100y, Tipp, Sft, Aug 5)
Boynton (USA) 113 1 (7f, Newj, GF, Jul 9)
Brave Anna (USA) 112 1 (6f, Newm, GF, Sep 24)
Brian The Snail (IRE) 95 1 (5f, Catt, Sft, Oct 25)
Brooklyn's Rose (IRE) 96 5 (7f, Leop, GF, Jul 21)
Brutal (IRE) 108 5 (1m, Donc, Gd, Oct 22)
Butterflies (IRE) 95 3 (1m, Curr, Gd, Aug 28)
Calare (IRE) 98 1 (1m, Curr, Gd, Oct 9)
Callender (IRE) 97 1 (5f, Nava, Sft, Sep 3)
Capri (IRE) 113 1 (1m, Curr, Hvy, Sep 25)
Caravaggio (USA) 117 1 (6f, Curr, GF, Aug 7)
Churchill (IRE) 121 1 (7f, Newm, Gd, Oct 8)
Clem Fandango (FR) 100 2 (5f, Newm, GF, Oct 7)
Cliffs Of Moher (IRE) 104 1 (7f, Leop, Yld, Oct 29)
Commander Cole 101 1 (1m 141y, Wolw, SD, Nov 11)
Contrast (IRE) 96 4 (1m, Hayd, Sft, Sep 3)
Coronet 96 1 (1m 2f, Newm, Gd, Oct 8)
Courage Under Fire (USA) 104 2 (6f, Curr, GF, Aug 7)
Create A Dream (USA) 100 4 (6f, Asco, GS, Jun 17)
Cristal Fizz (IRE) 100 1 (7f, Newb, GS, Oct 22)
Cuff (IRE) 102 1 (6f, Naas, Gd, May 29)
Cunco (IRE) 100 2 (1m 2f, Newm, Gd, Oct 8)
Currency Converter (USA) 100 3 (7f, Leop, GF, Jul 21)
D'bai (IRE) 102 3 (7f, Donc, Gd, Sep 10)
Dainty Dandy (IRE) 95 3 (6f, Asco, GF, Jul 23)
De Boss Man (IRE) 97 4 (6f, York, Gd, Oct 8)
Delectation 105 1 (6f, Ayr, GS, Sep 17)
Diodorus (IRE) 101 2 (1m 1f, Leop, Yld, Oct 29)
Double Lady (FR) 96 5 (7f, Newm, GF, Oct 7)
Douglas Macarthur (IRE) 105 3 (1m, Leop, Gd, Sep 10)
Dream Of Dreams (IRE) 105 2 (6f, York, Gd, Oct 8)
Dreamfield 99 1 (6f 15y, Nott, GS, Oct 5)
Drumfad Bay (IRE) 98 5 (7f, Curr, Sft, Aug 21)
Dubai Sand (IRE) 102 1 (1m 1f, Leop, Yld, Oct 29)
Elusive Beauty (IRE) 95 3 (6f, Curr, Yld, Jun 26)
Eqtiraan (IRE) 99 3 (7f 16y, Sand, GS, Aug 20)
Equimou 97 3 (5f, Donc, GS, Sep 7)
Escobar (IRE) 100 1 (7f, Newb, GF, Aug 13)
Executive Force 101 2 (7f, Dunw, SD, Oct 7)
Exemplar (IRE) 110 3 (1m, Curr, Hvy, Sep 25)
Eziyra (IRE) 108 1 (7f, Curr, Hvy, Sep 25)
Fair Eva 110 1 (6f, Asco, GF, Jul 23)
Finn Mccool (IRE) 101 7 (1m, Donc, Gd, Oct 22)
Firey Speech (USA) 105 2 (1m, Leop, Gd, Sep 10)
Fly At Dawn (USA) 96 1 (1m, Newm, GF, Sep 22)
Forest Ranger (IRE) 96 3 (1m 4y, Pont, Sft, Oct 17)
Frankuus (IRE) 100 1 (1m, Hayd, Sft, Sep 3)

Glastonbury Song (IRE) 95 1 (7f, Dunw, SD, Sep 30)
Glitter Girl 102 2 (7f, Newm, GF, Oct 7)
Global Applause 103 1 (5f 6y, Sand, GF, May 26)
Grecian Light (IRE) 103 2 (7f, Curr, Hvy, Sep 25)
Grey Britain 97 5 (6f, York, Gd, Aug 20)
Grizzel (IRE) 96 3 (7f 16y, Sand, GF, Jul 21)
Harry Angel (IRE) 111 1 (6f 8y, Newb, GS, Sep 17)
Hit The Bid 100 1 (5f, Curr, Gd, Aug 20)
Horseplay 95 1 (1m 75y, Nott, Sft, Oct 12)
Hydrangea (IRE) 112 2 (1m, Newm, GF, Oct 7)
Intelligence Cross (USA) 110 2 (6f, Newj, GF, Jul 7)
Intricately (IRE) 113 1 (7f, Curr, Yld, Sep 11)
Isomer (USA) 99 2 (7f, Asco, GS, Jun 18)
Jackhammer (IRE) 97 7 (7f, Good, GF, Jul 26)
Kananee (USA) 101 1 (6f, Ncsw, SD, Nov 17)
Kilmah 104 1 (7f, Good, GF, Aug 27)
King Electric (IRE) 99 4 (7f, Leop, GF, Jul 21)
Kings Gift (IRE) 100 2 (7f, Newb, GS, Oct 22)
Koropick (IRE) 106 5 (6f, Newm, GF, Sep 24)
Lady Aurelia (USA) 123 1 (5f, Asco, Sft, Jun 15)
Lancaster Bomber (USA) 116 2 (7f, Newm, Gd, Oct 8)
Landfall (FR) 110 1 (1m, Leop, Gd, Sep 10)
Larchmont Lad (IRE) 109 1 (7f, Newm, GF, Sep 22)
Law And Order (IRE) 100 3 (7f, Newb, GS, Oct 22)
Legendary Lunch (IRE) 104 2 (5f, Donc, Gd, Sep 9)
Lockheed 108 3 (7f, Curr, Yld, Sep 11)
Lost At Sea 99 1 (6f, Donc, GS, Sep 7)
Madam Dancealot (IRE) 100 1 (6f, Sali, Gd, Sep 1)
Magical Fire (IRE) 103 2 (6f, Newj, GF, Jul 8)
Majeste 102 4 (7f, Donc, Gd, Sep 10)
Majoris (IRE) 95 4 (7f, Donc, Gd, Sep 9)
Make Time (IRE) 99 5 (6f 212y, Sali, Sft, Sep 28)
Making Light (IRE) 102 1 (7f, Leop, Yld, Oct 23)
Masham Star (IRE) 100 1 (1m 5y, Ncsw, SD, Nov 28)
Medici Banchiere 99 5 (6f, Newj, GF, Jul 7)
Medicine Jack 107 1 (6f, Curr, Yld, Jun 25)
Medieval (IRE) 99 1 (1m 114y, Epso, Gd, Sep 25)
Mehmas (IRE) 114 1 (6f, Good, GF, Jul 28)
Mirdif 100 3 (6f 63y, Curr, Yld, Jul 16)
Miss Infinity (IRE) 105 3 (7f, Newm, GF, Sep 23)
Mister Trader 99 2 (5f, Curr, Sft, May 21)
Mokarris (USA) 107 1 (6f 8y, Newb, GF, Jul 15)
Montataire (IRE) 105 1 (1m, Sali, Gd, Aug 19)
Monticello (IRE) 96 2 (7f, Asco, GF, Jul 23)
Moonlit Show 97 1 (6f, Fair, Hvy, Sep 27)
Mr Scaramanga 97 2 (7f, Newb, GF, Aug 13)
Mrs Danvers 106 1 (5f, Newm, GF, Oct 7)
Mubtasim (IRE) 102 1 (6f, Hayd, GF, Aug 4)
Mur Hiba (IRE) 96 2 (5f, Curr, Gd, Aug 20)
Mutawatheb (IRE) 95 1 (1m, Donc, Gd, Oct 21)
Mystic Dawn (IRE) 96 3 (6f, Newm, Gd, Oct 28)
Nations Alexander (IRE) 103 1 (7f, Newj, GF, Aug 6)
Nobly Born 95 2 (6f 8y, Newb, GF, Jul 15)
Nuclear Power 99 5 (5f, Newm, GF, Oct 7)
On Her Toes (IRE) 98 3 (7f, Newj, GF, Aug 6)
Packing Stones (IRE) 107 3 (6f, Newj, GF, Jul 7)
Paco's Angel 97 4 (7f, Newm, GF, Oct 7)
Peace Envoy (FR) 107 1 (6f 63y, Curr, Yld, Jul 16)
Percy (IRE) 99 4 (1m, Leop, Gd, Sep 10)
Perfect Angel (IRE) 100 2 (6f 8y, Newb, GS, Sep 17)
Permian (IRE) 99 3 (1m 2f, Newm, Gd, Oct 8)
Phijee 96 1 (6f, Ripo, Gd, Aug 13)
Pipes Of Peace (IRE) 96 5 (7f, Leop, Yld, Oct 23)
Pleaseletmewin (IRE) 106 1 (7f, Newb, GS, Oct 22)
Poet's Vanity 105 1 (7f, Newm, GF, Oct 7)
Prince Of Lir (IRE) 107 1 (5f, Asco, Sft, Jun 16)
Promise To Be True (IRE) 105 1 (7f, Leop, GF, Jul 21)
Promising (IRE) 103 2 (7f, Good, GF, Aug 27)
Psychedelic Funk 102 2 (6f 63y, Curr, Yld, Jul 16)
Queen Anne's Lace (USA) 96 3 (1m, Curr, Gd, Oct 9)
Queen Kindly 112 1 (6f, York, GF, Aug 18)
Radio Silence (USA) 105 2 (7f, Curr, Sft, Aug 21)

Raheen House (IRE) 111 4 (1m, Donc, Gd, Oct 22)
Rainbow Mist (IRE) 99 5 (5f, Donc, Gd, Sep 9)
Ready To Roc (IRE) 95 5 (6f, Curr, Yld, Jun 25)
Really Special 100 1 (1m, Newm, GF, Oct 29)
Rehana (IRE) 107 4 (7f, Curr, Yld, Sep 11)
Repton (IRE) 103 5 (7f, Good, GF, Jul 26)
Rhododendron (IRE) 117 1 (1m, Newm, GF, Oct 7)
Rich Legacy (IRE) 105 1 (1m, Donc, Gd, Sep 8)
Rivet (IRE) 116 1 (1m, Donc, Gd, Oct 22)
Rodaini (USA) 104 1 (7f, Donc, Gd, Sep 9)
Roly Poly (USA) 112 2 (6f, Newm, GF, Sep 24)
Rosebride 97 2 (6f, Ayr, GS, Sep 17)
Salouen (IRE) 111 3 (1m, Donc, Gd, Oct 22)
Salsabeel (IRE) 104 2 (7f, Donc, Gd, Sep 9)
Saltonstall 96 6 (1m 1f, Leop, Yld, Sep 17)
Sea Fox (IRE) 107 3 (1m, Newm, GF, Sep 24)
Sea Of Grace (IRE) 104 1 (1m, Curr, Gd, Aug 28)
Seafront 97 2 (6f, Curr, Yld, Jun 26)
Seven Heavens 105 7 (7f, Newm, Gd, Oct 8)
Silver Line (IRE) 106 4 (6f, Newj, GF, Jul 7)
Sir Dancealot (IRE) 107 1 (6f, York, Gd, Oct 8)
Sir John Lavery (IRE) 95 1 (1m, Gowr, Hvy, Oct 18)
Sobetsu 99 1 (1m, Newm, Gd, Sep 17)
Son Of Rest 104 4 (7f, Curr, Yld, Sep 11)
South Seas (IRE) 108 6 (7f, Newm, Gd, Oct 8)
Spain Burg (FR) 109 1 (7f, Newm, GF, Sep 23)
Spanish Tenor (IRE) 100 4 (7f, Leop, Yld, Oct 23)
Spirit Of Valor (USA) 102 2 (7f, Leop, Yld, Oct 23)
Spiritual Lady 103 1 (6f, Newm, Gd, Oct 28)
Sportsmanship (USA) 96 4 (5f, Good, Gd, Jul 27)

Spy Ring (IRE) 99 2 (6f, Newm, Gd, Oct 28)
Star Of Rory (IRE) 98 2 (1m, Hayd, Sft, Sep 3)
Stormy Clouds (IRE) 97 1 (6f, York, GF, Aug 18)
Sultan Baybars 95 6 (7f, Newb, GS, Oct 22)
Sutter County 103 2 (6f, Ncsw, SD, Nov 17)
Syphax (USA) 109 1 (7f, York, GF, Aug 17)
Taj Mahal (IRE) 101 3 (7f, Leop, Yld, Oct 23)
Take A Deep Breath 102 2 (7f, Leop, GF, Jul 21)
The Anvil (IRE) 109 2 (1m, Newm, GF, Sep 24)
The Last Lion (IRE) 118 1 (6f, Newm, GF, Sep 24)
Thunder Snow (IRE) 115 2 (7f, Donc, Gd, Sep 10)
Tiburtina (IRE) 96 5 (7f, Good, GF, Aug 27)
Tinder (IRE) 96 3 (6f, Naas, Hvy, Oct 16)
Tis Marvellous 95 1 (6f, Wind, GF, Jul 11)
Tomily (IRE) 97 2 (6f, Donc, Gd, Oct 22)
Tommy Taylor (USA) 100 4 (7f, York, GF, Aug 17)
Top Score 98 2 (7f, Newm, GS, Oct 19)
Ultimate Avenue (IRE) 97 6 (7f, Newm, GF, Sep 22)
Unforgetable Filly 99 3 (7f, Newm, GF, Oct 7)
Urban Fox 98 3 (1m, Newm, GF, Oct 7)
Van Der Decken 99 5 (6f, Asco, Sft, Jun 14)
Via Egnatia (USA) 97 1 (1m, Newm, GF, Oct 1)
War Decree (USA) 113 1 (7f, Good, GF, Jul 26)
Whitecliffsofdover (USA) 107 2 (7f, Newm, GF, Sep 22)
Yalta (IRE) 111 1 (5f, Good, Gd, Jul 27)
Youarewonder (IRE) 98 3 (1m 1f, Leop, Yld, Oct 29)
Yucatan (IRE) 112 2 (1m, Donc, Gd, Oct 22)
Yulong Baobei (IRE) 103 1 (5f, Tipp, Yld, Jul 9)
Zainhom (USA) 106 2 (1m, Newm, Gd, Oct 8)

RACING POST RATINGS: LAST SEASON'S TOP PERFORMERS 3YO+

A Shin Hikari (JPN) 112 6 (1m 2f, Asco, Sft, Jun 15)
Abdon 113 1 (1m 2f 95y, Hayd, GF, Aug 6)
Abe Lincoln (USA) 104 2 (1m, Asco, Sft, Jun 16)
Abingdon (USA) 111 1 (1m 4f, York, GF, Aug 18)
Above N Beyond 108 3 (1m, Hayd, GS, May 21)
Above The Rest (IRE) 106 1 (7f 2y, Ches, GS, Sep 24)
Absolutely So (IRE) 113 4 (6f, Asco, GS, Jun 18)
Abstraction (IRE) 106 2 (5f, Cork, GF, May 20)
Accession (IRE) 104 3 (7f, Newb, Sft, Sep 16)
Aclaim (IRE) 115 1 (7f, Newm, GF, Oct 7)
Across The Stars (IRE) 113 3 (1m 4f, York, GF, Aug 17)
Adaay (IRE) 115 2 (7f, Newj, Hvy, Jun 25)
Adventurous (IRE) 104 2 (1m, Kemw, SD, Apr 2)
Aeolus 112 2 (6f, Donc, GF, Nov 5)
Afjaan (IRE) 106 1 (1m, Kemw, SS, Sep 3)
Afonso De Sousa (USA) 107 2 (1m 2f, Chmf, SD, Jan 16)
Ainippe (IRE) 106 3 (7f, Curr, Sft, May 2)
Air Pilot 115 2 (1m 1f, Newm, GS, Apr 13)
Air Vice Marshal (USA) 111 4 (1m, Newm, GS, Apr 30)
Ajman Princess (IRE) 105 2 (1m 4f, Asco, Sft, Jun 16)
Al Jazi (IRE) 110 1 (7f, Good, GF, Jul 29)
Alben Star (IRE) 114 1 (6f 1y, Linw, SD, Mar 25)
Algaith (USA) 109 2 (1m 4y, Pont, GF, Jul 24)
Algometer 114 1 (1m 3f 5y, Newb, GS, Sep 17)
Alice Springs (IRE) 118 1 (1m, Newm, GF, Oct 1)
Almanzor (FR) 129 1 (1m 2f, Asco, Gd, Oct 15)
Almela (IRE) 110 2 (1m 4f, Leop, Gd, Aug 4)
Almodovar (IRE) 115 3 (1m 4f, Asco, GS, Jun 18)
Alpha Delphini 114 2 (5f 34y, Newb, GS, Sep 17)
Always Smile (IRE) 116 2 (1m, Newm, GF, Oct 1)
Amazing Maria (IRE) 110 6 (1m, Asco, Sft, Jun 14)
Amazour (IRE) 106 1 (6f, Ncsw, SD, Dec 30)
Amour De Nuit (IRE) 107 1 (1m 6f, Chmf, SD, May 4)
Ancient History (IRE) 105 6 (1m 4f, Newm, Gd, Oct 8)
Angel Gabrial (IRE) 106 8 (2m 2f 147y, Ches, Gd, May 4)
Anglophile 105 2 (1m 7f 169y, Linw, SD, Mar 25)
Antiquarium (IRE) 109 1 (2m 56y, Ncsw, SD, Jun 25)
Arab Spring (IRE) 116 1 (1m 4f, Kemw, SS, Sep 3)
Arabian Queen (IRE) 116 2 (1m 1f, Newm, Gd, May 1)
Arcanada (IRE) 109 1 (1m, York, Gd, Aug 19)

Arch Villain (IRE) 107 1 (2m, Asco, GF, Aug 6)
Architecture (IRE) 115 2 (1m 4f 10y, Epso, GS, Jun 3)
Ardhoomey (IRE) 116 1 (5f, Curr, Yld, Sep 11)
Arod (IRE) 114 3 (1m, Good, GF, Aug 27)
Arthenus 106 4 (1m 2f, Asco, GS, Jun 18)
Ashadihan 105 5 (1m, Newj, GF, Jul 8)
Astronereus (IRE) 114 1 (1m 4f 5y, Newb, Gd, May 14)
Autocratic 108 1 (1m 2f 88y, York, Gd, Oct 8)
Awtaad (IRE) 122 1 (1m, Leop, Yld, Sep 10)
Ayrad (IRE) 113 2 (1m 4f, Good, GF, Jul 29)
Baccarat (IRE) 114 3 (6f, Ripo, Gd, Aug 13)
Ballydoyle (IRE) 113 2 (1m, Newm, Gd, May 1)
Banksea 105 2 (1m, Donc, Gd, Sep 10)
Baraweez (IRE) 107 5 (7f, Galw, Yld, Jul 31)
Barracuda Boy (IRE) 105 2 (6f 1y, Linw, SD, Feb 20)
Barsanti (IRE) 114 1 (1m 4f, York, GF, Aug 19)
Barye 108 2 (1m 4f, Linw, SD, Dec 17)
Basem 113 5 (1m 2f 88y, York, Gd, Jul 9)
Bateel (IRE) 106 1 (1m 4f, Newj, Sft, Jun 25)
Battalion (IRE) 109 1 (1m 2f, Linw, SD, Nov 30)
Battersea 111 4 (1m 6f, York, Gd, Aug 20)
Battle Of Marathon (USA) 114 5 (1m, Asco, Sft, Jun 15)
Baydar 111 1 (1m 2f 6y, Newb, GS, Sep 17)
Beacon Rock (IRE) 109 2 (1m 4f, Asco, GS, Jun 17)
Beautiful Romance 114 1 (1m 2f 88y, York, GF, May 12)
Beauty Way 108 2 (1m 2f 95y, Hayd, GF, Aug 6)
Belardo (IRE) 122 2 (1m, Asco, Sft, Jun 14)
Belgian Bill 106 4 (1m, Good, GF, Jul 29)
Berkshire (IRE) 111 2 (1m 2f 6y, Newb, GF, Jul 16)
Best In The World (IRE) 105 2 (1m 2f, Curr, Yld, Sep 11)
Best Of Times 107 5 (1m 1f 192y, Good, GF, Jul 26)
Big Orange 119 1 (1m 4f, Newj, GF, Jul 7)
Birchwood (IRE) 110 1 (7f 2y, Ches, Sft, Jul 9)
Birdman (IRE) 109 4 (1m, Donc, Sft, Apr 2)
Black Cherry 105 7 (1m, Asco, GS, Jun 15)
Blond Me (IRE) 109 1 (1m, Good, Gd, Apr 30)
Blue De Vega (GER) 106 2 (7f, Leop, Yld, Oct 29)
Blue Rambler 106 3 (1m 6f, Hayd, Sft, Sep 3)
Bobby's Kitten (USA) 117 1 (6f, Cork, Hvy, Mar 28)
Bocca Baciata (IRE) 113 2 (1m 2f, Curr, Yld, Jun 26)

Bondi Beach (IRE) 114 3 (1m 4f, Leop, Gd, Sep 10)
Boom The Groom (IRE) 111 1 (5f 89y, York, GF, Aug 17)
Bossy Guest (IRE) 107 6 (1m, Asco, Sft, Jun 15)
Bowson Fred 107 3 (5f, Hayd, Sft, Sep 3)
Brando 119 1 (6f, Ayr, GS, Sep 17)
Bravo Zolo (IRE) 109 2 (1m, Donc, Sft, Apr 2)
Brendan Brackan (IRE) 107 1 (1m 100y, Cork, Yld, Oct 15)
Breton Rock (IRE) 116 1 (7f, Newj, Hvy, Jun 25)
Buckstay (IRE) 114 3 (7f, Asco, GF, May 7)
Buratino (IRE) 108 4 (6f, Hayd, Gd, May 28)
Burmese 111 5 (2m, Asco, GS, Apr 27)
Burnt Sugar (IRE) 106 6 (6f, Asco, GS, Jun 18)
Buying Trouble (USA) 106 2 (6f, Newj, GF, Aug 27)
California (IRE) 105 3 (1m 6f 132y, Donc, Gd, Sep 8)
Calling Out (FR) 107 2 (1m, Donc, Sft, Apr 2)
Cannock Chase (USA) 120 1 (1m 2f 75y, Ches, Gd, May 5)
Cape Cova (IRE) 105 3 (1m 4f, Donc, GF, Nov 5)
Captain Cat (IRE) 112 1 (1m, Kemw, SD, Feb 24)
Captain Colby (USA) 107 1 (5f 140y, Donc, Gd, Sep 10)
Captain Joy (IRE) 110 1 (1m 1y, Linw, SD, Mar 25)
Carnachy (IRE) 109 1 (1m 2f 60y, Donc, GF, Nov 5)
Carntop 106 5 (1m 4f, Asco, GS, Jun 17)
Carry On Deryck 111 2 (1m 1f, Newm, Gd, Oct 8)
Caspian Prince (IRE) 113 1 (5f, Dunw, SD, Oct 21)
Celestial Path (IRE) 110 2 (1m, York, Gd, Jul 9)
Central Square (IRE) 111 1 (1m 2f 60y, Donc, Gd, Sep 8)
Certificate 114 2 (7f, Redc, GF, Oct 1)
Chain Of Daisies 111 1 (1m 2f 7y, Wind, GF, Aug 27)
Charming Kitten (USA) 105 3 (1m 6f, Dowr, Gd, Jul 22)
Charming Thought 108 4 (6f, Sali, Gd, Jun 12)
Cheikeljack (FR) 107 6 (6f, Asco, GS, Jun 17)
Chemical Charge (IRE) 109 2 (1m 4f, Kemw, SS, Nov 23)
Chil The Kite 107 4 (1m 67y, Wind, Sft, Jun 25)
Chookie Royale 111 1 (6f, Kemw, SD, Jan 13)
Clear Spring (IRE) 106 5 (6f, Sali, Gd, Jun 12)
Clever Cookie 115 1 (1m 6f, York, GF, May 13)
Code Red 106 6 (7f, Good, Gd, Aug 28)
Convey 117 1 (1m 4y, Pont, GF, Jul 24)
Cotai Glory 117 2 (5f, Asco, Sft, Jun 14)
Cougar Mountain (IRE) 118 1 (1m, Newm, GF, Sep 23)
Coulsty (IRE) 111 1 (7f, Thir, GS, Jul 29)
Countermeasure 114 4 (1m 2f 7y, Sand, Sft, Jul 2)
Crazy Horse 115 1 (6f 212y, Sali, GS, Oct 10)
Creggs Pipes (IRE) 107 1 (1m 123y, Galw, Sft, Jul 26)
Crimean Tatar (TUR) 110 1 (1m 4f, Kemw, SS, Nov 23)
Curbyourenthusiasm (IRE) 114 2 (1m 6f, York, GF, May 13)
Custom Cut (IRE) 117 3 (1m 114y, Epso, GS, Jun 3)
Cymric (USA) 107 4 (1m, Asco, Sft, Jun 14)
Cymro (IRE) 108 1 (1m 3f 200y, Hayd, Gd, Sep 1)
Dal Harraild 114 1 (1m 4f, Newm, GF, Sep 23)
Dancing Star 113 1 (6f, Good, GF, Jul 30)
Danzeno 115 2 (6f, Sali, Gd, Jun 12)
Dark Emerald (IRE) 112 3 (7f, Newb, GF, Aug 13)
Dartmouth 121 1 (1m 4f, Asco, GS, Jun 18)
Deauville (IRE) 114 2 (1m 2f 88y, York, GF, May 12)
Decorated Knight 112 1 (1m 1f, Leop, GF, Jul 14)
Desert Encounter (IRE) 107 2 (1m 4f 66y, Ches, GS, Sep 10)
Devonshire (IRE) 110 1 (1m, Curr, Yld, May 21)
Diamond Fields (IRE) 105 2 (1m, Asco, Sft, Jun 15)
Dick Whittington (IRE) 109 1 (7f 20y, Leop, Sft, Jun 16)
Dinkum Diamond (IRE) 106 4 (7f, Asco, GF, May 7)
Diploma 113 1 (1m 2f 88y, York, GF, Jul 22)
Divine (IRE) 115 1 (6f, Curr, GF, Jun 4)
Don't Touch 116 5 (6f, Asco, Gd, Oct 15)
Donjuan Triumphant (IRE) 110 2 (6f, Hayd, Gd, May 28)
Donncha (IRE) 106 2 (1m 14y, Sand, Sft, Jul 2)
Double Up 110 4 (5f 140y, Donc, Gd, Sep 10)
Dougan 105 3 (5f 216y, Wolw, SD, Dec 16)
Dragon Mall (USA) 107 4 (1m, Good, GF, Jul 29)
Duchess Andorra (IRE) 106 1 (1m 1f 100y, Gowr, Sft, Sep 18)
Duke Of Firenze 107 2 (5f 89y, York, GF, Aug 17)
Duretto 111 1 (1m 4f 5y, Newb, GS, Oct 22)
Dutch Connection 119 1 (7f, Good, GF, Jul 26)
Eagle Top 105 4 (1m 4f 5y, Newb, Gd, May 14)

Early Morning (IRE) 107 2 (1m, Asco, GF, Sep 2)
Eastern Impact (IRE) 110 2 (6f, Curr, GF, Aug 7)
Easton Angel (IRE) 113 2 (5f, York, Gd, Jul 9)
Easy Road 111 1 (5f, Asco, Sft, Oct 1)
Educate 116 1 (1m 2f 88y, York, Gd, Jul 9)
Elbereth 105 2 (1m 2f 88y, York, Gd, Jul 9)
Elidor 114 1 (1m 6f, Good, GF, Jul 26)
Elite Army 113 2 (1m 4f, Asco, GS, Jun 17)
Emell 108 4 (7f, Good, Gd, Aug 28)
Encore D'or 108 1 (5f, Chmf, SD, Nov 21)
Encounter (IRE) 106 2 (7f, Chmf, SD, Apr 16)
Endless Drama (IRE) 118 3 (1m, Newb, Gd, May 14)
Endless Time (IRE) 111 1 (1m 3f 200y, Hayd, Sft, Jul 2)
Energia Davos (BRZ) 113 1 (1m 2f, Newm, GF, Oct 29)
Ennaadd 114 1 (1m, Kemw, SD, Nov 16) Erupt (IRE) 113 5 (1m 4f, Asco, GF, Jul 23)
Ervedya (FR) 114 3 (1m, Newm, GF, Oct 1)
Estidhkaar (IRE) 111 1 (1m, Newm, GF, Oct 29)
Eternally 107 1 (7f 140y, Ling, GF, Aug 13)
Euro Charline 116 2 (1m, Newb, Gd, May 14)
Even Song (IRE) 108 1 (1m 4f, Asco, Sft, Jun 16)
Exospheric 120 1 (1m 4f, Newm, GS, Apr 30)
Express Himself (IRE) 107 2 (1m, Ayr, GF, Jun 18)
Fanciful Angel (IRE) 105 4 (7f, Chmf, SD, Dec 22)
Fannaan (USA) 105 2 (7f, Newb, Sft, Sep 16)
Fascinating Rock (IRE) 125 1 (1m 2f 110y, Curr, Sft, May 22)
Felix Leiter 106 3 (1m 67y, Wind, Sft, Jun 26)
Festive Fare 111 2 (1m 2f, Linw, SD, Feb 6)
Final Venture 107 4 (5f, Beve, Gd, Aug 27)
Fire Fighting (IRE) 116 1 (1m 4f, Newj, GF, Aug 13)
Fireglow 110 4 (1m, Newm, Gd, May 1)
Firmament 114 3 (1m, Asco, Gd, Oct 15)
First Mohican 108 2 (1m 4f, Linw, SD, Jan 8)
First Selection (SPA) 105 6 (1m, Hayd, Sft, Sep 3)
First Sitting 109 1 (1m 2f, Newj, GF, Aug 6)
Flash Fire (IRE) 114 4 (7f, Asco, GF, Jul 23)
Flight Risk (IRE) 110 2 (6f, Curr, Hvy, Sep 25)
Flying Officer (USA) 117 3 (2m, Asco, GS, Apr 27)
Folkswood 107 2 (1m 2f 23y, Yarm, GF, Aug 28)
Forever Popular (USA) 105 1 (1m 4f, Newj, GF, Jul 16)
Forge 111 1 (7f, Hayd, Gd, Sep 1)
Forgotten Rules (IRE) 110 7 (2m, Asco, Gd, Oct 15)
Fort Del Oro (IRE) 108 1 (5f, Naas, Gd, Apr 25)
Found (IRE) 123 2 (1m 2f, Leop, Yld, Sep 10)
Foundation (IRE) 111 5 (1m 2f 95y, Hayd, GF, Aug 6)
Franklin D (USA) 112 1 (1m, Newj, GF, Jul 16)
Frontiersman 106 1 (1m 4f, Newm, GF, Sep 22)
Frosty Berry 105 1 (1m 6f 15y, Nott, Hvy, Apr 6)
Fun Mac (GER) 107 3 (2m 1f 216y, Pont, Sft, Oct 17)
Furia Cruzada (CHI) 111 2 (1m, Asco, Sft, Jun 15)
Gabrial (IRE) 117 5 (1m, Good, GF, Jul 27)
Galileo Gold 123 2 (1m, Good, GF, Jul 27)
Gamgoom 110 2 (6f 1y, Linw, SD, Feb 6)
Gang Warfare 107 1 (1m 5f 194y, Wolw, SD, Mar 25)
George Dryden (IRE) 108 2 (6f, Ripo, GS, Apr 23)
Get Knotted (IRE) 106 2 (6f, Donc, Gd, Oct 21)
Gifted Master (IRE) 114 1 (6f, Asco, GS, Apr 27)
Glen Moss (IRE) 109 1 (6f, Hayd, Sft, Jul 2)
Gm Hopkins 116 1 (1m, Asco, GS, Apr 27)
Goken (FR) 113 3 (5f, Asco, Sft, Jun 14)
Gold Land 109 1 (7f, Epso, GS, Jun 3)
Gold Mount 108 1 (1m 4f, Asco, Sft, Jun 16)
Gold Prince (IRE) 107 (2m, Asco, Gd, Oct 15)
Gold Trail (IRE) 113 1 (1m 4f, Donc, Gd, Sep 10)
Gold-fun (IRE) 117 2 (6f, Asco, GS, Jun 18)
Golden Steps (FR) 107 1 (7f, Newj, GF, Jul 9)
Goldmember 106 4 (2m, Newm, GF, Sep 22)
Goldream 115 3 (6f, Asco, GS, Jun 18)
Goodwood Zodiac (IRE) 106 1 (1m 2f 18y, Epso, Gd, Aug 29)
Gordon Lord Byron (IRE) 116 1 (7f, Curr, Gd, Jul 17)
Gracious John (IRE) 114 2 (5f, Ncsw, SD, Dec 17)
Gravity Flow (IRE) 108 2 (6f, Newm, Gd, Oct 8)
Great Hall 108 1 (1m 2f 50y, Nott, Sft, Oct 12)
Great Order (USA) 108 2 (1m 2f 88y, York, Gd, Oct 8)

Green Door (IRE) 106 1 (5f, Newj, Sft, Jun 23)
Grendisar (IRE) 115 1 (1m 2f, Linw, SD, Feb 27)
Growl 118 2 (6f, Asco, Gd, Oct 15)
Haalick (IRE) 108 2 (7f, Good, Gd, May 21)
Hamelin (IRE) 107 3 (2m, Kemw, SD, Apr 2)
Harbour Law 116 1 (1m 6f 132y, Donc, Gd, Sep 10)
Harlequeen 108 3 (1m 4f, Curr, Gd, Jul 16)
Harrison 106 3 (1m 5f, Newj, GF, Jul 7)
Harry Hurricane 105 1 (5f, Hayd, Gd, Sep 24)
Harzand (IRE) 124 1 (1m 4f 10y, Epso, GS, Jun 4)
Hasanour (USA) 106 2 (7f, Naas, Gd, May 29)
Hathal (USA) 117 1 (1m, Hayd, Sft, Sep 3)
Hawkbill (USA) 123 1 (1m 2f 7y, Sand, Sft, Jul 2)
Hawke (IRE) 106 1 (1m 2f 150y, Dunw, SD, Oct 14)
Hawksmoor (IRE) 106 3 (1m 1f, Curr, Gd, Jul 17)
Heartbreak City (FR) 115 1 (1m 6f, York, Gd, Aug 20)
Heaven's Guest (IRE) 110 2 (7f, Newj, GF, Jul 9)
Here Comes When (IRE) 111 3 (7f, Leic, GS, Apr 23)
Higher Power 106 1 (2m, Kemw, SD, Nov 16)
Highland Colori (IRE) 105 6 (1m, Asco, Gd, Oct 15)
Highland Reel (IRE) 123 2 (1m 2f 88y, York, GF, Aug 17)
Hillbilly Boy (IRE) 107 1 (6f 18y, Ches, Gd, Jul 31)
Hit It A Bomb (USA) 114 3 (1m, Leop, Yld, Sep 10)
Home Of The Brave (IRE) 118 1 (7f, Hayd, Gd, May 28)
Hoof It 105 1 (6f, Good, GF, Jul 30)
Hoofalong 105 1 (5f, Muss, Gd, Jun 11)
Hors De Combat 107 5 (1m, Asco, GS, Apr 27)
Housesofparliament (IRE) 115 3 (1m 6f 132y, Donc, Gd, Sep 10)
Humidor (IRE) 105 2 (5f 140y, Donc, Gd, Sep 10)
Humphrey Bogart (IRE) 107 1 (1m 3f 106y, Ling, Gd, May 7)
Ibn Malik (IRE) 112 1 (7f, Newm, GS, Apr 13)
Idaho (IRE) 120 2 (1m 4f, Curr, Yld, Jun 25)
Iffranesia (FR) 105 3 (5f, Curr, Yld, Sep 11)
Illuminate (IRE) 105 5 (6f, Asco, GS, Jun 17)
Imperial Aviator 105 3 (1m 2f 6y, Newb, GS, Sep 17)
In My Pocket (IRE) 107 3 (1m, Leop, Gd, May 8)
In Salutem 107 1 (5f, Asco, GF, Aug 6)
Instant Attraction (IRE) 106 2 (1m 114y, Epso, GS, Jun 3)
Intimation 110 1 (1m, Naas, Hvy, Oct 16)
Intisaab 110 1 (6f, York, Gd, Oct 8)
Intransigent 110 2 (6f, Kemw, SD, Jan 13)
Irish Rookie (IRE) 109 4 (1m, Newj, GF, Jul 8)
Jack Dexter 106 4 (5f, Asco, GF, Jul 9)
Jack Hobbs 122 3 (1m 2f, Asco, Gd, Oct 15)
Jallota 114 3 (7f, York, Gd, Aug 19)
Jamesie (IRE) 105 5 (5f 182y, Nava, Sft, Sep 3)
Jane's Memory (IRE) 106 1 (6f, Hayd, GS, May 21)
Jazzi Top 108 5 (1m, Asco, Sft, Jun 15)
Jemayel (IRE) 110 3 (1m 1f 192y, Good, GF, Jul 30)
Jet Setting (IRE) 120 1 (7f 100y, Tipp, Hvy, Oct 2)
Johannes Vermeer (IRE) 109 3 (1m 1f, Newm, Gd, Oct 8)
Johnny Barnes (IRE) 109 4 (7f, Leic, GS, Apr 23)
Journey 121 1 (1m 4f, Asco, Gd, Oct 15)
Judicial (IRE) 105 3 (5f, Hayd, Gd, Sep 24)
Jungle Cat (IRE) 114 2 (5f, Newm, GS, Apr 30)
Justice Good (IRE) 106 1 (6f, Kemw, SS, Nov 23)
Kachy 113 2 (6f, Asco, GS, Jun 17)
Kadrizzi (FR) 107 1 (6f, Asco, GF, Aug 6)
Kassia (IRE) 109 1 (6f, Newm, Gd, Oct 8)
Kelinni (IRE) 109 1 (7f, Thir, Sft, Apr 16)
Kentuckyconnection (USA) 108 5 (1m, Newm, GS, Apr 30)
Kicky Blue (GER) 105 9 (2m 4f, Asco, Sft, Jun 16)
Kimberella 113 1 (6f, Ripo, Gd, Sep 24)
Kinema (IRE) 109 1 (1m 4f, Asco, GS, Jun 17)
King Bolete (IRE) 107 1 (1m 3f 200y, Hayd, GF, Jun 8)
Kings Fete 114 1 (1m 4f, Good, GF, Jul 29)
Kingsgate Native (IRE) 111 1 (5f 13y, Nott, GF, Aug 9)
Kodi Bear (IRE) 113 9 (1m, Good, GF, Jul 27)
Kool Kompany (IRE) 110 2 (1m, Newm, GF, Oct 29)
Koora 111 2 (1m 2f 88y, York, GF, May 12)
La Rioja 106 3 (6f, Curr, Hvy, Sep 25)
Lady Of Camelot (IRE) 108 5 (1m 3f 200y, Hayd, Sft, Jul 2)
Laganore (IRE) 111 1 (1m 2f, Newm, GF, Oct 7)
Lamar (IRE) 108 3 (1m 2f, Linw, SD, Feb 6)

Lancelot Du Lac (ITY) 107 2 (6f 1y, Linw, SD, Mar 25)
Latharnach (USA) 116 1 (7f, Redc, GF, Oct 1)
Laugh Aloud 111 1 (1m, Newm, GF, Sep 23)
Librisa Breeze 117 1 (7f, Asco, Sft, Oct 1)
Lightning Spear 122 3 (1m, Asco, Gd, Oct 15)
Lightscameraction (IRE) 112 1 (5f 6y, Linw, SD, Feb 27)
Limato (IRE) 125 1 (6f, Newj, GF, Jul 9)
Limitless (IRE) 110 1 (1m, Asco, Sft, Jun 16)
Line Of Reason (IRE) 111 1 (5f, Beve, Gd, Jun 14)
Litigant 110 6 (2m, Asco, Gd, Oct 15)
Log Out Island (IRE) 112 1 (6f 8y, Newb, Gd, May 14)
Long Island Sound (USA) 108 1 (1m 2f 150y, Dunw, SD, Sep 30)
Lord Ben Stack (IRE) 106 1 (1m 3f 200y, Hayd, Gd, Sep 24)
Lord Of The Land (IRE) 114 1 (6f 1y, Linw, SD, Nov 12)
Loving Things 109 3 (1m 3f 200y, Hayd, Sft, Jul 2)
Lucida (IRE) 107 6 (1m, Asco, Sft, Jun 15)
Lucy The Painter (IRE) 105 3 (1m 14y, Sand, GS, Aug 20)
Lulu The Zulu (IRE) 105 1 (6f, Newj, Sft, Jun 24)
Lumiere 113 1 (1m, Newj, GF, Jul 7)
Maarek 111 5 (6f, Newm, GS, Apr 14)
Magical Memory (IRE) 116 1 (6f, York, Gd, May 11)
Magnus Maximus 111 1 (6f, Asco, GF, Sep 3)
Mahsoob 118 1 (1m 1f, Newm, GS, Apr 13)
Majeed 110 2 (1m 3f 135y, Wind, GF, Aug 27)
Majestic Moon (IRE) 107 2 (7f 1y, Linw, SD, Mar 4)
Maleficent Queen 108 1 (1m 2f, Ayr, GS, May 18)
Maljaa 109 7 (5f, Asco, GF, Jul 9)
Man Of Harlech 105 4 (1m 2f, Linw, SD, Mar 25)
Markaz (IRE) 116 1 (6f, Ncsw, SD, Jun 25)
Marsha (IRE) 114 1 (5f, York, Gd, Jul 9)
Massaat (IRE) 117 2 (1m, Newm, GS, Apr 30)
Master Carpenter (IRE) 111 3 (1m 2f 75y, Ches, Gd, May 5)
Master The World (IRE) 114 2 (1m, Good, GF, Jul 29)
Mattmu 112 3 (6f, Newm, GS, Apr 14)
Maverick Wave (USA) 113 (1m 2f, Asco, Gd, Oct 15)
Max Dynamite (FR) 106 3 (2m 78y, Sand, GF, May 26)
Mayfair Lady 111 1 (6f, York, Gd, Jun 10)
Mecca's Angel (IRE) 125 1 (5f, York, Gd, Aug 19)
Medicean Man 110 3 (5f, Dunw, SD, Oct 21)
Mehronissa 112 2 (6f, Asco, Sft, Oct 1)
Memorial Day (IRE) 110 1 (1m 2f 6y, Pont, GS, Sep 22)
Metropol (IRE) 109 3 (1m 2f, Linw, SD, Mar 25)
Midterm 117 7 (1m 2f, Asco, Gd, Oct 15)
Mille Et Mille 112 4 (2m 4f, Asco, Sft, Jun 16)
Minding (IRE) 123 1 (1m, Asco, Gd, Oct 15)
Mindurownbusiness (IRE) 114 1 (1m 141y, Wolw, SD, Feb 8)
Mirza 112 1 (5f, Leic, GF, Oct 11)
Mise En Rose (USA) 108 2 (7f, Donc, Gd, Sep 9)
Miss Temple City (USA) 113 4 (1m, Asco, Sft, Jun 15)
Mister Universe 112 1 (1m 1y, Linw, SD, Mar 5)
Mitchum Swagger 116 2 (1m, Hayd, Sft, Sep 3)
Mix And Mingle (IRE) 106 7 (1m, Newm, Gd, May 1)
Mizzou (IRE) 117 2 (2m 4f, Asco, Sft, Jun 16)
Mobsta (IRE) 111 1 (6f, Donc, Sft, Apr 2)
Mondialiste (IRE) 118 2 (1m 2f 88y, York, GF, Jul 23)
Mongolian Saturday (USA) 105 (6f, Newj, GF, Jul 9)
Monsieur Joe (IRE) 113 2 (5f 6y, Sand, Sft, Jul 2)
Moonlight Magic 115 6 (1m 2f, Leop, Yld, Sep 10)
Moonraker 107 2 (6f, Ncsw, SD, Jun 25)
Moonrise Landing (IRE) 110 1 (1m 6f, York, Gd, May 21)
Morando (FR) 109 7 (1m, Asco, Gd, Oct 15)
Motherland (IRE) 108 1 (1m 4f 84y, Galw, Gd, Jul 25)
Mount Logan (IRE) 114 1 (1m 2f 60y, Donc, GS, Sep 7)
Mountain Bell 107 2 (1m 4f 5y, Newb, GS, Oct 22)
Move In Time 111 5 (5f 6y, Linw, SD, Feb 27)
Move Up 116 1 (1m 4f, Asco, Sft, Oct 1)
Moviesta (USA) 112 2 (5f, Dunw, SD, Oct 21)
Mr Lupton (IRE) 111 9 (6f, York, GS, Jun 11)
Mr Owen (USA) 106 (1m, Asco, Sft, Jun 15)
Muffri'ha (IRE) 112 1 (1m 1f, Newm, Gd, Oct 8)
Muntahaa (IRE) 116 1 (1m 5f 89y, Ches, Gd, Aug 20)
Muntazah 106 4 (1m 2f 88y, York, GF, May 12)
Mustallib (IRE) 106 2 (6f, Kemw, SS, Sep 19)
Mustashry 109 4 (1m 14y, Sand, Gd, Sep 14)

Mutakayyef 122 3 (1m 2f 88y, York, GF, Aug 17)
Mutawathea 107 3 (7f, Newj, GF, Jul 9)
Muthmir (IRE) 116 3 (5f 6y, Linw, SD, Feb 27)
Muwaary 110 3 (1m 14y, Sand, Gd, Sep 14)
My Dream Boat (IRE) 122 1 (1m 2f, Asco, Sft, Jun 15)
Mythmaker 111 2 (6f 1y, Linw, SD, Nov 12)
Naadirr (IRE) 111 3 (6f, Wind, Gd, May 23)
Nakeeta 105 2 (1m 7f, Leop, Yld, Oct 29)
Nameitwhatyoulike 111 1 (6f, York, GS, Sep 4)
Namhroodah (IRE) 107 1 (1m, Asco, GF, Jul 22)
Nathra (IRE) 109 1 (7f, Newm, GS, Apr 12)
Nearly Caught (IRE) 114 5 (2m, Asco, Gd, Oct 15)
Nemoralia (USA) 114 1 (7f, York, Gd, Aug 19)
New Bay 117 4 (1m 2f, Leop, Yld, Sep 10)
Nezwaah 111 2 (1m 2f 23y, Yarm, GF, Sep 14)
Nightflower (IRE) 108 4 (1m 3f 200y, Hayd, Sft, Jul 2)
Ninjago 107 4 (5f, York, Gd, May 21)
Not So Sleepy 105 3 (1m 2f 6y, Newb, GS, Oct 22)
Notarised 107 3 (1m 6f, Good, GS, May 21)
Now Or Never (IRE) 108 4 (1m, Asco, GS, Jun 17)
Oasis Fantasy (IRE) 109 5 (1m 2f 7y, Sand, GS, Aug 20)
Oceanographer 109 1 (1m 2f 60y, Donc, Gd, Jul 30)
Ode To Evening 107 2 (1m 1f 192y, Good, GF, Jul 28)
Oh This Is Us (IRE) 109 1 (7f, Donc, GF, Nov 5)
One Word More (IRE) 106 3 (1m, York, Gd, Jul 9)
Onenightidreamed (IRE) 114 1 (7f, Curr, Hvy, Apr 3)
Only Mine (IRE) 111 1 (6f, Naas, Gd, May 29)
Opal Tiara (IRE) 109 1 (7f, Good, Gd, Aug 28)
Order Of St George (IRE) 121 1 (2m 4f, Asco, Sft, Jun 16)
Oriental Fox (GER) 107 1 (2m 1f 216y, Pont, Sft, Oct 17)
Orion's Bow 111 2 (6f, Good, GF, Jul 30)
Ornate 109 2 (6f, Asco, Gd, Sep 30)
Our Channel (USA) 107 4 (1m 1f 103y, Wolw, SD, Dec 26)
Out Do 106 3 (5f, Asco, GF, Aug 6)
Outback Traveller (IRE) 112 1 (6f, Asco, GS, Jun 18)
Pacify 108 2 (1m 2f 88y, York, Gd, May 11)
Pallasator 116 2 (2m, Good, GF, Jul 28)
Pearl Secret 111 7 (5f, Good, GF, Jul 29)
Perfect Pasture 112 2 (5f 13y, Nott, Gd, Nov 2)
Persuasive (IRE) 113 1 (1m 14y, Sand, GS, Aug 20)
Pinzolo 108 1 (1m 4f, Linw, SD, Dec 17)
Pipers Note 105 1 (5f, Ripo, Gd, Aug 30)
Pirouette 105 2 (1m, Newm, GF, Sep 23)
Platitude 110 1 (1m 6f, Good, GF, Aug 27)
Poet's Word (IRE) 111 2 (1m 2f 60y, Donc, Gd, Sep 8)
Polarisation 106 2 (1m 4f 10y, Epso, GS, Jun 4)
Port Douglas (IRE) 112 2 (1m 4f 66y, Ches, Gd, May 5)
Portage (IRE) 115 1 (1m, Asco, Sft, Jun 15)
Postponed (IRE) 126 1 (1m 2f 88y, York, GF, Aug 17)
Poyle Vinnie 106 3 (6f 18y, Ches, Sft, Jul 9)
Pretend (IRE) 113 2 (6f, Ncsw, SD, Jun 25)
Pretty Perfect (IRE) 113 2 (1m 6f 132y, Donc, Gd, Sep 8)
Priceless 107 1 (5f, Donc, GS, Sep 7)
Prize Money 116 1 (1m 4f, Donc, GF, Nov 5)
Profitable (IRE) 120 1 (5f, Hayd, GS, May 21)
Projection 110 3 (6f, Newj, GF, Aug 13)
Promising Run (USA) 107 5 (1m, Asco, GS, Jun 17)
Qatari Hunter (IRE) 107 4 (1m 4f, Good, GF, Jul 27)
Qemah (IRE) 114 1 (1m, Asco, GS, Jun 17)
Qewy (IRE) 112 2 (1m 6f, Good, GF, Jul 26)
Quebee 106 1 (1m 14y, Sand, Gd, Sep 14)
Queen Blossom (IRE) 106 1 (1m, Curr, Sft, Mar 20)
Queen Catrine (IRE) 106 1 (7f, Fair, Yld, Jul 10)
Queen's Trust 115 3 (1m 4f, York, GF, Aug 18)
Quest For More (IRE) 116 2 (2m, Asco, Gd, Oct 15)
Quick Jack (IRE) 109 1 (1m 6f, Leop, Gd, Sep 10)
Quiet Reflection 120 1 (6f, Hayd, Sft, Sep 3)
Racing History (IRE) 117 6 (1m 2f, Asco, Gd, Oct 15)
Raucous 109 3 (6f, Asco, Sft, Oct 1)
Raymonda (USA) 107 1 (7f, Fair, GF, Jun 8)
Razor Wind (IRE) 107 2 (1m 1f 103y, Wolw, SD, Feb 15)
Realize 109 1 (7f, Chmf, SD, Dec 22)
Red Box 105 2 (1m, Asco, GF, Jul 22)
Red Verdon (USA) 114 4 (1m 4f, Curr, Yld, Jun 25)

Remarkable 110 2 (1m, Asco, Gd, Oct 15)
Rene Mathis (GER) 106 4 (7f 122y, Ches, Gd, May 28)
Renneti (FR) 105 (1m 7f, Leop, Yld, Oct 29)
Restorer 105 3 (1m 4f, Kemw, SS, Nov 2)
Revolutionist (IRE) 112 3 (1m 2f, Asco, GS, Jun 18)
Ribchester (IRE) 124 2 (1m, Asco, Gd, Oct 15)
Richard Pankhurst 117 1 (7f, Newb, GF, Aug 13)
Ridge Ranger (IRE) 113 2 (6f, Pont, Gd, Aug 14)
Right Touch 106 2 (7f 122y, Ches, Gd, Aug 20)
Rivellino 108 1 (6f 1y, Linw, SD, Feb 6)
Robin Of Navan (FR) 112 2 (1m 4f, Kemw, SS, Sep 3)
Rockspirit (IRE) 107 1 (1m 2f, Chmf, SD, Oct 6)
Rose De Pierre (IRE) 105 1 (1m, Cork, Yld, Aug 2)
Roseburg (IRE) 115 3 (1m 4f 10y, Epso, GS, Jun 4)
Rosental 108 2 (1m 2f 95y, Hayd, GS, Sep 3)
Roudee 107 1 (6f, Ayr, GS, Sep 17)
Royal Artillery (USA) 117 1 (1m 2f 95y, Hayd, GF, Aug 6)
Royal Birth 107 1 (5f, Chmf, SD, Jun 15)
Russian Soul (IRE) 105 6 (6f 1y, Linw, SD, Mar 25)
Sagaciously (IRE) 107 1 (1m 1f 192y, Good, GF, Jul 27)
Salateen 108 1 (7f, Newm, GF, Sep 24)
Sandro Botticelli (IRE) 110 1 (2m 78y, Sand, Sft, Jul 2)
Scarlet Dragon 112 1 (1m 4f, Newm, GF, Oct 7)
Scotland (GER) 108 2 (1m 4f, Asco, GF, May 7)
Scottish (IRE) 119 1 (1m 208y, York, Gd, Aug 20)
Scrutineer (IRE) 106 1 (6f 6y, Hami, Hvy, Sep 26)
Sea Of Flames (IRE) 105 1 (1m 1y, Linw, SD, Mar 25)
Sea Wolf (IRE) 105 1 (1m, Curr, Gd, Aug 28)
Seamour (IRE) 110 2 (1m 6f 132y, Donc, Gd, Sep 9)
Second Step (IRE) 113 3 (1m 6f, York, GF, May 13)
Second Wave (IRE) 112 4 (1m 1f 192y, Good, GF, Jul 26)
Secret Brief (IRE) 109 1 (1m, Donc, Sft, Apr 2)
Secret Number 112 1 (1m 2f, Ayr, Sft, Sep 15)
Seismos (IRE) 106 7 (2m 56y, Ncsw, SD, Jun 25)
Seventh Heaven (IRE) 121 1 (1m 4f, York, GF, Aug 18)
Shalaa 115 1 (6f, Asco, Sft, Oct 1)
Shamreen (IRE) 106 1 (1m 2f, Curr, Yld, Sep 11)
Shanghai Glory (IRE) 105 1 (6f, Curr, Yld, Oct 9)
Sharja Queen 112 1 (1m 2f, Newm, GF, Oct 1)
She Is No Lady 105 2 (2m 78y, Sand, Sft, Jul 2)
Sheikhzayedroad 117 1 (2m, Asco, Gd, Oct 15)
Shogun (IRE) 109 4 (1m 4f, Leop, Gd, Aug 4)
Shrewd 106 2 (1m 6f, York, Gd, Aug 20)
Signs Of Blessing (IRE) 117 3 (6f, Asco, GS, Jun 18)
Silver Rainbow (IRE) 106 1 (6f, Newj, GF, Jul 16)
Simple Verse (IRE) 115 2 (1m 4f, Newm, GS, Apr 30)
Sir Isaac Newton 117 4 (1m 2f 88y, York, GF, Aug 17)
Sir Maximilian (IRE) 114 1 (5f 16y, Ches, Gd, May 4)
Siyoushake (IRE) 110 4 (1m, Newm, GF, Oct 1)
Sky Hunter 116 1 (1m 1f 192y, Good, GS, Sep 21)
Sloane Avenue (USA) 110 2 (1m, Kemw, SD, Feb 24)
So Beloved 117 1 (7f, Hayd, Gd, May 7)
So Mi Dar 118 1 (1m 2f 23y, Yarm, GF, Sep 14)
Soie D'leau 105 1 (5f, Donc, Gd, Oct 22)
Solar Deity (IRE) 111 3 (1m 2f, Chmf, SD, Jan 3)
Solar Flair 106 2 (6f, Newj, GF, Aug 5)
Soldier In Action (FR) 108 1 (1m 4f, Good, Gd, Oct 9)
Sole Power 111 8 (6f, Newj, GF, Jul 9)
Somehow (IRE) 114 1 (1m 1f, Curr, Gd, Aug 28)
Sound Advice 108 1 (7f 122y, Ches, Gd, May 28)
Sovereign Debt (IRE) 115 2 (7f, Curr, Gd, Jul 17)
Spangled 111 1 (7f, Donc, Gd, Sep 9)
Spark Plug (IRE) 115 1 (1m 1f, Newm, GF, Sep 24)
Speedy Boarding 115 2 (1m 4f, Asco, Gd, Oct 15)
Spirit Quartz (IRE) 112 4 (5f, Newm, GS, Apr 30)
Spirit Raiser (IRE) 105 1 (1m 75y, Nott, GF, Jun 1)
Spring Loaded (IRE) 110 1 (5f 216y, Wolw, SD, Dec 26)
Squats (IRE) 109 3 (7f, Asco, Sft, Oct 1)
Sruthan (IRE) 114 1 (1m, Curr, Sft, Mar 20)
St Michel 113 3 (2m 2f, Donc, Gd, Sep 9)
Star Storm (IRE) 111 2 (1m 4f, Kemw, SS, Nov 2)
Stars Over The Sea (USA) 109 2 (1m 3f 200y, Hayd, Gd, Sep 1)
Steel Of Madrid (IRE) 110 7 (1m 4f, Newm, GF, Oct 7)
Steip Amach (IRE) 109 1 (1m, Leop, Gd, May 8)

Stellar Mass (IRE) 114 1 (1m 4f, Leop, Gd, Aug 4)
Steve Rogers (IRE) 105 2 (2m, Kemw, SD, Nov 16)
Stormy Antarctic 116 1 (1m, Newm, GS, Apr 14)
Strath Burn 109 3 (6f, Donc, Gd, Jul 30)
Success Days (IRE) 116 1 (1m 2f, Curr, Yld, Aug 21)
Suedois (FR) 118 2 (6f, Newj, GF, Jul 9)
Suegioo (FR) 110 4 (2m, Asco, GS, Apr 27)
Sumbal (IRE) 105 4 (1m 4f 5y, Newb, GS, Oct 22)
Suzi's Connoisseur 105 2 (7f, Good, GF, Aug 27)
Sweeping Up 106 2 (1m 3f 200y, Hayd, Gd, May 28)
Sword Fighter (IRE) 114 5 (2m, Good, GF, Jul 28)
Tabarrak (IRE) 108 1 (7f, Asco, GF, May 6)
Take Cover 117 1 (5f, Good, GF, Jul 29)
Tanaza (IRE) 110 1 (7f 100y, Tipp, Sft, Aug 25)
Taneen (USA) 106 6 (6f, Newj, GF, Jul 7)
Tashaar (IRE) 109 3 (1m 3f 5y, Newb, GS, Sep 17)
Tasleet 107 1 (7f, Chmf, SD, Apr 16)
Tawdeea 109 1 (1m 3f 183y, Leic, Gd, Oct 24)
Team Talk 111 1 (1m 2f, Linw, SD, Nov 12)
Tempus Temporis (USA) 105 4 (1m 1f 103y, Wolw, SD, Feb 29)
Tennessee Wildcat (IRE) 107 2 (1m 2f, Leop, Gd, Jul 7)
Tepin (USA) 120 1 (1m, Asco, Sft, Jun 14)
Teruntum Star (FR) 105 1 (6f, Newm, GS, Apr 12)
The Grey Gatsby (IRE) 119 5 (1m 2f, Asco, Gd, Oct 15)
The Gurkha (IRE) 124 1 (1m, Good, GF, Jul 27)
The Happy Prince (IRE) 114 2 (7f, Donc, Gd, Sep 10)
The Major General (IRE) 110 2 (1m 4f, Good, GF, Jul 27)
The Tin Man 121 1 (6f, Asco, Gd, Oct 15)
Thesme 109 5 (5f, York, Gd, Aug 19)
Thikriyaat (IRE) 109 1 (1m, Good, GF, Jul 29)
Third Time Lucky (IRE) 106 5 (1m, Asco, Gd, Oct 15)
Time Test 124 1 (1m 2f 7y, Sand, GF, May 26)
To Be Wild (IRE) 106 1 (1m 4f, Donc, Gd, Oct 22)
Togoville (IRE) 105 2 (6f, Dunw, SD, Feb 19)
Tony Curtis 106 4 (1m, Sali, GF, Aug 11)
Toormore (IRE) 120 1 (1m 14y, Sand, GS, Apr 22)
Top Notch Tonto (IRE) 108 2 (1m 123y, Galw, Sft, Jul 26)
Top Tug (IRE) 105 3 (1m 4f, York, Gd, Jul 8)

Toscanini (IRE) 114 1 (6f, Curr, GF, Aug 7)
Travertine (IRE) 106 3 (1m 2f, Curr, Yld, Jun 26)
Treasury Notes (IRE) 106 1 (1m, Ripo, GS, Aug 29)
Tree Of Knowledge (IRE) 110 4 (1m 4f, Leop, Gd, Sep 10)
Tribal Beat (IRE) 114 1 (1m, Leop, GF, Aug 11)
Trip To Paris (IRE) 108 4 (2m 88y, York, GF, Aug 19)
Tryster (IRE) 112 5 (1m 2f, Asco, Sft, Jun 15)
Tullius (IRE) 113 (1m, Asco, Gd, Oct 15)
Tupi (IRE) 113 2 (6f, Newm, GS, Apr 14)
Turret Rocks (IRE) 106 5 (1m 4f, York, GF, Aug 18)
Twilight Payment (IRE) 109 2 (1m 6f, Curr, Gd, Aug 20)
Twilight Son 118 1 (6f, Asco, GS, Jun 18)
Ulysses (IRE) 113 2 (1m 2f 7y, Wind, GF, Aug 27)
Undrafted (USA) 110 6 (6f, Asco, GS, Jun 18)
Us Army Ranger (IRE) 122 2 (1m 4f 10y, Epso, GS, Jun 4)
Usherette (IRE) 119 1 (1m, Asco, Sft, Jun 15)
Ventura Storm (IRE) 115 2 (1m 6f 132y, Donc, Gd, Sep 10)
Very Special (IRE) 113 2 (1m, Newj, GF, Jul 8)
Waady (IRE) 113 3 (5f, Newm, GS, Apr 30)
Wall Of Fire (IRE) 110 1 (1m 6f 132y, Donc, Gd, Sep 9)
Washington Dc (IRE) 115 2 (5f, Good, GF, Jul 29)
Watchable 112 2 (6f, Wind, Gd, May 23)
Waterloo Bridge (IRE) 105 7 (6f, Asco, GS, Jun 17)
Watersmeet 107 1 (1m 5f 194y, Wolw, SD, Dec 3)
Western Hymn 118 2 (1m 2f 7y, Sand, GF, May 26)
What About Carlo (FR) 105 3 (1m 2f 18y, Epso, Sft, Apr 20)
White Lake 105 6 (1m 14y, Sand, Sft, Jul 2)
Wicklow Brave 115 1 (1m 6f, Curr, Yld, Sep 11)
Willytheconqueror (IRE) 107 2 (5f, Beve, Gd, Aug 27)
Windfast (IRE) 111 1 (6f, Newj, GF, Aug 27)
Wings Of Desire 119 2 (1m 4f, Asco, GF, Jul 23)
Winning Story 109 1 (2m 56y, Ncsw, SD, Dec 21)
Yorker (SAF) 116 2 (1m 208y, York, Gd, Aug 20)
You're Fired (IRE) 111 2 (7f, Hayd, Gd, May 7)
Yuften 110 1 (1m, Asco, Gd, Oct 15)
Zhui Feng (IRE) 106 6 (1m 2f 6y, Newb, GS, Sep 17)
Zhukova (IRE) 117 1 (1m 2f, Naas, Sft, May 11)
Zonderland 114 2 (1m, Good, GF, Aug 27)

TOPSPEED: LAST SEASON'S LEADING TWO-YEAR-OLDS

KEY: Horse name, best Topspeed figure, finishing position when earning figure, (details of race where figure was earned)

Afandem (IRE) 98 2 (5f, York, Gd, Aug 20)
Ajman King (IRE) 84 2 (1m 75y, Nott, GS, Oct 12)
Al Johrah 87 2 (5f, Asco, Sft, Jun 15)
Alicante Dawn 86 1 (6f, Ripo, GS, Aug 29)
Amabilis 87 2 (7f, Newj, GF, Jul 9)
Andok (IRE) 83 2 (7f, Donc, Gd, Oct 22)
Aneen (IRE) 85 1 (7f, Curr, Yld, Oct 10)
Apex King (IRE) 88 1 (7f, Asco, GF, Jul 23)
Ardad (IRE) 100 1 (5f, Asco, Sft, Jun 14)
Atty Persse (IRE) 85 1 (1m 14y, Sand, Gd, Sep 14)
Baashiq (IRE) 82 1 (1m, Redc, GS, Oct 14)
Bahamas (IRE) 83 5 (7f, Asco, Gd, Jul 23)
Barney Roy 82 1 (1m, Hayd, Gd, Sep 24)
Barrington (IRE) 85 1 (5f 10y, Wind, Gd, May 23)
Battaash (IRE) 97 3 (5f, Newm, GF, Oct 7)
Bear Valley (IRE) 83 1 (7f, Good, GF, Jul 28)
Best Of Days 96 2 (7f, York, GF, Aug 17)
Best Solution (IRE) 93 1 (1m, Newm, Gd, Oct 8)
Big Time Baby (IRE) 96 1 (5f, York, Gd, Aug 20)
Bletchley 88 2 (6f, Asco, GS, Jun 17)
Blue Point (IRE) 108 1 (6f, York, Gd, Aug 20)
Blushing Rose 83 1 (7f, Kemw, SS, Aug 22)
Bohemian Flame (IRE) 85 3 (5f 6y, Sand, GF, May 26)
Boynton (USA) 95 1 (7f, Newj, GF, Jul 9)
Brave Anna (USA) 97 1 (6f, Newm, GF, Sep 24)
Brian The Snail (IRE) 92 1 (5f, Catt, Sft, Oct 25)
Brutal (IRE) 91 5 (1m, Donc, Gd, Oct 22)

Callender (IRE) 84 7 (5f, Dunw, SD, Oct 21)
Caravaggio (USA) 109 1 (6f, Asco, Sft, Jun 14)
Century Dream (IRE) 86 1 (1m 75y, Nott, GS, Oct 12)
Churchill (IRE) 104 1 (7f, Curr, Yld, Sep 11)
Clem Fandango (FR) 96 2 (5f, Newm, GF, Oct 7)
Cliffs Of Moher (IRE) 104 1 (7f, Leop, Yld, Oct 29)
Comedy School (USA) 87 1 (6f, York, Gd, Oct 7)
Coronet 92 1 (1m 2f, Newm, Gd, Oct 8)
Count Calabash (IRE) 87 1 (1m 1f, Newm, GF, Oct 29)
Courage Under Fire (USA) 85 5 (7f, York, GF, Aug 17)
Cracksman 91 1 (1m, Newm, GS, Oct 19)
Create A Dream (USA) 84 4 (6f, Asco, GS, Jun 17)
Cuff (IRE) 84 1 (6f, Naas, Sft, May 11)
Cunco (IRE) 96 2 (1m 2f, Newm, Gd, Oct 8)
Dabyah (IRE) 89 1 (7f, Newj, Gd, Jul 9)
Dainty Dandy (IRE) 87 3 (6f, Asco, GF, Jul 23)
De Boss Man (IRE) 85 1 (6f, Curr, Gd, Aug 20)
Delectation 85 1 (6f, Ayr, GS, Sep 17)
Doctor Geoff (IRE) 88 1 (1m, Naas, Yld, Sep 21)
Dream Of Dreams (IRE) 87 2 (6f, Good, GF, Oct 8)
Eartha Kitt 84 1 (6f, Hayd, Gd, Oct 14)
Equinox 86 2 (5f, York, GF, Jul 23)
Escobar (IRE) 83 1 (7f, Newb, GF, Aug 13)
Eziyra (IRE) 92 2 (1m, Curr, Gd, Aug 28)
Fair Eva 106 1 (6f, Asco, GF, Jul 23)
Final Reckoning (IRE) 86 1 (6f, Good, GF, Jul 29)
Finn Mccool (IRE) 82 7 (1m, Donc, Gd, Oct 22)
Firefright (IRE) 82 3 (7f, Newj, GF, Aug 12)
Fly At Dawn (USA) 91 1 (1m, Newm, GF, Sep 22)

Frankuus (IRE) 87 1 (1m, Hayd, Sft, Sep 3)
Full Intention 84 4 (5f, Asco, Sft, Jun 14)
Gheedaa (USA) 84 2 (6f, Donc, GF, Nov 5)
Giovanni Battista (IRE) 83 1 (7f, Newm, Gd, Oct 28)
Glitter Girl 83 2 (7f, Newm, GF, Oct 7)
Global Applause 98 1 (5f 6y, Sand, GF, May 26)
Grey Britain 84 5 (6f, York, Gd, Aug 20)
Grizzel (IRE) 83 8 (5f, Donc, Gd, Sep 9)
Harbour Master 86 1 (7f 16y, Sand, GS, Aug 20)
Harry Angel (IRE) 104 1 (6f 8y, Newb, GS, Sep 17)
Hurricane Rush (IRE) 82 3 (1m 3y, Yarm, GF, Sep 13)
Hydrangea (IRE) 97 2 (7f, Curr, Yld, Sep 11)
Ice Canyon 83 2 (6f, Curr, Gd, Aug 20)
Intelligence Cross (USA) 99 2 (6f, Newj, GF, Jul 7)
Intrepidly (USA) 82 1 (7f, Kemw, SS, Oct 5)
Intricately (IRE) 98 1 (7f, Curr, Yld, Sep 11)
Isomer (USA) 89 2 (7f, Asco, GS, Jun 18)
Istan 82 1 (6f, Curr, Gd, Jul 17)
Kananee (USA) 88 1 (7f, Kemw, SS, Nov 2)
Kazimiera 82 2 (1m, Newm, GF, Oct 29)
Khafoo Shememi (IRE) 85 1 (6f, Newj, GF, Aug 27)
Kilmah 90 2 (6f, Asco, GF, Jul 23)
Kings Gift (IRE) 86 1 (7f, Redc, Gd, Sep 6)
Kyllang Rock (IRE) 85 2 (5f, Hayd, Gd, Sep 23)
Lady Aurelia (USA) 115 1 (5f, Asco, Sft, Jun 15)
Lancaster Bomber (USA) 96 2 (7f, Newm, Gd, Oct 8)
Landfall (FR) 87 1 (1m, Leop, Gd, Sep 10)
Larchmont Lad (IRE) 89 1 (7f, Newm, GF, Sep 22)
Law And Order (IRE) 83 1 (7f, Newj, GF, Aug 26)
Legendary Lunch (IRE) 96 2 (5f, Donc, Gd, Sep 9)
Leontes 85 1 (6f 18y, Ches, Gd, Jul 31)
Lockheed 94 3 (7f, York, GF, Aug 17)
Looting 82 1 (6f, Ffos, Gd, Aug 26)
Magical Fire (IRE) 87 2 (6f, Newj, GF, Jul 8)
Mailshot (USA) 84 5 (6f, Good, GF, Jul 29)
Majeste 85 1 (6f 8y, Newb, GF, Jul 16)
Majoris (IRE) 90 1 (7f, Newj, GF, Aug 6)
Make Time (IRE) 95 1 (6f 212y, Sali, Sft, Sep 28)
Making Light (IRE) 91 1 (7f, Leop, Yld, Oct 23)
Maldonado (FR) 83 2 (7f, Newj, GF, Aug 12)
Mandarin (GER) 82 1 (1m 5y, Ncsw, SD, Sep 30)
Masham Star (IRE) 90 1 (7f, Donc, Gd, Oct 22)
Max Zorin (IRE) 82 1 (7f 122y, Ches, Gd, Sep 9)
Mazyoun 84 2 (6f, Newj, GF, Aug 27)
Medici Banchiere 85 1 (5f, Carl, GF, May 23)
Medicine Jack 83 1 (6f, Curr, Yld, Jun 25)
Medieval (IRE) 89 4 (6f, Asco, Sft, Jun 14)
Mehmas (IRE) 103 1 (6f, Good, GF, Jul 28)
Middle Kingdom (USA) 86 1 (1m 5y, Ncsw, SD, Nov 25)
Mister Trader 86 2 (5f, Curr, Sft, May 21)
Mokarris (USA) 96 2 (6f, York, Gd, Aug 20)
Montataire (IRE) 92 1 (1m, Sali, Gd, Aug 19)
Monticello (IRE) 87 2 (7f, Asco, GF, Jul 23)
Mr Black 84 1 (5f, Kemw, SS, Sep 19)
Mr Scaramanga 84 4 (7f, Asco, GS, Jun 18)
Mrs Danvers 102 1 (5f, Newm, GF, Oct 7)
Mubtasim (IRE) 83 1 (6f, Hayd, GF, Aug 4)
Mutahaady (IRE) 84 2 (7f, Kemw, SS, Nov 2)
Mutawatheb (IRE) 88 1 (1m, Donc, Gd, Oct 21)
Mystic Dawn (IRE) 85 3 (6f, Newm, Gd, Oct 28)
Naseem (IRE) 89 1 (1m, Chmf, SD, Dec 22)
Nations Alexander (IRE) 86 3 (6f, Newj, GF, Jul 8)
Nautical Haven 85 1 (6f, York, GF, Jul 23)
Nayyar 84 1 (5f 34y, Newb, GF, Aug 23)
Nobly Born 82 2 (6f 8y, Newb, GF, Jul 15)
Novoman (IRE) 85 3 (7f, Donc, Gd, Oct 22)
Now Children (IRE) 87 1 (1m, Ayr, GS, Sep 17)
Nuclear Power 92 5 (5f, Newm, GF, Oct 7)
Orderofthegarter (IRE) 87 2 (7f, Leop, Yld, Oct 29)
Orewa (IRE) 83 1 (5f, Beve, GS, Aug 28)
Outre Mer (IRE) 82 1 (1m 2f 50y, Nott, Gd, Sep 28)
Packing Stones (IRE) 95 3 (6f, Newj, GF, Jul 7)

Parnassian (IRE) 86 2 (6f, Souw, SD, Nov 10)
Pedestal (IRE) 86 3 (5f, Asco, Sft, Jun 14)
Perfect Angel (IRE) 91 2 (6f 8y, Newb, GS, Sep 17)
Permian (IRE) 95 3 (1m 2f, Newm, Gd, Oct 8)
Phijee 85 1 (6f, Ripo, Gd, Aug 13)
Pipes Of Peace (IRE) 83 5 (7f, Leop, Yld, Oct 23)
Pleaseletmewin (IRE) 87 1 (7f, Newj, GF, Jul 9)
Poet's Society 85 1 (6f, Chmf, SD, Sep 22)
Poet's Vanity 86 1 (7f, Newm, GF, Oct 7)
Prince Of Lir (IRE) 85 7 (5f, Donc, Gd, Sep 9)
Promise To Be True (IRE) 85 5 (7f, Curr, Yld, Sep 11)
Promising (IRE) 86 2 (6f, Good, Gd, Jul 27)
Psychedelic Funk 90 3 (6f, Asco, Sft, Jun 14)
Queen Anne's Lace (USA) 90 1 (1m, Gowr, Sft, Sep 18)
Queen Kindly 106 1 (6f, York, GF, Aug 18)
Raheen House (IRE) 95 4 (1m, Donc, Gd, Oct 22)
Rainbow Mist (IRE) 90 5 (5f, Donc, Gd, Sep 9)
Rajar 84 1 (6f, Newj, Gd, Jul 30)
Really Special 90 1 (1m, Newm, GF, Oct 29)
Rehana (IRE) 89 4 (7f, Curr, Yld, Sep 11)
Rhododendron (IRE) 97 1 (1m, Newm, GF, Oct 7)
Rich Legacy (IRE) 83 1 (7f, Newj, GF, Aug 12)
Rivet (IRE) 102 1 (1m, Donc, Gd, Oct 22)
Roly Poly (USA) 106 2 (6f, York, GF, Aug 18)
Ronald R (IRE) 83 1 (7f 3y, Yarm, GF, Jul 13)
Rosabelle 87 1 (5f 110y, Ches, GS, Sep 24)
Rusumaat (IRE) 90 2 (6f, Good, GF, Jul 29)
Salouen (IRE) 96 3 (1m, Donc, Gd, Oct 22)
Saltonstall 86 1 (7f, Lime, Sft, Oct 8)
Sea Of Grace (IRE) 93 1 (1m, Curr, Gd, Aug 28)
Seven Heavens 83 7 (7f, Newm, Gd, Oct 8)
Silver Line (IRE) 94 4 (6f, Newj, GF, Jul 7)
Sir Dancealot (IRE) 90 1 (6f, York, Gd, Oct 8)
Sobetsu 96 1 (1m, Newm, Gd, Sep 17)
Son Of Rest 85 4 (7f, Curr, Yld, Sep 11)
South Seas (IRE) 86 6 (7f, Newm, Gd, Oct 8)
Spain Burg (FR) 83 1 (6f, Ripo, Gd, Aug 13)
Spanish Tenor (IRE) 88 4 (7f, Leop, Yld, Oct 23)
Spirit Of Valor (USA) 91 2 (7f, Leop, Yld, Oct 23)
Spiritual Lady 95 1 (6f, Newm, Gd, Oct 28)
Sportsmanship (USA) 92 4 (5f, Good, Gd, Jul 27)
Spy Ring (IRE) 89 2 (6f, Newm, Gd, Oct 28)
Star Archer 88 1 (1m, Hayd, Gd, Sep 1)
Star Of Rory (IRE) 85 2 (1m, Hayd, Sft, Sep 3)
Stormy Clouds (IRE) 90 1 (6f, York, GF, Aug 18)
Super Julius 84 1 (5f 16y, Ches, Gd, Jun 11)
Sutter County 87 2 (6f, Ncsw, SD, Nov 17)
Syphax (USA) 97 1 (7f, York, GF, Aug 17)
Taamol (IRE) 84 1 (7f, Newj, Sft, Jun 25)
Tahoo (IRE) 84 1 (5f, York, GF, Jul 23)
Taj Mahal (IRE) 90 3 (7f, Leop, Yld, Oct 23)
Talaayeb 86 1 (7f, Newm, GF, Sep 24)
The Last Lion (IRE) 97 2 (5f, Good, Gd, Jul 27)
Thunder Snow (IRE) 93 4 (7f, Newm, Gd, Oct 8)
Tibr (USA) 85 1 (5f, Ling, Gd, May 7)
Tis Marvellous 83 9 (5f, Donc, Gd, Sep 9)
Tomily (IRE) 86 3 (6f, York, Gd, Oct 7)
Tommy Taylor (USA) 87 4 (7f, York, GF, Aug 17)
Top Score 86 3 (6f, Good, GF, Jul 29)
Town Charter (USA) 86 1 (6f, Ayr, GS, Jul 4)
Van Der Decken 88 5 (6f, Asco, Sft, Jun 14)
Via Egnatia (USA) 95 1 (1m, Newm, GF, Oct 1)
War Decree (USA) 91 7 (7f, Good, Gd, Jul 26)
Wayside Flower 83 2 (6f, Naas, Sft, May 11)
Whitecliffsofdover (USA) 87 2 (7f, Newm, GF, Sep 22)
Wild Tempest 87 2 (1m, Newm, Gd, Oct 19)
Wings Of Eagles (FR) 87 4 (1m 2f, Newm, Gd, Oct 8)
Wolf Country 88 1 (1m 3y, Yarm, GS, Oct 10)
Yalta (IRE) 109 1 (5f, Good, Gd, Jul 26)
Yucatan (IRE) 97 2 (1m, Donc, Gd, Oct 22)
Yulong Baobei (IRE) 86 1 (5f, Tipp, Yld, Jul 9)
Zainhom (USA) 87 2 (1m, Newm, Gd, Oct 8)

TOPSPEED: LAST SEASON'S TOP PERFORMERS 3YO+

Abdon 96 1 (1m 2f 95y, Hayd, GF, Aug 6)
Abe Lincoln (USA) 96 2 (1m, Asco, Sft, Jun 16)
Above N Beyond 98 3 (1m, Hayd, GS, May 21)
Above The Rest (IRE) 92 1 (7f 2y, Ches, GS, Sep 24)
Absolutely So (IRE) 104 4 (6f, Asco, GS, Jun 18)
Accession (IRE) 90 2 (7f, Newj, GF, Aug 6)
Aclaim (IRE) 97 1 (7f, Newm, GF, Oct 7)
Across The Stars (IRE) 87 3 (1m 4f, York, GF, Aug 17)
Adaay (IRE) 97 4 (7f, Curr, Gd, Jul 17)
Aeolus 95 5 (5f, Hayd, GS, May 21)
Air Force Blue (USA) 89 (6f, Newj, GF, Jul 9)
Air Vice Marshal (USA) 96 4 (1m, Newm, GS, Apr 30)
Al Jazi (IRE) 99 1 (7f, Good, GF, Jul 29)
Al Mohalhal (IRE) 89 2 (7f 20y, Leop, Sft, Jun 16)
Alben Star (IRE) 91 1 (6f 1y, Linw, SD, Mar 25)
Aleef (IRE) 92 3 (5f, Catt, Sft, Oct 15)
Alfred Hutchinson 96 2 (1m 1y, Linw, SD, Nov 12)
Algometer 93 2 (1m 2f 7y, Sand, GS, Apr 22)
Alice Springs (IRE) 106 1 (1m, Leop, Yld, Sep 10)
Almanzor (FR) 100 1 (1m 2f, Leop, Yld, Sep 10)
Almela (IRE) 88 2 (1m 4f, Leop, Gd, Aug 4)
Almodovar (IRE) 92 3 (1m 4f, Asco, GS, Jun 18)
Alpha Delphini 106 2 (5f 34y, Newb, GS, Sep 17)
Alveena (IRE) 88 2 (1m 4f, Curr, Yld, May 21)
Always Smile (IRE) 101 3 (1m, Newj, GF, Jul 8)
Alyssa 90 1 (1m 6f 21y, Sali, GF, Aug 11)
Amazing Maria (IRE) 90 7 (1m, Newj, GF, Jul 8)
An Saighdiur (IRE) 90 1 (7f, Curr, Gd, Aug 20)
Anamba 89 1 (7f, Naas, Gd, May 29)
Arab Spring (IRE) 90 3 (1m 2f 95y, Hayd, GF, Aug 6)
Arcanada (IRE) 94 1 (7f 2y, Ches, Gd, Jun 25)
Architecture (IRE) 107 2 (1m 4f 10y, Epso, GS, Jun 3)
Ardhoomey (IRE) 103 1 (5f, Curr, Yld, Sep 11)
Arnold Lane (IRE) 87 1 (7f, Good, GF, Jun 5)
Arod (IRE) 101 3 (1m, Good, Gd, Aug 27)
Arthenus 91 4 (1m 2f, Asco, GS, Jun 18)
Ashadihan 96 6 (1m, Asco, GS, Jun 17)
Ashpan Sam 90 2 (6f, Epso, Gd, Aug 30)
Awake My Soul (IRE) 98 4 (1m 2f 88y, York, Gd, May 11)
Awtaad (IRE) 101 4 (1m, Asco, Gd, Oct 15)
B Fifty Two (IRE) 96 4 (6f 8y, Newb, GS, May 13)
Baadi 87 1 (1m 3f 135y, Wind, Gd, May 23)
Baccarat (IRE) 101 3 (6f, Ripo, Gd, Aug 13)
Ballybacka Queen (IRE) 87 8 (1m 4f, Curr, Yld, May 21)
Ballydoyle (IRE) 94 2 (1m, Newm, Gd, May 1)
Baraweez (IRE) 91 5 (7f, Galw, Yld, Jul 31)
Barleysugar (IRE) 89 2 (1m, Chmf, SD, Jun 1)
Barracuda Boy (IRE) 89 4 (6f, Hayd, Gd, May 7)
Barsanti (IRE) 88 1 (1m 4f, York, GF, Aug 19)
Barwick 89 1 (1m 4f 10y, Epso, Sft, Apr 20)
Basil Berry 91 4 (7f 3y, Yarm, GF, Aug 2)
Battersea 92 4 (1m 6f, York, Gd, Aug 20)
Baydar 94 1 (1m 2f 6y, Newb, GS, Sep 17)
Beauty Way 93 2 (1m 2f, Asco, GF, Jul 9)
Belardo (IRE) 94 4 (1m 14y, Sand, GS, Apr 22)
Belgian Bill 95 4 (1m, Good, GF, Jul 29)
Benkei (IRE) 90 6 (1m 6f, Leop, Gd, Sep 10)
Berkshire (IRE) 104 1 (1m 3f 135y, Wind, GF, Aug 27)
Bermondsey 88 1 (1m 2f 7y, Sand, Gd, Jun 10)
Besharah (IRE) 96 2 (6f, York, Gd, Jul 8)
Best In The World (IRE) 89 1 (1m 4f, Cork, Yld, Aug 2)
Best Of Times 90 5 (1m 1f 192y, Good, GF, Jul 26)
Bint Dandy (IRE) 93 4 (1m, Chmf, SD, Jun 1)
Birdman (IRE) 96 6 (1m 2f, Redc, GF, May 30)
Blaine 93 1 (6f, Epso, GS, Jun 4)
Blair House (IRE) 87 2 (1m 114y, Epso, Gd, Sep 25)
Blithe Spirit 89 6 (5f 110y, Ches, Gd, Aug 20)
Blond Me (IRE) 91 1 (1m, Good, Gd, Apr 30)
Bobby Wheeler (IRE) 91 2 (7f, Good, GF, Jul 30)
Bobby's Kitten (USA) 87 1 (6f, Cork, Hvy, Mar 28)
Bocca Baciata (IRE) 94 1 (1m 1f, Curr, Gd, Jul 17)
Bondi Beach (IRE) 89 3 (1m 4f, Leop, Gd, Sep 10)

Boom The Groom (IRE) 105 1 (5f 89y, York, GF, Aug 17)
Boomerang Bob (IRE) 90 1 (6f, Chmf, SD, Oct 26)
Booming Delight (IRE) 87 1 (7f, Hayd, Gd, May 28)
Boomshackerlacker (IRE) 92 5 (1m, Good, GF, Jul 29)
Bosham 88 1 (5f, Chmf, SD, Feb 4)
Botany Bay (IRE) 89 1 (1m 5f, Leop, Gd, Jul 7)
Both Sides 87 3 (1m 2f 7y, Sand, Gd, Sep 14)
Bowson Fred 101 3 (5f, Hayd, Sft, Sep 3)
Brando 111 3 (6f, Asco, Gd, Oct 15)
Bravo Zolo (IRE) 87 3 (1m 1y, Linw, SD, Feb 13)
Breakable 89 1 (1m, Ripo, Gd, Aug 13)
Breton Rock (IRE) 95 3 (1m 14y, Sand, GS, Apr 22)
Brother Tiger 90 1 (5f, Chmf, SD, Feb 7)
Buckstay (IRE) 100 5 (6f, Asco, GS, Jun 18)
Buratino (IRE) 97 4 (6f, Hayd, Gd, May 28)
Burmese 95 5 (2m 4f, Asco, Sft, Jun 16)
Burnt Sugar (IRE) 96 6 (6f, Asco, GS, Jun 18)
C Note (IRE) 92 1 (7f, Leic, GF, Oct 11)
California (IRE) 93 3 (1m 6f 132y, Donc, Gd, Sep 8)
California Whip (USA) 95 2 (1m, Hayd, GS, May 21)
Calvinist 87 1 (1m 6f, York, Gd, Oct 7)
Candelisa (IRE) 87 2 (6f, Pont, Hvy, Apr 5)
Cannock Chase (USA) 96 1 (1m 2f 75y, Ches, Gd, May 5)
Cape Cova (IRE) 91 4 (1m 6f 132y, Donc, Gd, Oct 21)
Capo Rosso (IRE) 96 2 (1m 1y, Linw, SD, May 7)
Captain Colby (USA) 100 1 (5f 140y, Donc, Gd, Sep 10)
Captain Joy (IRE) 93 1 (1m 1y, Linw, SD, Mar 25)
Carnachy (IRE) 89 1 (1m 2f 60y, Donc, GF, Nov 5)
Carnival King (IRE) 88 1 (7f 3y, Yarm, GF, Aug 28)
Carry On Deryck 102 2 (1m 1f, Newm, GF, Sep 24)
Cartago 87 2 (1m 2f 6y, Newb, Gd, May 14)
Caspian Prince (IRE) 106 1 (5f, Dunw, SD, Oct 21)
Celestial Path (IRE) 104 2 (1m, York, Gd, Jul 9)
Central Square (IRE) 90 2 (1m 2f, Redc, GF, May 30)
Certificate 102 1 (7f, Donc, GF, Aug 13)
Chain Of Daisies 101 1 (1m 2f 7y, Wind, GF, Aug 27)
Charles Molson 89 5 (6f, Good, GF, Jul 30)
Chelsea Lad (IRE) 88 1 (1m, Newm, GF, May 21)
Chestnut Fire 92 3 (7f, Dunw, SD, Dec 23)
Chiclet (IRE) 91 5 (5f, Dunw, SD, Oct 21)
Classic Seniority 88 1 (6f, Ayr, GS, Sep 16)
Claudio Monteverdi (IRE) 88 1 (1m, Leop, Hvy, Apr 6)
Clear Spring (IRE) 99 1 (6f 8y, Newb, GS, May 13)
Clever Cookie 92 7 (2m 4f, Asco, Sft, Jun 16)
Cloudberry 90 1 (1m 7y, Newb, GS, Oct 21)
Colour Blue (IRE) 95 1 (7f 20y, Leop, Yld, Sep 10)
Confessional 92 2 (5f, Catt, Sft, Oct 15)
Continuum 89 2 (1m 5f 61y, Newb, GF, Aug 12)
Convey 97 2 (1m, York, GF, May 12)
Cornwallville (IRE) 94 2 (6f, Ayr, Gd, Jun 17)
Cotai Glory 107 1 (5f 34y, Newb, GS, Sep 17)
Cote D'azur 88 2 (1m 1f, Newm, GF, Sep 23)
Cougar Mountain (IRE) 91 5 (7f, Newm, GF, Oct 7)
Coulsty (IRE) 93 2 (7f, Leic, GS, Apr 23)
Countermeasure 87 4 (1m 2f 7y, Sand, Sft, Jul 2)
Cradle Mountain (IRE) 88 2 (2m, Curr, Gd, Oct 9)
Creggs Pipes (IRE) 90 1 (1m 123y, Galw, Sft, Jul 26)
Custom Cut (IRE) 106 3 (1m 114y, Epso, GS, Jun 3)
Cymraeg Bounty 88 1 (6f, Redc, GF, Aug 6)
Cymric (USA) 90 2 (1m, Newj, GF, Jul 7)
Dal Harraild 98 3 (1m 4f, Asco, Gd, Sep 3)
Dance Of Fire 87 2 (1m, Hayd, Hvy, Jul 1)
Dance The Dream 88 1 (1m 3f 183y, Leic, GS, Oct 4)
Dancing Star 101 1 (6f, Good, GF, Jul 30)
Danehill Kodiac (IRE) 90 2 (1m 4f, Asco, Gd, Sep 3)
Danzeno 106 3 (6f, York, Gd, May 11)
Dark Emerald (IRE) 93 3 (7f, Newb, GF, Aug 13)
Darshini 87 2 (1m 2f 6y, Pont, GF, Jun 19)
Dartmouth 100 1 (1m 4f, Asco, Gd, Jun 18)
Deauville (IRE) 106 2 (1m 2f 88y, York, GF, May 12)
Decorated Knight 102 2 (1m 114y, Epso, GS, Jun 3)
Demora 89 1 (5f 11y, Bath, Sft, Apr 15)

Desert Encounter (IRE) 91 3 (1m 3f 200y, Hayd, Sft, Jul 2)
Desert Haze 88 2 (1m, Dunw, SD, Oct 28)
Desert Law (IRE) 92 3 (5f, Curr, Yld, Jun 26)
Devonshire (IRE) 89 5 (1m 1f, Curr, Gd, Jul 17)
Dick Whittington (IRE) 102 1 (7f 20y, Leop, Sft, Jun 16)
Dinkum Diamond (IRE) 90 4 (7f, Asco, GF, May 7)
Distant Past 89 3 (5f, Asco, Sft, Oct 1)
Divine (IRE) 99 2 (6f 8y, Newb, GF, Jul 16)
Doctor Sardonicus 94 2 (6f, Chmf, SD, Oct 26)
Dommersen (IRE) 89 2 (1m 1f, Sand, GF, Jun 11)
Don't Touch 108 5 (6f, Asco, Gd, Oct 15)
Donjuan Triumphant (IRE) 99 2 (6f, Hayd, Gd, May 28)
Donncha (IRE) 96 3 (1m, Good, GF, Jul 29)
Dont Bother Me (IRE) 91 1 (7f, Leop, Gd, May 8)
Double Up 101 4 (5f 140y, Donc, Gd, Sep 10)
Dougan 91 3 (6f 8y, Newb, GS, May 13)
Downforce (IRE) 91 5 (5f, Curr, Hvy, Sep 25)
Dragon Mall (USA) 87 4 (1m, Good, GF, Jul 29)
Dream Dubai 92 2 (6f, Asco, GS, Apr 27)
Dubai Fashion (IRE) 89 1 (1m 114y, Epso, Gd, Sep 25)
Duke Of Firenze 101 2 (5f 89y, York, GF, Aug 17)
Dutch Connection 100 2 (1m 14y, Sand, GS, Apr 22)
Dutch Destiny 88 1 (6f, Hayd, Sft, Jul 15)
Dutch Law 92 1 (7f, Asco, GF, Sep 3)
Dutch Masterpiece 95 2 (5f, Asco, Sft, Oct 1)
Early Morning (IRE) 90 1 (1m 1y, Linw, SD, Apr 20)
Earring (USA) 91 2 (1m 1f, Curr, Gd, Jul 17)
East Street Revue 90 2 (5f, Hayd, Gd, Sep 24)
Eastern Impact (IRE) 101 6 (6f, Newj, GF, Jul 9)
Easton Angel (IRE) 106 2 (5f, York, Gd, Jul 9)
Easy Road 93 1 (5f, Asco, Sft, Oct 1)
Eddystone Rock (IRE) 87 2 (1m 2f, Curr, Yld, Jun 26)
Educate 97 5 (1m 2f, Asco, GS, Jun 18)
Elidor 100 1 (1m 6f, Good, GF, Jul 26)
Elite Army 90 2 (1m 4f, Asco, GS, Jun 17)
Encore D'or 98 1 (5f, Chmf, SD, Nov 21)
Epsom Icon 89 1 (1m 114y, Epso, GS, Jun 4)
Erik The Red (FR) 96 3 (1m 2f 88y, York, Gd, May 11)
Estidhkaar (IRE) 91 1 (1m, Newm, GF, Oct 29)
Eternally 91 1 (7f, Asco, GS, Oct 1)
Exospheric 100 5 (1m 2f 88y, York, GF, Aug 17)
Express Himself (IRE) 98 2 (1m, Ayr, GF, Jun 18)
Fabricate 88 1 (1m 3f 183y, Leic, GS, Oct 4)
Fannaan (USA) 89 2 (7f, Newb, Sft, Sep 16)
Father Bertie 89 2 (1m, Ayr, Sft, Sep 15)
Fendale 88 2 (6f, Ayr, GS, Sep 16)
Final Venture 97 2 (5f, Asco, GF, Jul 22)
Fire Fighting (IRE) 98 1 (1m 1f 192y, Good, GF, Jul 26)
Fireglow 94 2 (1m 2f 88y, York, Gd, May 11)
Firmament 99 2 (7f, Asco, GF, Sep 3)
First Sitting 99 1 (1m 2f, Newj, GF, Aug 6)
Flash Fire (IRE) 99 1 (7f, Asco, GF, May 7)
Flight Risk (IRE) 93 5 (7f, Curr, Gd, Jul 17)
Flowers On Venus (IRE) 88 3 (6f, Asco, GF, Jul 8)
Flying Officer (USA) 93 6 (2m 4f, Asco, Sft, Jun 16)
Flying Pursuit 90 2 (6f, York, GS, Sep 4)
Folkswood 98 2 (1m 2f 23y, Yarm, GF, Aug 28)
Forge 90 2 (1m, Good, GF, Jul 29)
Fort Bastion (IRE) 91 3 (1m, Thir, Sft, Apr 30)
Found (IRE) 98 2 (1m 2f, Leop, Yld, Sep 10)
Foundation (IRE) 103 3 (1m 2f 88y, York, GF, May 12)
Franklin D (USA) 102 1 (1m, Good, GF, Jul 29)
Gabrial (IRE) 91 3 (1m, Asco, GF, Jul 9)
Gabrial's Kaka (IRE) 92 1 (1m, Ayr, GF, Jun 18)
Galileo Gold 109 1 (1m, Newm, GS, Apr 30)
Gamesome (FR) 94 2 (5f, York, Gd, Jul 8)
Gamgoom 96 2 (5f, Chmf, SD, Jan 2)
Garcia 93 1 (1m, Hayd, GS, May 21)
George Cinq 93 2 (7f, Thir, GS, Jul 30)
George Dryden (IRE) 91 5 (6f, Ripo, Gd, Aug 13)
Get Knotted (IRE) 93 3 (7f, Donc, GF, Aug 13)
Gifted Master (IRE) 104 1 (6f, Asco, GS, Apr 27)
Glen Moss (IRE) 98 3 (6f, Asco, GS, Jun 18)
Glory Awaits (IRE) 89 4 (1m, York, GF, May 12)
Goken (FR) 95 (6f, Newj, GF, Jul 9)
Gold Mount 100 1 (1m 4f, Asco, Sft, Jun 16)

Gold Prince (IRE) 91 2 (1m 3f 200y, Hayd, Sft, Jul 2)
Gold Trail (IRE) 104 1 (1m 4f, Donc, Gd, Sep 10)
Gold-fun (IRE) 110 2 (6f, Asco, GS, Jun 18)
Golden Steps (FR) 89 1 (7f, Newj, GF, Jul 9)
Goldream 103 7 (5f, York, Gd, Aug 19)
Gordon Lord Byron (IRE) 104 1 (7f, Curr, Gd, Jul 17)
Gothic Empire (IRE) 90 1 (7f, Asco, Gd, Sep 30)
Gracious John 100 1 (5f 13y, Nott, Gd, Nov 2)
Gratzie 89 1 (1m 5y, Bath, Fm, Jun 11)
Gravity Flow (IRE) 89 1 (6f, Wind, GF, Aug 7)
Great Hall 93 1 (1m 2f 18y, Epso, Gd, Sep 25)
Green Door (IRE) 90 1 (5f, Newj, Sft, Jun 23)
Grendisar (IRE) 93 1 (1m 2f, Linw, SD, Feb 27)
Grey Mirage 92 3 (1m 1y, Linw, SD, Nov 12)
Growl 112 2 (6f, Asco, Gd, Oct 15)
Guishan 89 1 (6f, Newj, Sft, Jun 23)
Haalan 89 3 (1m 2f 23y, Yarm, GF, Aug 28)
Haalick (IRE) 99 2 (7f, Good, Gd, May 21)
Haley Bop (IRE) 91 2 (1m, Ayr, GS, Sep 17)
Harbour Law 109 1 (1m 6f 132y, Donc, Gd, Sep 10)
Harlequeen 96 3 (1m 4f, Curr, Gd, Jul 16)
Harry Hurricane 100 1 (5f, Hayd, Gd, Sep 24)
Harzand (IRE) 115 1 (1m 4f 10y, Epso, GS, Jun 4)
Hasanour (USA) 94 2 (7f, Naas, Gd, May 29)
Havana Beat (IRE) 89 7 (2m 88y, York, GF, Aug 17)
Have A Nice Day 94 2 (7f, Rosc, Gd, Aug 15)
Hawkbill (USA) 93 1 (1m 2f 7y, Sand, Sft, Jul 2)
Hawksmoor (IRE) 93 3 (1m 1f, Curr, Gd, Jul 17)
Hay Chewed (IRE) 94 1 (5f, Leic, GS, Sep 6)
Heartbreak City (FR) 95 1 (1m 6f, York, Gd, Aug 20)
Heaven's Guest (IRE) 92 2 (7f, Newj, GF, Jul 9)
Here Comes When (IRE) 92 3 (7f, Leic, GS, Apr 23)
Higher Power 90 2 (1m 6f 132y, Donc, Gd, Oct 21)
Highland Acclaim (IRE) 90 1 (6f, Epso, Gd, Aug 30)
Highland Reel (IRE) 107 2 (1m 2f 88y, York, GF, Aug 17)
Highly Sprung (IRE) 88 1 (6f 3y, Yarm, GF, Sep 14)
Hit The Jackpot (IRE) 94 6 (1m 2f 88y, York, Gd, May 11)
Holler (AUS) 89 7 (6f, Asco, GS, Jun 18)
Home Cummins (IRE) 94 1 (1m, York, Gd, Jul 9)
Home Of The Brave (IRE) 101 1 (7f, Leic, GS, Apr 23)
Hoof It 90 1 (6f, Good, GF, Jul 30)
Hoofalong 96 1 (5f, Muss, Gd, Jun 11)
Hornsby 90 4 (7f, Good, GF, Jul 30)
Housesofparliament (IRE) 106 3 (1m 6f 132y, Donc, Gd, Sep 10)
Humidor (IRE) 97 2 (5f 140y, Donc, Gd, Sep 10)
Humphrey Bogart (IRE) 93 5 (1m 4f 10y, Epso, GS, Jun 4)
Huntsmans Close 93 5 (5f, Epso, Gd, Aug 29)
Ibn Malik (IRE) 95 1 (7f, Newm, GS, Apr 13)
Ice Slice (IRE) 89 3 (1m, Hayd, Hvy, Jul 1)
Idaho (IRE) 109 3 (1m 4f 10y, Epso, GS, Jun 4)
Iffranesia (FR) 91 3 (5f, Curr, Yld, Sep 11)
Ifwecan 90 3 (7f 3y, Yarm, GF, Aug 28)
Imperial Aviator 90 1 (1m 2f 6y, Newb, Gd, May 14)
In Salutem 94 2 (6f, Curr, Yld, Jun 24)
Innocent Touch (IRE) 90 1 (1m 2f 18y, Epso, Gd, Aug 29)
Instant Attraction (IRE) 94 2 (1m, Thir, Sft, Apr 30)
Intense Tango 94 1 (1m 6f, Leop, Gd, Sep 10)
Intisaab 103 1 (6f, York, Gd, Oct 8)
Irish Rookie (IRE) 96 4 (1m, Newj, GF, Jul 8)
Jack Dexter 94 8 (6f, Asco, Gd, Oct 15)
Jailawi (IRE) 92 1 (1m 1y, Linw, SD, May 7)
Jallota 90 1 (7f, Asco, GF, Aug 28)
Jemayel (IRE) 92 3 (1m 1f 192y, Good, GF, Jul 30)
Jennies Jewel (IRE) 93 5 (2m, Curr, Gd, Oct 9)
Jet Setting (IRE) 110 1 (7f 100y, Tipp, Hvy, Oct 2)
Johnny Barnes (IRE) 90 4 (7f, Leic, GS, Apr 23)
Journey 112 1 (1m 4f, Asco, Gd, Oct 15)
Judicial (IRE) 100 3 (5f, Hayd, Gd, Sep 24)
Jungle Cat (IRE) 93 2 (5f, Newm, GS, Apr 30)
Just Glamorous (IRE) 88 8 (5f, Good, GF, Jul 28)
Justice Good (IRE) 92 1 (6f, Kemw, SS, Nov 23)
Kachy 93 6 (5f, York, Gd, Jul 9)
Kadra (IRE) 91 1 (1m, Dunw, SD, Oct 28)
Kadrizzi (FR) 94 1 (6f, Asco, GF, Aug 6)
Kasbah (IRE) 94 1 (5f, Dunw, SD, Mar 4)
Kassia (IRE) 94 2 (5f, Good, Gd, Jul 28)

Kelinni (IRE) 94 1 (7f, Thir, Sft, Apr 16)
Kentuckyconnection (USA) 92 5 (1m, Newm, GS, Apr 30)
Keystone 89 4 (1m 1y, Linw, SD, Nov 12)
Kickboxer (IRE) 92 5 (6f 8y, Newb, GS, May 13)
Kimberella 98 1 (6f, York, GF, Jul 23)
Kings Fete 88 3 (1m 4f, Asco, GS, Jun 17)
Kingsgate Native (IRE) 88 1 (5f 13y, Nott, GF, Aug 9)
Knights Table 88 1 (1m 4f 10y, Ripo, Gd, Jul 16)
Kool Kompany (IRE) 90 2 (1m, Newm, GF, Oct 29)
La Rioja 91 3 (6f, York, Gd, Jul 8)
Lady Macapa 97 1 (6f, Good, Gd, Oct 9)
Lady Of Camelot (IRE) 88 1 (1m 3f 183y, Leic, GF, May 30)
Lancelot Du Lac (ITY) 99 1 (5f, Chmf, SD, Jan 2)
Lat Hawill (IRE) 96 2 (1m, Hayd, GF, Aug 6)
Lathom 90 5 (5f, Good, GF, Jul 28)
Laugh Aloud 93 1 (1m, Newm, GF, Sep 23)
Lexington Abbey 94 2 (6f, York, Gd, Oct 8)
Librisa Breeze 102 6 (6f, Asco, Gd, Oct 15)
Light And Shade 95 1 (1m, Asco, GF, May 7)
Lightning Spear 108 3 (1m, Asco, Gd, Oct 15)
Lightscameraction (IRE) 97 5 (5f, Hayd, Gd, Sep 24)
Limato (IRE) 118 1 (6f, Newj, GF, Jul 9)
Limitless (IRE) 100 1 (1m, Asco, Sft, Jun 16)
Lincoln (IRE) 95 6 (5f, Hayd, Gd, Sep 24)
Line Of Reason (IRE) 100 1 (5f, Beve, Gd, Jun 14)
Linguistic (IRE) 91 2 (1m 2f 75y, Ches, Gd, May 6)
Log Out Island (IRE) 101 1 (6f 8y, Newb, Gd, May 14)
Lord Of The Land (IRE) 93 1 (6f 1y, Linw, SD, Nov 12)
Lumiere 103 1 (1m, Newj, GF, Jul 7)
Lunar Deity 89 1 (1m 1y, Linw, SD, Feb 13)
Maarek 92 4 (5f, Curr, Yld, Sep 11)
Magical Memory (IRE) 112 1 (6f, York, Gd, May 11)
Magnus Maximus 100 1 (6f, Asco, GF, Sep 3)
Majeed 103 2 (1m 3f 135y, Wind, GF, Aug 27)
Majestic Hero (IRE) 89 2 (5f, Asco, Gd, Sep 3)
Majestic Moon (IRE) 93 2 (7f 1y, Linw, SD, Mar 4)
Maleficent Queen 89 1 (1m 2f, Ayr, GS, May 18)
Maljaa 96 7 (5f, Asco, GF, Jul 9)
Maneen 93 1 (1m 2f, Curr, Sft, May 22)
Markaz (IRE) 99 1 (6f, Ncsw, SD, Jun 25)
Marsha (IRE) 107 1 (5f, York, Gd, Jul 9)
Massaat (IRE) 104 2 (1m, Newm, GS, Apr 30)
Master Speaker (IRE) 89 (5f, Dunw, SD, Oct 21)
Master The World (IRE) 106 2 (1m, Good, GF, Jul 29)
Maverick Wave (USA) 91 2 (1m 2f, Linw, SD, Feb 27)
Maybelater 95 3 (1m 1f 198y, Sali, GF, Aug 10)
Mayfair Lady 103 1 (6f, York, Gd, Jun 10)
Meadway 90 1 (5f, Muss, Gd, Jun 11)
Mecca's Angel (IRE) 121 1 (5f, York, Gd, Aug 19)
Medicean Man 103 3 (5f, Dunw, SD, Oct 21)
Mehronissa 102 2 (6f, Asco, Sft, Oct 1)
Memorial Day (IRE) 98 1 (1m 2f 6y, Pont, GS, Sep 22)
Midterm 96 1 (1m 2f 7y, Sand, GS, Apr 22)
Mille Et Mille 98 4 (2m 4f, Asco, Sft, Jun 16)
Minding (IRE) 111 1 (1m 4f 10y, Epso, GS, Jun 3)
Mindurownbusiness (IRE) 88 3 (1m 1y, Linw, SD, Mar 25)
Miracle Of Medinah 92 2 (6f 110y, Donc, Gd, Sep 9)
Mirsaale 91 3 (1m 5f 14y, Hami, Sft, May 1)
Mirza 104 1 (5f, Leic, GF, Oct 11)
Mise En Rose (USA) 94 2 (7f, Good, GF, Jul 29)
Mister Universe 98 1 (7f 32y, Wolw, SD, Mar 12)
Misterioso (IRE) 89 1 (6f, Asco, GF, Jul 8)
Mizzou (IRE) 104 2 (2m 4f, Asco, Sft, Jun 16)
Molly Dolly (IRE) 91 2 (7f, Curr, Yld, Jun 25)
Mongolian Saturday (USA) 94 (6f, Newj, GF, Jul 9)
Monsieur Joe (IRE) 102 4 (5f, York, Gd, Jul 9)
Mont Kiara (FR) 90 1 (6f, Newj, GF, Jul 23)
Moonlight Magic 88 6 (1m 2f, Leop, Yld, Sep 10)
Moonraker 90 2 (6f, Ncsw, SD, Jun 25)
Morando (FR) 101 1 (1m, Ayr, GS, Sep 17)
More Mischief 89 1 (1m 2f 60y, Donc, Sft, Apr 3)
Move Up 95 1 (1m 2f, Asco, GF, Jul 9)
Moviesta (USA) 105 2 (5f, Dunw, SD, Oct 21)
Mr Lupton (IRE) 106 1 (6f, York, GS, Jun 11)
Muhadathat 95 3 (5f, Good, GF, Jul 28)
Muir Lodge 88 1 (6f, Asco, GF, May 6)

Mujassam 88 3 (6f, Newm, GF, May 21)
Muntadab (IRE) 91 1 (7f, Thir, GS, Jul 30)
Muntahaa (IRE) 88 1 (1m 4f, Kemw, SD, Jun 2)
Muntazah 97 4 (1m 2f 88y, York, GF, May 12)
Mustashry 91 2 (1m, York, GF, Aug 18)
Mutakayyef 105 3 (1m 2f 88y, York, GF, Aug 17)
Mutawathea 92 2 (7f, Asco, GF, May 7)
Muthmir (IRE) 106 3 (5f, York, Gd, Jul 9)
My Dream Boat (IRE) 91 5 (1m 2f, Leop, Yld, Sep 10)
My Name Is Rio (IRE) 89 3 (5f, Muss, Gd, Jul 29)
My Reward 89 9 (2m 88y, York, GF, Aug 17)
My Target (IRE) 89 1 (1m 1y, Linw, SD, Nov 12)
Mythmaker 90 2 (6f 1y, Linw, SD, Nov 12)
Naadirr (IRE) 91 3 (6f, Wind, Gd, May 23)
Nakeeta 95 2 (2m 88y, York, GF, Aug 17)
Nameitwhatyoulike 94 1 (6f, York, GS, Sep 4)
Namhroodah (IRE) 97 1 (1m, Asco, GF, Jul 22)
Nayel (IRE) 90 1 (1m 2f 88y, York, Gd, May 11)
Nemoralia (USA) 103 2 (1m, Asco, GS, Jun 17)
New Bay 92 4 (1m 2f, Leop, Yld, Sep 10)
New Caledonia (IRE) 89 1 (1m 4f, Asco, Gd, Sep 3)
Ninjago 99 4 (5f, York, Gd, May 21)
Normandy Barriere (IRE) 94 1 (6f 110y, Donc, Gd, Sep 9)
Not Never 92 2 (1m 4f 5y, Newb, Sft, Sep 16)
Notarised 90 3 (1m 6f, Good, GF, Jul 26)
Now Or Never (IRE) 100 4 (1m, Asco, GS, Jun 17)
Nuno Tristan (USA) 93 3 (6f, Good, GF, Jul 30)
Oasis Fantasy (IRE) 93 2 (1m 1f 192y, Good, GF, Jul 26)
Ocean Sheridan (IRE) 90 1 (5f, Catt, Sft, Oct 15)
Ode To Evening 92 2 (1m 1f 192y, Good, GF, Jul 28)
Off Art 89 7 (1m 2f 88y, York, Gd, May 11)
One Word More (IRE) 99 3 (1m, York, Gd, Jul 9)
Opal Tiara (IRE) 97 1 (7f, York, GF, Aug 18)
Order Of St George (IRE) 107 1 (2m 4f, Asco, Sft, Jun 16)
Orion's Bow 99 2 (6f, Good, GF, Jul 30)
Ornate 96 2 (6f, Asco, Gd, Sep 30)
Out Do 90 7 (6f, Asco, GF, Sep 3)
Outback Traveller (IRE) 105 1 (6f, Asco, GS, Jun 18)
Outrage 90 1 (5f, Kemw, SD, Dec 20)
Pacify 103 2 (1m 2f 88y, York, Gd, May 11)
Pearl Secret 96 4 (5f, Hayd, GS, May 21)
Perfect Pasture 105 1 (6f 63y, Curr, Yld, Jul 16)
Peril 88 2 (7f 14y, Ncsw, SD, May 17)
Persuasive (IRE) 96 2 (1m, Leop, Yld, Sep 10)
Pipers Note 92 4 (6f, York, Gd, Oct 8)
Platitude 97 2 (1m 4f, Asco, Sft, Jun 16)
Poet's Word (IRE) 89 1 (1m 3f, Good, GF, Jul 29)
Polarisation 90 2 (1m 4f 10y, Epso, GS, Jun 4)
Political Policy (IRE) 92 2 (1m 2f 150y, Dunw, SD, Sep 30)
Port Douglas (IRE) 88 2 (1m 4f 66y, Ches, Gd, May 5)
Postponed (IRE) 110 1 (1m 2f 88y, York, GF, Aug 17)
Poyle Vinnie 97 3 (5f 110y, Ches, Gd, Aug 20)
Predominance (IRE) 92 1 (7f, Hayd, Gd, Apr 23)
Pretend (IRE) 95 2 (6f, Ncsw, SD, Jun 25)
Pretty Perfect (IRE) 100 4 (1m 4f, Asco, Gd, Oct 15)
Priceless 97 2 (6f, Newj, GF, Jul 23)
Primo Uomo (IRE) 90 1 (5f, Curr, Yld, Oct 9)
Prize Money 98 2 (1m 2f, Newm, Gd, May 1)
Profitable (IRE) 107 1 (5f, Hayd, GS, May 21)
Projection 97 3 (6f, Newj, GF, Aug 13)
Promising Run (USA) 98 5 (1m, Asco, GS, Jun 17)
Qemah (IRE) 108 1 (1m, Asco, GS, Jun 17)
Qewy (IRE) 98 2 (1m 6f, Good, GF, Jul 26)
Queen Catrine (IRE) 90 1 (7f, Fair, Yld, Jul 10)
Queen's Trust 102 3 (1m 4f, Asco, Gd, Oct 15)
Quest For More (IRE) 99 2 (2m 2f, Donc, Gd, Sep 9)
Quick Jack (IRE) 106 1 (1m 6f, Leop, Gd, Sep 10)
Quiet Reflection 108 1 (6f, Hayd, Gd, May 28)
Race Day (IRE) 95 2 (1m 1y, Linw, SD, Mar 25)
Raucous 100 3 (6f, Asco, Sft, Oct 1)
Realize 92 3 (7f 32y, Wolw, SD, Mar 12)
Red Baron (IRE) 95 2 (5f, Thir, GF, May 14)
Red Box 93 2 (1m, Asco, GF, Jul 22)
Red Pike (IRE) 91 2 (5f, Beve, Gd, Jun 14)
Red Verdon (USA) 89 6 (1m 4f 10y, Epso, GS, Jun 4)
Reflektor (IRE) 89 2 (5f 16y, Ches, Sft, Jun 11)

Regal Monarch 89 2 (1m 6f, York, Gd, Aug 20)
Related 95 2 (6f, Good, GF, Jul 30)
Remarkable 93 2 (1m, Asco, Gd, Oct 15)
Restorer 92 3 (1m 4f, Kemw, SS, Nov 2)
Revolutionist (IRE) 103 1 (1m 2f, Redc, GF, May 30)
Rex Imperator 88 3 (6f, Ripo, Gd, Aug 13)
Ribchester (IRE) 111 2 (1m, Asco, Gd, Oct 15)
Richard Pankhurst 98 1 (7f, Newb, GF, Aug 13)
Ridge Ranger (IRE) 104 1 (6f, York, Gd, Jul 8)
Ringside Humour (IRE) 89 3 (1m 2f, Curr, Yld, Sep 11)
Rivellino 91 6 (6f, Good, GF, Jul 30)
Robot Boy (IRE) 96 1 (5f, York, Gd, Oct 7)
Rockspirit (IRE) 91 1 (1m 2f 23y, Yarm, GF, Aug 28)
Roll On Rory 93 2 (6f, Newm, Gd, Oct 28)
Roudee 93 1 (6f, Ayr, GS, Sep 17)
Royal Artillery (USA) 92 1 (1m 2f 95y, Hayd, GF, Aug 6)
Royal Birth 99 1 (5f, Chmf, SD, Jun 15)
Ruscombe 88 3 (1m 5f 61y, Newb, GF, Jul 15)
Russian Soul (IRE) 90 5 (7f, Dunw, SD, Dec 23)
Sagaciously (IRE) 97 2 (1m 1f 198y, Sali, GF, Aug 10)
Salateen 91 1 (7f, Ling, Gd, Sep 10)
Scarlet Dragon 93 2 (1m 2f 6y, Newb, GS, Sep 17)
Scottish (IRE) 104 1 (1m 208y, York, Gd, Aug 20)
Scottish Glen 90 3 (1m 1y, Linw, SD, May 7)
Sea Of Flames 98 1 (1m 1y, Linw, SD, Mar 25)
Sea Wolf (IRE) 89 1 (7f, Curr, Yld, Jun 26)
Seanie (IRE) 89 5 (7f 32y, Wolw, SD, Mar 12)
Second Step (IRE) 92 3 (1m 3f 135y, Wind, GF, Aug 27)
Second Wave (IRE) 96 2 (1m 2f, Asco, GS, Jun 18)
Seventh Heaven (IRE) 105 1 (1m 4f, Curr, Gd, Jul 16)
Shalaa (IRE) 107 1 (6f, Asco, Sft, Oct 1)
Shamshon (IRE) 95 1 (5f, Asco, Sft, Oct 1)
Shanghai Glory (IRE) 89 2 (6f, Newj, GS, Jun 18)
Shared Equity 88 2 (6f, Epso, GS, Jun 4)
Sharja Queen 94 1 (1m 1f 198y, Sali, GF, Jul 9)
Sheikhzayedroad 101 3 (2m 4f, Asco, Sft, Jun 16)
Show Stealer 88 1 (6f, Newm, GF, May 14)
Si Senor (IRE) 91 2 (1m 1y, Linw, SD, Feb 27)
Sign Of The Kodiac (IRE) 97 1 (6f, Chmf, SD, Jun 1)
Signs Of Blessing (IRE) 109 4 (6f, Asco, Gd, Oct 15)
Silvanus (IRE) 88 3 (5f, Thir, GF, May 14)
Silver Rainbow (IRE) 96 1 (6f, Newj, GF, Jul 16)
Silvery Moon (IRE) 90 1 (1m, Ayr, Sft, Sep 15)
Simannka (IRE) 89 7 (1m 2f, Curr, Yld, Sep 11)
Simple Verse (IRE) 104 1 (1m 6f 132y, Donc, Gd, Sep 8)
Sir Isaac Newton 101 4 (1m 2f 88y, York, GF, Aug 17)
Sir Maximilian (IRE) 97 1 (5f 16y, Ches, Gd, May 4)
Sir Robert Cheval 94 2 (6f, Newm, GF, May 21)
Sir Roderic (IRE) 88 1 (7f 16y, Sand, GS, Jul 2)
Skiffle 91 1 (1m 1f 192y, Good, Gd, May 19)
Sky Hunter 90 1 (1m 1f 192y, Good, GS, Sep 21)
Snap Shots (IRE) 92 1 (6f, Ripo, Gd, Aug 1)
Snoano 93 1 (1m 4f, York, GS, Jun 11)
So Beloved 95 4 (1m, Ayr, GF, Jun 18)
So Mi Dar 102 1 (1m 2f 88y, York, Gd, May 11)
Soie D'leau 95 1 (5f, Hayd, Sft, Sep 3)
Solar Flair 93 1 (6f 15y, Nott, Gd, Jul 1)
Soldier In Action (FR) 95 1 (1m 4f, Good, Gd, Oct 9)
Sole Power 101 8 (5f, York, Gd, Aug 19)
Somehow (IRE) 88 2 (1m 4f, Cork, Yld, Aug 2)
Sors (IRE) 91 1 (6f, Curr, Gd, Aug 28)
Sound Advice 95 4 (1m, Ayr, GF, Jun 18)
Southern Belle (IRE) 88 1 (6f 15y, Nott, Gd, Aug 2)
Sovereign Debt (IRE) 102 2 (7f, Curr, Gd, Jul 17)
Spanish Squeeze (IRE) 91 8 (1m 2f 88y, York, Gd, May 11)
Spark Plug (IRE) 108 1 (1m 1f, Newm, GF, Sep 24)
Speedy Boarding 104 2 (1m 4f, Asco, Gd, Oct 15)
Spirit Quartz (IRE) 100 1 (5f, Tipp, Sft, Aug 25)
Split The Atom (IRE) 88 3 (5f, Dunw, SD, Mar 4)
Spring Loaded (IRE) 94 1 (5f 216y, Wolw, SD, Dec 26)
Spring Offensive (IRE) 91 3 (1m, Hayd, GF, Aug 6)
Squats (IRE) 95 4 (7f, Asco, GF, Sep 3)
St Michel 94 3 (2m 2f, Donc, Gd, Sep 9)
Stake Acclaim (IRE) 89 1 (5f 10y, Wind, Sft, Apr 18)
Star Storm (IRE) 100 2 (1m 4f, Kemw, SS, Nov 2)
Stargazer (IRE) 92 5 (1m 4f, Asco, Gd, Sep 3)

Stars Over The Sea (USA) 98 1 (1m 4f 8y, Pont, GF, Aug 3)
Steel Train (FR) 90 1 (7f, Donc, GF, Nov 5)
Stellar Mass (IRE) 89 1 (1m 4f, Leop, Gd, Aug 4)
Stepper Point 88 8 (5f, Asco, GF, Jul 9)
Stormy Antarctic 89 6 (1m, Asco, Gd, Oct 15)
Strath Burn 88 4 (6f, Wind, Gd, May 23)
Suedois (IRE) 110 2 (6f, Newj, GF, Jul 9)
Suegioo (FR) 91 8 (2m 4f, Asco, Sft, Jun 16)
Suqoor 88 2 (6f, Chmf, SD, Jun 1)
Tabarrak (IRE) 90 1 (7f, Asco, GF, May 6)
Taexali (IRE) 88 2 (5f 7y, Hami, Sft, May 1)
Take Cover 108 3 (5f, York, Gd, Aug 19)
Tanaza (IRE) 90 8 (1m, Asco, GS, Jun 17)
Taneen (USA) 93 6 (6f, Newj, GF, Jul 7)
Tang Fleming 88 3 (7f, Good, Gd, May 21)
Taqdeer (IRE) 91 1 (1m 2f, Newm, Gd, May 1)
Tashaar (IRE) 91 4 (1m 3f 135y, Wind, GF, Aug 27)
Taurean Star (IRE) 88 1 (1m, Asco, GF, May 6)
Tawdeea 98 1 (1m 3f 200y, Hayd, Sft, Jul 2)
Teruntum Star (FR) 98 1 (6f, Newm, GS, Apr 12)
The Black Princess (IRE) 89 2 (1m 1f 192y, Good, Gd, May 19)
The Grey Gatsby (IRE) 88 6 (1m 2f 88y, York, GF, Aug 17)
The Gurkha (IRE) 97 2 (1m, Asco, Sft, Jun 14)
The Happy Prince (IRE) 102 4 (5f, Dunw, SD, Oct 21)
The Tin Man 116 1 (6f, Asco, Gd, Oct 15)
Thesme 103 5 (5f, York, Gd, Aug 19)
Thikriyaat (IRE) 92 1 (1m, Good, GF, Jul 29)
Third Time Lucky (IRE) 90 4 (1m 1f, Newm, GF, Sep 24)
Time Test 106 1 (1m 2f 7y, Sand, GF, May 26)
Tony Curtis 88 4 (1m 2f 7y, Wind, GF, Aug 27)
Tony The Gent (IRE) 89 2 (1m 2f, Cork, Yld, Oct 15)
Toofi (FR) 90 8 (6f, Asco, GS, Jun 18)
Toormore (IRE) 104 1 (1m 14y, Sand, GS, Apr 22)
Top Beak (IRE) 89 2 (1m, Hayd, Gd, Sep 23)
Top Notch Tonto (IRE) 88 2 (1m 123y, Galw, Sft, Jul 26)
Toscanini (IRE) 88 3 (7f, Curr, Gd, Jul 17)
Travertine (IRE) 95 3 (1m 2f, Curr, Yld, Jun 26)
Treasury Notes (IRE) 95 1 (1m, Hayd, GF, Aug 6)
Tullius (IRE) 103 1 (1m 114y, Epso, GS, Jun 3)
Tupi (IRE) 88 6 (6f, York, Gd, May 11)
Turret Rocks (IRE) 88 4 (1m 4f, Curr, Gd, Jul 16)
Tutu Nguru (USA) 91 2 (1m, Asco, GF, May 7)
Twilight Son 111 1 (6f, Asco, GS, Jun 18)
Ulysses (IRE) 105 2 (1m 2f 7y, Wind, GF, Aug 27)
Undrafted (USA) 99 6 (6f, Asco, GS, Jun 18)
Unicorn (IRE) 90 3 (1m 6f, York, Gd, Aug 20)
Union Rose 96 2 (5f 6y, Sand, Sft, Jul 1)
Us Army Ranger (IRE) 112 2 (1m 4f 10y, Epso, GS, Jun 4)
Usherette (IRE) 91 6 (1m, Newj, GF, Jul 8)
Valley Of Fire 89 1 (7f, Hayd, Gd, Sep 2)
Ventura Storm (IRE) 107 2 (1m 6f 132y, Donc, Gd, Sep 10)
Very Dashing 88 4 (1m 1f 198y, Sali, GF, Aug 10)
Very Special (IRE) 102 2 (1m, Newj, GF, Jul 8)
Very Talented (IRE) 91 3 (1m 1f, Newm, GF, Sep 24)
Viren's Army (IRE) 92 1 (5f, Hayd, GS, May 6)
Von Blucher (IRE) 88 3 (7f, Asco, GF, Sep 3)
Waady (IRE) 97 3 (5f, Hayd, GS, May 21)
Wall Of Fire (IRE) 98 1 (1m 6f, York, Gd, Aug 20)
Washington Dc (IRE) 102 5 (6f, Newj, GF, Jul 9)
Watchable 93 3 (6f, Hayd, Gd, May 7)
Western Hymn 101 1 (1m 4f, Kemw, SS, Nov 2)
What About Carlo (FR) 91 3 (1m 2f 18y, Epso, GS, Jun 3)
Wicklow Brave 100 1 (1m 6f, Curr, Yld, Sep 11)
Willytheconqueror (IRE) 94 1 (5f 6y, Sand, GS, Apr 22)
Windsor Beach (IRE) 89 1 (1m 2f, Cork, Yld, Oct 15)
Wings Of Desire 107 1 (1m 2f 88y, York, GF, May 12)
Withernsea (IRE) 94 2 (7f, Hayd, Gd, Apr 23)
Yangtze 89 3 (1m 6f, York, Gd, Oct 7)
Yattwee (USA) 93 5 (1m, Asco, Sft, Jun 16)
Yorker (SAF) 100 2 (1m 208y, York, Gd, Aug 20)
You're Fired (IRE) 96 1 (1m, Hayd, Gd, Apr 23)
You're Hired 90 1 (1m 3f 104y, Yarm, GF, Sep 13)
Yuften 94 1 (1m, Asco, Gd, Oct 15)
Zhui Feng (IRE) 92 5 (1m 1f, Newm, GF, Sep 24)
Zhukova (IRE) 90 1 (1m 4f, Leop, Gd, Sep 10)
Zonderland 100 2 (1m, Good, GF, Aug 27)

INDEX OF HORSES

INDEX OF HORSES